To J. J. —
A great friend +
ballplayer. Very valuable
during road trips.
Best always,
Theo

11 July 08

MAXIMUM HORSEPOWER

How to Strengthen Your Sales Force Quickly

OCEAN PALMER

FIRST EDITION

Book cover design by Stacey Lane, Stacey Lane Design LLC, Denver, Colorado

Edited by Charol Messenger, Centennial, Colorado

Library of Congress Cataloging-in-Publication Data

Simendinger, Theodore J.
    Maximum Horsepower (How to Strengthen Your Sales Force Quickly)/Theodore J. Simendinger as "Ted Simendinger." 1st edition.

    ISBN: 0-9765485-1-8

    1. Non-fiction   2. Business   3. Sales   4. Management   5. Title

    Library of Congress Control Number: TXu 1-575-468

        10 9 8 7 6 5 4 3 2 1

Published by Airplane Reader Publishing Company, Denver, Colorado U.S.A.

Printed in the United States of America

DEDICATION

MAXIMUM HORSEPOWER is dedicated to all the sales leaders around the world who drive good business forward. Thank you for honoring the world's greatest profession.

TABLE OF CONTENTS

TABLE OF CONTENTS

SELLING IN A DECLINING ECONOMY

As markets tighten and the economy shifts from mass consumption to specific selection, sustained success requires recalibration and course correction. To professional salespeople, a tightening economy has a silver lining: It weeds out the amateurs.

How people who sell for a living view a toughening marketplace will dramatically differ, based on skill level and personal choice. Some salespeople, the amateurs, will press the doom-and-gloom button at every cause of stress. Others, more skilled, will say with a shrug, "It's a stabilizing market." Rather than overreact, professional salespeople step back, reassess the viable market, pick a new path, and keep moving forward. After all, one person's mess is another's opportunity to clean up.

From a personality standpoint, optimists and pessimists will react differently to soft-market adversity. Optimists see problems as temporary inconveniences. Pessimists consider derailments validation.

But when the economy grunts and groans, customer actions and reactions will change, too. Smart salespeople will adjust.

How Customers Change: Wants versus Needs

Throughout the up-and-down ride of an economic rollercoaster, a customer's *need* to change remains relentless. The *velocity* of change may increase or decrease, but markets continually contract and expand. Since a tight economy shifts purchasing patterns from accumulation to selective acquisition, customers react by changing their buying priorities. They move from what they *want* and are willing to accept, to a sharper focus centered solely on what they truly *need*. Wants and needs are dramatically different, so this increased selectivity will arise whenever the customer perceives that an unnecessary gap exists between the two.

Behaviorally, expect customers to continue to commoditize whatever they can. Also, expect them to carefully and selectively *invest* in valued solutions. Due to increased accountability for chosen expenditures, "spent" money, the borderline purchases that typified the days of plenty, will decrease. Customers will buy cheap when they can, and buy value when they must, but as things worsen, the mid-market soft-spend will evaporate.

Value buys must help the customer operate a better business, so customer expectations will rise. In exchange, there will be increased receptivity to professionals and subject matter experts. A tight economy forces decision-makers to manage out the operational mistakes of acquisition and utilization. Along with those decisions, risk increases commensurate with the pressure to improve. Customers will reject desperate salespeople, opting instead to lean on true professionals for counsel, advice, and collaborative problem solving. They will insist on (and expect) "equity interactions" and won't have time or patience for low-equity meetings that do not advance an initiative. As a result, customers will invest more time and resources with valued suppliers and waste less of both with everyone else.

As the economic pendulum swings, don't be surprised when customers modify buying tactics, too. New decision-making layers, influencers, political buy-ins, signoffs, and contract terms—everything gets tossed into the salad bowl of possible change. In some cases, the entire slate of people you've traditionally dealt with will be wiped clean.

Given these economically induced market force changes, the challenge for salespeople is how to keep flourishing while others around them begin to fail.

HOW SKILLED SALESPEOPLE WILL ADAPT

The rules of engagement during a robust economy are different from those in weakening times. New rule #1: Take nothing for granted. If new players are introduced on the customer's side, they are there for a reason—to instigate change. Trust this: Change agents *will* make change. Might be right, might be wrong, but they will implode the status quo. This is good news if you're on the outside looking in. Bad news if it's your relationship to lose. When your champion has left the building, so has your relationship.

As things tighten, the natural temptation is to sell harder, more aggressively. Be cautious. Expect customers, especially new ones, to study, doubt, and test alternatives with increased diligence. To improve your chances, *teach* first and *sell* second as you advance methodically through the selling cycle. *Solve* more, too. Those two things, teaching insight and solving problems, will advance your differentiated offering faster toward the close than unempathetic sales pressure.

The tighter the market, the more vital it becomes to fill the prospect funnel and keep *more* deals percolating. Some will unexpectedly fall out. Others will be lost. Reps must keep opportunities *moving*. Expect heightened competition. Price, margin, and terms all will face increased pressure. Pending deals will undergo increased scrutiny, horizontally *and* vertically, prior to signature. And, as customer stress increases, shorter fuses will burn on the customer's side of the desk. Coach your people to sell better, more *thoroughly*, in order to minimize objections, which are negative emotional reactions to what a customer sees and hears. Under stress, objections cause collateral damage.

As times toughen, field salespeople must close better (and more often), even if what they are closing for is one baby step up an endless spiral staircase en route to a deal's conclusion. This takes discipline and patience, especially as the stakes rise for both sides.

Creativity always pays off in selling, especially so in a tough market. I heard a story in London recently about a British rep who kept getting screened from seeing a prospect he thought had the potential to become a great customer. The rep boxed up two pieces from a mannequin and shipped the box to the customer's office. Curious, the customer opened it. Inside was a note written on the back of the rep's business card, taped to one of the plastic appendages. His message read simply, "I'd give an arm and a leg for twenty minutes of your time."

The bold move worked. The rep got the appointment, was perfectly prepared, and nailed the presentation. So began a robust relationship that's proven beneficial for both sides.

In a tight economy, differentiation is a vital challenge, and creativity can help at every stage of the sales cycle, not just the approach. Cleverly sell beyond the boundaries of what's expected, and sometimes that one special idea will help tip the deal. Smart sales leaders will grow increasingly more open-minded to suggestions from the field, since the sales force is closest to the customer. The best, most creative ideas sometimes come from new and innovative deal-structures that break the traditional mold of how a company does business. Rental instead of lease or outright sale, customized fleet management services, and second-life product placement into untapped, cost-sensitive vertical markets are examples in the capital equipment space. If an idea is ethical and profitable, consider it.

From a leadership perspective, urge your people to maintain a "how can we" attitude. Don't let them get sucked into the negative vortex of "can't because." Coach them to think bigger, not smaller, and to see—and sell—what is *possible*. Don't let them dwell on what is broken, internally within the company or externally in the marketplace. This is important because of a vital sales truism: Salespeople tend to find what they are looking for. If what they see in a tight market are additional opportunities to win under level conditions that fairly reward better selling, then *that* is what they will aggressively chase. If they are half-beaten—and looking for reasons why a customer *won't* be buying in a contracting market—then *that* fatalistic validation will doom them to fail. Fussing about market noise will impede results but will not keep the economy from changing.

Successful salespeople embrace a winner's outlook and take that vision to the street every day. Customers reward them for it. Conversely, customers penalize reps who come across as wounded or defeated, or who choose to play a "blame game." Pity does not (and will not) sell. Customers, after all, have options. In tight times, they reward those who deserve it most—the positive professionals whose diligent work has earned the business.

WHAT WINNERS DO DURING A TIGHT MARKET

Here are five snapshots of how great reps adjust in a softening economy. These and many more are amplified in great detail throughout MAXIMUM HORSEPOWER.

1. *Performers have a great discipline on staying productive, not just busy.* The art comes in knowing the difference between the two. Hallmark enablers: smarter time decisions and the flawless execution of tested strategic plans.

2. *Performers vet opportunities by differentiating quickly, and then test the value the prospect places on that differentiation.* If the value validates, good salespeople will invest in the opportunity. If the customer refuses to see value, the reps will cut the cord. Top producers will *not* waste time on pipe-dream opportunities. Their choices are determined by close-rate probability, measured against potential reward. Good, winnable deals are pursued. Others are abandoned.

3. *Performers work harder than ever to become increasingly relevant to the customer's business.* Vertical market insight, expertise, and problem-solving all add value.

4. *Performers work for results, not by a wristwatch.* Pro selling is not a punch-the-time-clock career choice. It is a *results* profession. When the rules of the game change, so will how the winners play. Reps must stay flexible, willing to adapt on the fly. If they don't, they will be outsold by people who do. When they pursue a deal but lose, top performers will perform an unemotional, analytical post-mortem to learn the true reasons why. Loss reviews illuminate what must change in order to avoid being beaten the same way twice. "Price," they realize, is a loser's crutch. Sometimes they got outsold.

Typically these loss analyses reveal an error caused by "the reflexive loop" (being behaviorally predictable), and illustrate the value of "contrarian thinking." Contrarian thinking occurs when the salesperson turns everything he or she assumed to be true right back around and assumes it's false. This diametrically different perspective enables the rep to understand a totally opposite point of view. New insight often sheds light on the *real* reasons the deal was lost. More often than not in major account selling, the real deal-breaker is not price.

5. *Most important of all, top performers—those who continue to flourish when others flail in frustration—are relentlessly willing to invest in themselves.* They get and stay fit, remain upbeat, and keep learning. As others become discouraged by serial disappointments and grow weaker, great salespeople stay cool under fire and grow stronger. This steeled temperance comes by design, not by accident.

For sales leaders, a tightening economy also serves to help stratify their sales pool. Lines of demarcation are more clearly drawn between professionals, journeymen, and amateurs. Pros win, amateurs lose, and journeymen do some of both, depending who they face off against. Journeymen beat amateurs, lose to pros, and toss a coin when competing within their peer group. Because of that, sustaining solid performance in a decelerating economy requires companies to capitalize on maximizing desired matchups and avoiding bad ones. Smart sales leaders orchestrate these. They do not leave their team's performance to evolving-market coverage models that rely on convenience, tradition, hope, luck, or random chance.

So, when the marketplace tightens its belt a notch, make a competitor be the one who's forced to skip the meal. Recognize what the changing market is giving you—and has taken away—and act accordingly. Plan smart and work smarter with a better, more talented sales force, and you will *win*. MAXIMUM HORSEPOWER teaches how.

CHAPTER

THE CHANGING MARKETPLACE

THE FOUR VITAL REASONS TO STRENGTHEN YOUR SALES FORCE NOW

IN THIS CHAPTER

- **How the market is moving**

- **The impact of blue-chip rightsizing**

- **How technology is changing pro selling**

- **The sales impact of cultural diversity**

The fourth Thursday of every November is an American holiday, with forty-five million turkeys meeting their destinies as honored centerpieces on Thanksgiving Day dinner tables.

Some are cooked well, some aren't. Some are carved well, most aren't. Because preparing and serving a stuffed turkey is a once or twice-a-year ritual, millions of Americans live their entire lives without learning how to properly cook or carve one.

I grew up resenting turkeys because my dad made all four of us kids dress up in church clothes just to eat one. Each Thanksgiving my dad turned showman, standing at the head of the table, dramatically holding aloft his special long-bladed turkey knife and matching silver fork. He commenced the avian dissection with deliberate drama, carefully peeling off slice after slice of juicy breast meat with thin cut, layering precision. I never asked him where he learned to carve a turkey so well, but there was no question he knew what he was doing. He always finished with a mound of meat, perfectly stacked and shingled, and a bare-boned skeleton.

Shortly after I finished college, I was in a relationship that required me to eat two Thanksgiving turkeys in one day. The first came in early afternoon at my girlfriend's home. It was the first time I witnessed a turkey savagely attacked. I winced as I watched, since it never dawned on me that people with knives might not know the exact placement of bone and cartilage throughout every square inch of a large bird's frame.

After we left, I learned a valuable lesson: Never laugh at a woman's father who is cluelessly hacking up a dead bird, since doing so is hurtful to romantic ambition.

Metaphorically speaking, that Thanksgiving turkey is what MAXIMUM HORSEPOWER is all about: To teach companies how to carve the bird better than their competition. With that in mind, four impact factors drive the urgent need for strategic sales talent development:

1. A changing market domestically, a blossoming one abroad
2. Blue chip downsizing and widespread corporate repositioning
3. The use, misuse, and increasing abuse of evolving technology
4. Immigration and the changing face of field sales personnel

4 IMPACT FACTORS
1. A CHANGING MARKET
2. BLUE CHIP DOWNSIZING
3. EVOLVING TECHNOLOGY
4. IMMIGRATION

IMPACT FACTOR #1: THE CHANGING MARKETPLACE

As the corporate business climate continues to dramatically move toward increased commoditization, companies must either sell cheaply or create saleable value. Businesses that stand still and do nothing will lose. Adaptation is the dance partner of survival.

No longer can a company stay mid-priced and quasi-consultative, since lukewarm pricing and minimal value leave you unprotected against a pummeling by rival gangs of worthy competitors. Bestselling author and sales thought leader Neil Rackham calls this the "dead mice" conundrum. "What are you selling," he asks, "A better mousetrap or dead mice cheap?"

Modern corporate survival dictates the need to commit to one strategy or the other, neither a convenient choice. Competitors and buyer alternatives are mushrooming, so businesses that do nothing—neither acting nor reacting—are getting crushed. Entire business segments are being squeezed into extinction: the corner stockbroker, the neighborhood travel agent, the local airlines ticket office, the independent grocer, pet shop or bookstore. More will follow.

Market evolution is causing corporate sales growth to hinge on doing one of two things well: converting a cheap cost model into a cheap pricing structure to push volume sales, or selling a differentiated, premium-priced value proposition at a sustainable margin. Many American companies lean on low-cost production nations and offshore outsourcing to deliver a lower cost basis for goods and services. For increasing numbers of major corporations, these moves are a survival necessity. To avoid downsizing or extinction, sales velocity must offset shrinking margins. The easiest way to accelerate sales velocity is to increase decisions and order rates by decreasing price. Expect the velocity emphasis to continue.

Today's customers are conditioned to change. Armed with a better idea of what they want, they shop with a shorter, sizzling fuse. Thanks to a proliferation of alternatives, decision-makers have increasing options to choose from. Chances are good they will find what they want at the price they are willing to pay, at terms they demand.

To thrive in this changing market, sales organizations must reposition their reps to win with a new go-to-market approach. If your solutions aren't cheap, value propositions must strengthen, as must the proficiency of the sales force chartered with delivering your message. Better value propositions delivered by better talent will win more deals. Winning more deals assures sustainability.

THE WAL-MART FACTOR

The locomotive behind these seismic changes is headquartered in Bentonville, Arkansas, a small town of 30,000 in northwest Arkansas and home to the world's largest retailer. During an average day, twenty-five million customers spend nearly one billion dollars in Wal-Mart's 6,800 stores worldwide. These numbers will continue to grow, as the company plans to open 500 supercenters across the United States by 2010. International expansion is planned to be even more aggressive. *(source: Wal-Mart Stores, Inc.)*

What Wal-Mart has done to the marketplace, of course, is to build a framework of commodity pricing, thanks to the company's near-fanatical pressure on its 61,000 suppliers to lower cost. In turn, Wal-Mart buys in bulk and resells around the world. I visited a textile plant in southern India and witnessed 200 employees machining an endless assembly line of the exact same item: an olive-colored skirt. The customer? Wal-Mart.

The impact of the Wal-Mart approach—driving down the cost of sales by pressuring suppliers—goes way beyond retailing. Increasing numbers of corporations are making their own attempts at commoditizing goods and services, some of which are not commodity solutions. Salespeople are perplexed. How can they fill out a bid for a complex service that ignores the significant differences between their solution and others in the marketplace?

Bid issuance has expense ramifications on both sides of the negotiation desk, the sum of which can outweigh the savings a buyer will realize or the profits the surviving winner hopes to make. Squeezing contract blood out of a supplier renewal agreement that was squeezed dry the last time around has obvious limitations.

On the customer side, there are direct and indirect costs tied to every step: issuing, clarifying, responding, evaluating, deciding, implementing, and monitoring. Change, of course, is disruptive. Factoring in the ancillary costs of change, what are the true net savings after the quantification of direct and indirect expenses?

Some companies have turned to outsourcing the bid function, tossing things over the wall to hungry consultants who want to bid *everything,* because split-share commission checks are contingent on the hard-dollar savings they generate. This is pure win/lose procurement, an adversarial buy/sell opportunity environment that an increasing number of service suppliers are deciding to walk away from, because services can't be commoditized like widgets, pencils or ping-pong balls. This reluctance to compete is frustrating for both buyers and sellers. What is often unspoken is that buyers want the best solution at the best price—not necessarily the cheapest, although the bid documents purport to say that—and the sellers want more business; they just want to make sure they can make a buck while delivering it.

The bid process, of course, is designed to equate as many goods and services as possible to help drive down price. Diminished (or no) value is placed on tangible or intangible benefits, as well as indirect cost. Salespeople despise the arrival of a thick bid package unless they helped the buyer write it. But once the bid arrives, the sales organization must decide what to do: respond, don't respond, or push back on the rules, trying to create a more winnable opportunity with more favorable terms.

Recipient supplier companies struggle with this decision—what to do with the phone book-sized set of bid specs. Some companies have a "respond no matter what" culture. Years ago at Xerox, I worked for a guy who made us do that. The futility of the exercise reached the molten earth's core when one of my teammates had to try to convince McDonald's restaurants—who were bidding cash registers—that Xerox machines were a better alternative.

Compared to what a good salesperson can accomplish through direct selling, bid responses eat up disproportionate amounts of time and have low success rates. Even the wins are thin, with prices shaved and contract prices whittled to the bone. Since the rules are written for the benefit of the buyer, not the seller, winning often means having to agree to less-than-desirable margins, along with risky terms and conditions. Both are gambles that can hog-tie internal resources. If neither price nor terms are in your favor, sometimes a loss is really a win in disguise.

Smart sales reps seek to avoid commoditization. They prefer to differentiate their offerings from competitors and take their chances aggressively selling those differences. Value creators do this tremendously well, much preferring to win or lose on the open battlefield.

SHOPPERS VS. CUSTOMERS: OUR "DO IT YOURSELF" SOCIETY

Spurred by the complex combustion of global responses to the rise of the Wal-Mart juggernaut, commoditization has resulted in dangerous price decisions for product and service providers whose primary retention strategy is slashing prices. Margins erode unless infrastructure support services are slashed in tandem, too. Neither of these decisions bodes well for a long-term relationship. Both behaviors feed a non-reliant "shopper" mentality, where the buyer is allegiant not to the supplier but to the price.

Value creators work differently. They nurture "customer" (not shopper) relationships, since *customers* are loyal to companies. *Shoppers*, on the other hand, are not loyal to companies; shoppers are loyal to price.

WE APPRECIATE YOUR BUSINESS. DO IT YOURSELF.

Spurred on by the Wal-Mart factor, the wildfire spread of the shopper model has crossed all industries. It is the music by which we march toward our "do it yourself" society. Need airplane tickets, a boarding pass, hotel room, rental car, or theater tickets? *Do it yourself.* Need directions or have to pump gas? *Do it yourself.* Need to check bank balances, transfer money, pay a bill or trade a stock? *Do it yourself.* Need to check out an overflowing cart at the grocery or home improvement store? *Do it yourself.* Hurry, please. Scan everything, one by one, often repeatedly, since the scanner only beeps when it feels like it. Then bag everything yourself, one item at a time, and pay for it with uncrumpled face-up dollars fed in the right direction. But before you do, check the bottom of your cart in case you forgot something. If you are too slow the computer voice will badger you, loudly urging you to hurry. After all, others are impatiently waiting to do it themselves, too.

Much of what used to be done for us by others we now must do for ourselves via computer. Our on-line lives are becoming an alpha-numeric soup of multiple passwords, user ID's, credit card numbers, months and years of expiration, and security codes. We share our favorite pet's name, the cities we were born, our elementary school, and our mother's maiden name. Passwords are four, six, or eight digits, alpha only or alphanumeric. They are case sensitive, expiring when someone else decides they should. If the computer decides the password we've chosen is easy to guess, it chides us to do better. All rules are set for the convenience of the site's programmers. None are designed by customers.

Zero of these keystroking, lifeless business interactions create a positive emotional event in the mind of a customer. Each is tedious, repetitious, and time-consuming. Companies don't care, trading our inconveniences for a behavior conditioning that's designed to massage the perception that what we get in the end are lower prices. Whether that's fact or fiction is debatable. Are prices *really* lower? Or is the only thing that's lower the vendor's cost of goods sold? Draped around a do-it-yourself environment, the phrase "We want to earn your business" has never been so oxymoronic.

What are the ramifications of the compounding frequency of such a marching army of depersonalized experiences? Who are we supposed to be loyal to? A machine which monotones that even though we are serving ourselves we are too slow, too inept, and simply must hurry up?

Contrasted with this depersonalized shopper approach, the catering-to-the-customer model is a different emotional experience, one that hinges on creating customer value. Successful value creation depends on the salespeople creating as many positive emotional experiences as possible, while whittling down the number of negative ones as low as possible. The net difference between the two *(positive interactions minus negative ones)* determines the quality of the customer experience. Companies that work hard to create positive emotional experiences, and teach their people how to minimize negative ones, are in a good position to succeed.

Publix Super Markets, for example, caters to *customers*. They worry less about situational cheap pricing than they do about catering to the long-term wants and needs of a loyal repeat customer base. Employees focus on the creation of positive emotional experiences, both verbal and non-verbal. Theirs is a complex multi-faceted strategy that has enabled the company to maintain a solid presence in a wickedly tough market space.

Winn-Dixie, a long-time Publix competitor, went the other way, choosing not to invest in maximizing the customer experience. They got caught in the middle, the death zone between price and value, and now finds itself on the financial ropes. The Winn-Dixie cost model isn't cheap enough to compete with Wal-Mart superstores, and their stores aren't nice enough to compete with Publix. Customers have options. Given these options, customers aren't choosing Winn-Dixie.

WIN BY PRICE, LOSE BY PRICE

Going low works when you've got a cost basis low enough to sustain a tolerable margin. If price moves your product, less-skilled salespeople are all you need. Developing talent in a commodity world is a dubious investment since the shoppers don't care. Price, not the person, makes the sale. Raise your price and shoppers go elsewhere.

Customers, on the other hand, demand more. Customers expect premium value for a premium price and will pay for it. Hence the heightened marketplace demand for skilled sales and support professionals who are adept at creating, building, and sustaining value.

Companies can't achieve value pricing if they don't have people skilled enough to create and harvest it.

Strategy, organizational thought, relevance, clarity of high impact messaging, and flawless delivery are absolute *musts* in the competitive world of value creation. All are scarce in this changing business climate, where the relentless hunt to stockpile top sales talent can mean the difference between P&L heaven and P&L purgatory.

BUYERS ARE IMPATIENT

In corporate dealings, our business customers are under rising amounts of pressure and growing increasingly impatient with the salespeople who call on them. Back in the Xerox heyday, we were taught to chitchat ("build rapport" it was called) and then segue into the sales call with "Tell me about your business."

Open with that today and you'll get the bum's rush right out the door. Customer expectations are higher and their taximeter starts running the moment you sit down. Decision-makers have tight calendars, which means every minute is valuable.

Clients today expect relevant dialogue focused on their businesses, not yours. Competence and relevance are the coupled cost of entry. Better, deeper, and smarter pre-call prep is essential.

Today's decision-makers couldn't care less about what something does. What they want to know is what it does *for them,* a focus they expect you to have when you walk through their door. Today customers are armed with more information than ever before, so salespeople enter meetings facing an existing bias, pro or con, rather than sitting down with someone who's open-minded. During the meeting the client will process what he or she sees, learns, and surmises against that bias. They need to be sold, not persuaded. *The new sales challenge is changing views, rather than creating them.*

Keep this in mind when building your talent development strategy: The object is to leapfrog the competition, not stay even. Understand today's market but aim your adaptations into the future. Build for two, three, or five years out. Improvement will be relentless but not instantaneous. By the time you install comprehensive positive change throughout your sales organization, the calendar will have rolled. Build for where the market is going, not for where it's been.

CHANGING GLOBAL DYNAMICS

Money doesn't sleep, so global change is flying at light speed. Europe, the Middle East, Africa, and the Far East are undergoing phenomenal metamorphosis, each for different combinations of reasons than what's happening domestically. So while the scenarios and backdrops are different, the selling skills needed to succeed are very much the same. The net impact on the professional sales force is the same: there simply aren't enough value creators, enough strategic sales leaders, to go around.

In Europe, especially Central and Eastern Europe, the interweaving machinations between members and neighbors of the evolving European Union have impacted life and business dramatically. The domino effect will continue as the euro extends its muscle to an increasing number of strengthening, open border nations. Opportunities, big ones, are rising from the ashes of suppression. Suppressed economies with good, motivated, and often portable workforces are awakening.

Consequently, the knocking down of traditional economic, political, and social silos has created a massive need for strategic thinkers and talented sales professionals. The price of finding them, hiring them, and keeping them relentlessly escalates. Europe is burgeoning with great opportunities for pros with global aspirations.

The Middle East is undergoing a sonic boom, the nature of which is unmatched anywhere in the world, totally different than what's going on in China and India. The Middle East oil projects are staggering in scale, creating a dire need for experienced leadership talent available to think big, sell big, and execute big. As with Europe, the Middle East can't find the talent fast enough to hire it. The money is flying.

Africa is a different story. At a meeting global workforce summit in the Netherlands recently, Africa was described as a puzzle, with each country being a different piece.

South Africa is the continent's business heartbeat. Selling in Africa is situational management at it its best, offering selective opportunity for those with the courage and will to pursue it. Working in Africa, especially outside of South Africa, is extraordinarily stressful, in some place life threatening. It takes street smarts to sell well there. Book smarts won't carry you much beyond the bus stop on the corner.

Asia, of course, is radically different as India explodes and China continues to evolve. Both are team environments so in order to succeed you must flourish as part of the team. It's a different skill set than lone gun revenue generators of the U.S. marketplace typically operate under. The upside of flourishing in those market spaces is, of course, enormous.

In summary, just like the repositioning economy of the United States, changing sales climates around the globe are driving the expanding need for more value creators, more sales leaders, and more strategic revenue-driving sales professionals. The demand is far greater than anything we've seen before. The money at stake is unprecedented, as well.

Whether your aspirations focus domestically or globally, now is a great time to be skilled in our profession.

IMPACT FACTOR #2: BLUE CHIP DOWNSIZING AND CORPORATE REPOSITIONING

The moving marketplace is driving the need for relentless corporate reconfigurations. As mammoth companies continue to contract via divestitures, layoffs, and attempts to flatten hierarchical structures, mid-market opportunities are expanding, as are market niches for start-ups and innovators. For them, time is of the essence. Windows of opportunity fly open and slam shut, so flawless execution is crucial.

Leaner companies must rely, more than ever before, on high-performance salespeople who can orchestrate major success. Far more disposable are the grinders who provide market or territory coverage but not market control. Companies need profit generators, not overhead.

WHY IS THERE A TALENT SHORTAGE?

The marketplace demand for skilled sales talent is expanding but the available pool of clever value creators remains flat. The big question, of course, is why. Why isn't the talent pool of top-notch sales pros growing commensurate with the horizontally expanding global and domestic marketplace opportunity?

One reason is that the traditional "blue chips" have changed their approach to inventorying, nurturing, developing, and stockpiling white-collar sales talent. The blue chip environment today is nothing like it was in the seventies, eighties or nineties. Corporate restructures and downsizing decisions have abolished the bench strength assembly line of some former powerhouse sales pro suppliers like Xerox and IBM. Their globally respected learning labs of relentless critique and strict expectation have been shuttered, closed in deference to a leaner workforce.

Wholesale cutbacks and reconfigurations mean that few companies are willing to invest in what they perceive to be migrant talent loyal to themselves but not the company. Conversely, the abolition of the blue chip's historic enticement—the promise of a safe, solid, financially appealing, long-term career—has made an entire generation of sales pros quite comfortable leaving the blue chips and migrating from opportunity to opportunity, something that was unheard of a decade or two ago. Pro talent is less trusting of big business than they are of their own ability to carve out a good living wherever they choose to work. Most believe that the safest career consists of a series of different sales experiences as opposed to just one long loyal one. The key to attracting and retaining this type of sales professional is creating an environment that encourages relentless professional growth. The promise of emotional equity can lure them in; the delivery of positive emotional equity helps keep them.

THESE ARE NOT THE GOOD OLD DAYS

Gone are the corporate diamond mines, where blue chip companies stockpiled talent in the rough, then systematically cut and polished those human gemstones via an assembly-line process that invested skill and emotional equity in exchange for long-term performance.

Today there is diminished allegiance in both directions, long-term loyalty from both sides of the desk replaced by mistrust, re-orgs, and job-hopping. People leave, they get replaced; but the harsh reality of trying to recruit sales rainmakers is that it's a lot easier to find a flawed talent running *from* something than it is to find a skilled one running *toward* your particular business.

Most sales candidates with experience are unpolished, with limited talent, a low ceiling, or little professional training. Stars, on the other hand, are very difficult to lure away without overpaying, so most sales organizations settle for less-skilled talent, second or third-tier, as a compromise. When this happens, the company is doomed to lackluster results, since all good intentions are worthless when sales results are substandard. Expecting second or third-tier talent to deliver top tier results is unrealistic. It will not happen.

One Godzilla-sized but invisible villain of the Wal-Mart effect is the dramatic impact tight cost-containment can have on sales organizations. The list of reasons why is long, but here are six common problems that stem from looking at improving sales as an unnecessary expense, rather than as a strategic investment:

1. *Bench strength is eliminated.*

    Gone are the luxury days of investing in eager new hires anxious to learn professional selling. Companies are hiring in a reactionary mode, acting only when it's time to fill an open territory. Hiring costs, as a rule of thumb, average about six months' pay per new hire, not factoring in the cost of lost revenue or the raised ire of customer dissatisfaction. It takes time to get a new rep functionally proficient. Each second the onboarding clock ticks, revenue leaks.

    Bench strength also motivates the existing sales force to get out of bed, hit the streets, make the calls, and close the business. When a rep knows there's someone trained and waiting in the wings, eager for a chance and ready to replace him or her, motivation remains omni-present. Eliminate the bench strength and you lose that Big Brother motivation.

2. Reactionary hiring is less selective.

Too many pressured sales managers make quick, reactive personnel decisions because "any body is better than no body." Empty territories cause substandard team performance, ratcheting up the pressure. They also increase the manager's burden of additional work. Consequently, the manager is tempted to hire the first close fit he or she finds. Rarely do reactionary hires produce an impact player.

3. Reactionary hiring managers tend to overestimate previous sales experience.

This frustrating "snap-the-pencil" problem is far more widespread than it should be, because "Plug and play" hiring expectations fail more often than they succeed. Why? Everybody needs to ramp up, regardless how easy a transition seems, but not all managers have the patience to wait. Welcome aboard, here's your budget, where's your forecast?

REACTIONARY HIRING MANAGERS TEND TO OVERESTIMATE PREVIOUS SALES EXPERIENCE.

Unrealistic plug-and-play expectations are mushrooming coast-to-coast, industry-to-industry, due to ever-increasing pressure on sales managers to deliver absolute results. These unrealistic expectations squeeze the rep from both ends because (1) reactionary hires create a managerial urgency for immediate results to offset open territory losses and (2) excessive turnover hurts customer relationships and tempts customer defection.

Sales experience is only good for two things, leadership and performance.

Just because someone has sold before doesn't mean he or she can role model the profession's critical success factors. There are *millions* of experienced salespeople walking the streets who can't create value in a competitive marketplace, much less build, sustain, protect, or communicate that value under pressure. The number of skilled *value creators* is far smaller than the demand. The odds of finding one whenever you want one are very, very slim.

4. Cutbacks don't mean "cut corners."

As more and more publicly traded firms use the term "shareholder value" as a code word for "stock price on Wall Street at this exact minute," revenue shortfalls are offset by knee-jerk reactionary expense controls.

Companies operate with either a marketing-oriented philosophy or from an expense-managed point of view. Because of that, sales organizations sometimes fall into a tar pit of cut corners. This is especially common in high-turnover organizations. Stability matters in selling, especially with customers. Erase the rep, erase the relationship. It's important to insulate your customer relationships during times of belt-tightening. Never think that substituting face-to-face sales calls with emails and phone calls is seamless. It's not. It's a very risky strategic downgrade.

Companies view the money involved at bettering its revenue generators in one of two ways, either an investment or expense. Non-revenue generators see it as an expense. Revenue generators see it as the required "preventive maintenance" that must be done to keep the pistons firing. Investing in better techniques means better work every day. Better work every day helps produce better results.

If you sell cheaply or have a "lifer" work force that supports the product more so than sells it, or if price, not talent, moves what you sell, then save a nickel.

But if your goal is to maximize profitable revenue growth, invest. *Don't be shy about holding your salespeople to a "best in class" standard.* Raise the bar, invest what's needed, cull the weak, and reward the overachievers.

This Alphonse and Gaston dance over whether money spent on sales talent development is an expense or an investment can put a governor on a company's sales engine. Great sales pros are made, not born. Objectively measuring what they *know* is easy—just give them a test and grade it. Measuring what makes them *great* is a heck of a lot harder.

Measurement is a hot topic these days, especially in Six Sigma-driven cultures, and is a topic we will expand upon later. Too many companies get all knotted up trying to objectively measure a subjective, invisible thing.

5. *Paper-shuffling managers weaken the onboarding process.*

Virtual teams are increasing, span of control is widening (too wide in many cases), effective coaching is a dying art, and rep development is, more often than not, an oxymoron that's left to the ingenuity and survival instincts of the salesperson. While pulling people out of the field to coach them and make them better is seen by sales leadership as an investment in people with a multiplicative upside payback, accounting views it as a direct expense.

There are four onboarding steps every new sales rep must travel en route to successfully integrating to a level of contributory proficiency. Since this topic is elaborated on in great detail later in the book, for now suffice it to say there are very specific reasons some companies onboard talent well and get good production quickly, while others flail.

When onboarded successfully, with expectations matching reality, a good rep will perform at a consistent level of performance. At this stage—the fourth step of the road they must travel—you finally receive a positive return on your money, time, and resource investment.

When preconceived expectations do not match reality, reps are vulnerable to de-commit emotionally. Bailouts happen here, some forced, some voluntary. Early exits cost a ton of money. A company I worked with was losing $24 million a year here, losing one-third of thousands of new hires within six months. They blamed it on the people, which was silly. Each exiting rep was basically a bad debt expense—

uncollectible. Until the company owned its cost of turnover, it didn't step up to deal with the true causes of exodus.

Companies that struggle with sales integration and retention must increase the hiring manager's accountability. Managers must own the success of their people, especially during a new hire's ascension through the four-step onboarding process. Too many field managers hire someone on Monday, give him or her an ID badge and territory list on Tuesday, and call to ask for a forecast on Wednesday. This is especially common with remote reps, where distance and expense combine to make it financially and logistically cumbersome for a hiring manager to maintain personal interaction. Disengaged managers track activities and blame the rep for a performance shortfall. Browbeats, threats, and cajoling are not the furniture of a motivated environment.

TOO MANY FIELD MANAGERS HIRE SOMEONE ON MONDAY, GIVE HIM OR HER AN ID BADGE AND TERRITORY LIST ON TUESDAY, AND CALL TO ASK FOR A FORECAST ON WEDNESDAY.

Onboarding smartly, especially in tough financial environments, is more science than art. Doing it right is never an accident, the byproduct of which pays off in better retention and a quicker zoom up the effectiveness curve. Accelerated assimilation yields more profit, faster.

6. *Line of sight.*

Racehorses require equine vets, not neighborhood vets, so sales talent development belongs in sales, not in Human Resources or Organizational Development. There is little chance that even a great H.R. or O.D. team could dissect and fix a sales problem or talent development issue, since revenue shortfalls are rarely solved by tactics in lieu of strategies. Cleaning house, recruiting in a slew of new people, and watching wide-eyed new hires trying to ramp up the effectiveness curve won't deliver the numbers. Well intended or not, H.R. and O.D. don't know the ropes. Sales is a profession, doubly so at the value creation level, and the development of revenue generators needs to stay housed inside the profession.

THE CARNEGIE HALL FACTOR

A lost tourist stops an old man on a Manhattan street corner and asks, "How do you get to Carnegie Hall?"

The old man squints at the tourist, then rubs his chin. "Practice," the old man decides. "Practice, practice, practice."

The same holds true for selling. Gone are the corporate mother lodes, the traditional process of sourcing, hiring, shaping, molding, and relentlessly coaching the next generation of assembly line, white collar salespeople virtually extinct. In its place is a mad scramble for talented mercenary job-hoppers whose proven skills make them hot commodities for recruiters, the ongoing targets of very competitive courtships.

Today talent comes wherever you find it, typically in small numbers rather than *en masse*. Post an important position on an electronic job board and watch what happens: An avalanche of unqualified people will bury the handful of applicants who might be. The funnel overflows with suspects. Who among them is worthy of Carnegie Hall? Top-shelf salespeople hired to succeed in a politically charged world of high stakes business-to-business relationships must exercise, and act upon, sophisticated thought-processes on a disciplined basis. These men and women are the Carnegie Hall musicians of their chosen profession. With polished professional bench strength now a corporate dinosaur, where will companies find its next generation of talents skilled enough to play at this level?

> **WHERE WILL COMPANIES FIND ITS NEXT GENERATION OF TALENTS SKILLED ENOUGH TO PLAY AT THIS LEVEL?**
>
> **EASY: STEAL IT OR DEVELOP IT!**

The answer is easy: steal it or develop it.

In lieu of the old blue chip talent factory, a sleeper

source for developing next generation sales talent could be the military. Exiting veterans might supplant the traditional blue chip incubation farms as the most fertile source of new mid-market sales professionals because servicemen and women will be emerging with three disciplines and one big X-factor that smart sales talent developers can quickly be able to build upon: They are accustomed to working together in pursuit of a shared vision, have disciplined work habits, and understand the importance of flawless execution. The X-factor is that many will be hungrily motivated by the opportunity to earn multiples of what they used to make, raising the standard of living they and their families enjoy. Vets like driving company cars and BMWs just as much as civilians.

College business schools, another possible source of future sales impact players, are missing the market because fewer than two-dozen American universities offer professional selling as a concentrated area of study. Smart sales recruiters will focus on the schools that do.

IMPACT FACTOR #3: THE USE, MISUSE, AND INCREASING ABUSE OF EVOLVING TECHNOLOGY

The *good* news: More info than ever before is at our fingertips.

The *bad* news: Most folks aren't good at managing it. Workers are finding themselves increasingly busy but decreasingly productive, overwhelmed by everything available; unable to synthesize the merger of tools and information into high impact messages, professionally delivered. All the information available via the Internet means nothing unless its bounty can be sifted, with the trash thrown out and the salient data parlayed to a salesperson's strategic benefit.

This is obviously a hot topic, since everyone is entitled to their own opinion concerning the pluses and minuses of emerging technology and its impact on behavior.

"Before we relied on computers, we had to learn things," said billionaire tech entrepreneur Mark Cuban. "Now you simply have to know where to find it."

Not everyone share's Cuban's view that a computer is a handy substitute for a brain.

"The Internet is like one of those garbage dumps in Bombay," said retired M.I.T. scientist Joseph Weizenbaum. "There are people, most unfortunately, crawling all over it, and maybe they can find a bit of aluminum, or perhaps something they can sell. But mainly it's garbage." Weizenbaum, obviously, champions independent thought.

One of the world's richest men sees things differently. In interviews, Bill Gates often underscores Microsoft's determination to bring computers much closer to people than they are today. Gates predicts computers will evolve with a level of personal interaction and dependence that few can visualize. "Operating a computer by speaking to it is likely in the future," he said to BBC interviewer Jeremy Paxman. "One of the things you'll be able to select is the personality."

Among future visions is the Tablet PC, a device with handwriting recognition software that Gates believes will replace the need for pencil and paper. Such innovation will continue to reshape behavior. The debate rages whether this is a good or bad thing. Sales professionals make their living by influencing behavior. Having computers change human behavior might make selling even more difficult.

The less rosy flip side to Gates' future vision was voiced by Fresno State chemistry major David Cano after a date text-messaged him nineteen times in one night to ask about the state of their relationship.

"That's being hooked on texting," he said, "not hooked on me. When I talked to her on the phone, conversations lasted two minutes."

Like it or not, sales leaders will inherit Cano's girlfriend's peer group in the next wave of entry level candidates. The Next Generation is the Text Generation, so it's vital to ponder the impact of evolving technology and behaviors on your current and future sales force.

THE NEXT GENERATION IS THE TEXT GENERATION, SO IT'S VITAL TO PONDER THE IMPACT OF EVOLVING TECHNOLOGY AND BEHAVIORS ON YOUR CURRENT AND FUTURE SALES FORCE.

A quick, practical example of the pluses and minuses of sales technology is online learning. The pluses are several: It is an easy, convenient way to archive specific content that can be easily monitored, added to, subtracted from, or modified. Trackable testing programs help make sure sales reps learn what they are expected to know.

Web reliance leaves salespeople open to distraction and wasted time, since sites can be the gateway to as much info as a site owner can load. Content, links, and half the immediate world are accessible via keystrokes. Depending on the robustness of the site, content can be tightly managed or seemingly limitless. Archives can be current and relevant or obsolete and irrelevant.

The pitfall for salespeople is that online dependence creates a silent black hole of endless information down which to disappear. MAXIMUM HORSEPOWER sales organizations know the difference between being busy and being productive. *Busy* nets activity but produces sub-optimum results. *Productive*—defined as "selling more"—is what matters. So, if your sales organization uses online learning, make sure the information is current, essential, tested, and retested. The retest is vital. There is a world of difference between memorization and knowledge. If you tie your people to a video screen, verify they've learned what you're paying them to learn. Never assume that salespeople learn anything by clicking boxes. Test them and retest them.

Keeping with computer terms, the mind space that accompanies our use of technology tools preoccupies our brain's RAM—Random Access Memory. Digital page skimming fuels short-term thinking, best suited for one-dimensional knowledge transfer. It will not inspire reflective, contemplated thought.

The problem comes when companies expect online learning modules to be efficient for anything besides what RAM reading can deliver: knowledge transfer. As a skill development tool, online learning is worth very little. No one gets to Carnegie Hall by reading about playing a violin. They get there by taking lessons and practicing.

Salespeople have one of three preferred learning styles—audio, visual, and kinesthetic—and RAM reading silently (and one-dimensionally) caters to the visual one of those three. Its convenience is superb but its skill impact will be negligible. Over-reliance on computers will actually hinder selling skills, since professional salespeople earn their livings with their ears first and mouths second. Their eyes rank third.

OVERRELIANCE ON COMPUTERS WILL ACTUALLY HINDER SELLING SKILLS, SINCE PROFESSIONAL SALESPEOPLE EARN THEIR LIVINGS WITH THEIR EARS FIRST AND MOUTHS SECOND.

A national team of relationship managers I recently worked with is responsible for the protection and growth of multi-million-dollar customer relationships. Their account visits have been curtailed to reduce expenses, so electronic interactions have skyrocketed. Each relationship manager receives over 100 emails a day, the majority generated internally. Many include forwarded messages and low-value attachments. Consequently, their external relationships have been depersonalized, their influence is weakening, and they are increasingly vulnerable to competition. The account managers see it, feel it, and fear it. Their problems, unfortunately, are predictable; you cannot get closer to a customer by distancing yourself from them.

Email does some things well, other things dreadfully. Relaying finite "need to know" information is good. Using email as a substitute for the telephone is bad. Compared to interactive dialogue, email message creation is slow and it does not transfer tone or emotion. It is also word choice reliant.

Sales is a dialog profession, not a written one, and few salespeople write well. In fact, the vast majority write poorly; it's why they're in sales. That's not a knock—it's a stark reality. This limitation will increase, since spell-check and automatic grammar correction enable workers to duck the work it takes to write better. *This pronounced shift in sales communication channels—from the spoken word to the typed one (from an area of strength to an area of weakness)—is a dramatic sales detriment.* Selling is a voice business, a verbal exchange business, a voice-and-tone and body language business. This shift away from the spoken word to the typed one has ominous ramifications. These relationship managers showcase the repercussions: Depersonalized by a reduction in live interactions, their account influence is eroding, value perception diminishing, competitive advance dissipating. In short order they've become firefighters, not account managers.

THIS PRONOUNCED SHIFT IN SALES COMMUNICATION CHANNELS—FROM THE SPOKEN WORD TO THE TYPED ONE (FROM AN AREA OF STRENGTH TO AN AREA OF WEAKNESS)—IS A DRAMATIC SALES DETRIMENT.

Why? As Pogo said, "I have seen the enemy and it is us."

Emotionally, emails in selling suffer from being *inhuman* interactions that lack a two-way dialogue. Tack on the sedentary and voiceless emotional daily toll from dealing one by one with a hundred emails, and the negative impact is many-fold. Being sedentary slows metabolism, increases susceptibility to weight gain, changes eating habits and/or coffee consumption, weakens self-image, lowers self-esteem, saps energy, and diminishes motivation. It is a very negative spiral.

The problems these relationship managers face aren't theirs alone. They are spreading. In many businesses interpersonal dialogue is being replaced, by choice or mandate, by a dramatic shift toward the electronic exchange of staccato, lifeless text. From a sales point of view, this trend is a harbinger of far more harm than good. Emoticons do not advance strategic dialogue. People do.

TOOL ABUSE: WHY IT STYMIES CAREER DEVELOPMENT

A recent research study underwritten by Hewlett-Packard in the United Kingdom quantified in street terms the impact of chronic email dependence. People addicted to email, the study reported, demonstrate a cognitive loss that is equivalent to someone who has smoked two marijuana cigarettes. Such findings do not bode well for those with a problem who aspire to sell in the complex sale environment.

Are these relationship managers dealing with their hundred emails daily staying busy? Heck, yes, they're busy.

Are they productive? Not nearly as productive as many have vocalized they want to be. Good talent wants to get results. Busy makes them frustrated. Productive makes them proud.

An additional problem the growing misuse of technology creates is that it provides salespeople an easy way to waste a ton of precious time. People speak 180 words a minute. When typing an email, message creation speed plummets. On a words-per-minute basis, the "net pace" of message creation drops to a fraction of what it could be via interactive dialogue. Texting is even worse. Texting is digital shorthand, a "dumbed down" version of email. It's instantly spontaneous, can't convey emotion, and slow. The texting world record-holder is a New Zealand teenager who, blindfolded, accurately typed and sent a 160-character message in forty-five seconds—half the speed of a skilled typist (who's half the speed of an average talker).

 THE TEXTING WORLD RECORD-HOLDER IS A NEW ZEALAND TEENAGER WHO, BLINDFOLDED, ACCURATELY TYPED AND SENT A 160-CHARACTER MESSAGE IN FORTY-FIVE SECONDS—HALF THE SPEED OF A SKILLED TYPIST (WHO'S HALF THE SPEED OF AN AVERAGE TALKER).

Forced to play ping-pong with 500 business-related emails each week, how easy is it for someone immersed in that environment to stay busy? *Simple,* of course! You'll be cross-eyed by Friday but busy all week. How motivating is it to wake up Monday morning, facing another week of the same inefficient monotony? It isn't. Slogging through such tedium does not fulfill a salesperson's life, nor will his or her skills improve. Their talent level will be an endless but eroding plateau.

Over time, as the account managers have experienced, depersonalized communication will weaken value relationships with customers. Behaviors are triggered by feelings and emotions. Since email does not transfer either of those—voice and tone do—attempts to do so electronically are empty or misinterpreted. The strength of the relationship erodes.

Other implications have ominous long-term ramifications for next generation selling. Technology dependence creates reliance; over-reliance leads to misuse. Misuse negatively reshapes behavior both cognitively and physically. Chronic misuse turns into full-blown abuse. Technology abuse, of course, manifests in addictive behavior. David Cano's college dating experience exemplified the problem.

Our brains, as small as they are compared to the rest of our bodies, require 20-percent of the body's blood. Like our limbs, our brains work best with exercise. It's very difficult to hop around hour after hour from thought-bite to thought-bite, immersed in flash after flash of Random Access Memory, and then shift to solving complex, multi-layered business problems when competing against people who think that way all the time. Repetitive, task-oriented RAM thinking reconditions how the mind thinks, acts, and reacts. RAM thinkers challenged with the stresses of complex, competitive, strategic selling is an organizational recipe for disaster.

This growing behavioral conditioning trend inhibits learning and stifles the ability to concentrate and focus on complex problems. I see this as a growing trend in the classroom and it's not good. Strategic salespeople must be able to focus and concentrate, blocking aside distractions. Behaviorally, people are skimming more and studying less.

BlackBerries and similar-functioning products—portable email and cell phone devices—conveniently enable folks to stay in touch "on the fly" wherever they travel. BlackBerries have spawned digital shorthand and two-thumb typing, which abbreviates the email user's RAM memory/messaging process even more.

I have worked with scores of business people who are "addicted" to the tools, to the extent that they cannot focus for an extended period of time on complex business issues that require more than a RAM attention span. These obsessive-compulsive behaviors are impediments to professional growth—and alarming to me. Anytime someone's ability to think, observe, reflect, concentrate, or deduce evaporates in favor of an unknown digital message on a tiny LCD screen, there is obvious behavioral risk.

Used properly, PDAs and BlackBerriers are terrific tools that save time, improve communication, and increase productivity. Misused, they waste time and keep people busy but harm potential efficiency. Chronically abused, they change behaviors, dull attention spans, and create impassable barriers to skill development. In the hands of the chronically addicted, I have seen the tool dictate the behaviors of the person, not vice-versa. My saddest testimony to tool addiction is the car wreck of a friend and coworker whose life has forever changed in the aftermath of a near-fatal car crash. He was multitasking as he drove, absorbed with his PDA, and drifted off the road. Upon impact, his gifted life exploded into a nightmare. Technology will never replace his life today, restore his cognitive capabilities, nor free him from his wheelchair. Gone is the life he used to live.

In the context of professional sales development, improving people becomes almost impossible when the chronic abuse symptoms arise: ruptured attention spans, poor listening, rushed and assumptive conclusions, and ill-thought-out answers. All of these reflexive behaviors, individually and collectively, erode someone's chances of developing high-level selling skills and degrade their strategic sales effectiveness.

In the classroom, technology addicts struggle to concentrate and lack focus. They make substandard skill development students with low learning retention rates and have little probability of behavioral change. While they might be quick to grasp a concept, the idea is typically RAM-processed, usually forgotten and not internalized. Since their retention levels are low, their demonstrated ability to prove the mastery of key concepts is usually below that of better-focused, less-distracted students.

THE GOOD NEWS ABOUT CHRONIC TECHNOLOGY ABUSE

On the flip side, technology distraction creates a great sales opportunity for people smart enough to guard against it. When your people insulate themselves against traps their competitors are falling into, your people will gain a competitive edge. With the chasm between the addicted RAM-thinkers and controlled strategic-thinkers widening, the opportunity to behaviorally separate from competitors continues to grow. Teach your people to control their mind space and behaviors, and they will have a big edge when competing against others who don't.

So, if you and your sales organization are tethered to technology, the key question you must answer is whether those tools are keeping your people *busy* or *productive*. With the trend toward busy, hold your team accountable to a higher standard. Insist that they control their own behaviors. Be firm if you have to.

As more and more companies archive and gateway everything imaginable while dumping half the planet onto their own intranets, the lure of getting buried beneath it all will stay ever-present. There exists, of course, great value to be gleaned from relevant information critical to advancing a sale. Finding it, however, tends to be the art form. Distilling, synthesizing, packaging, and presenting what you need to advance the sale can mean there are more decisions than ever before on what to keep and what not to. At every stage there's the chance to stay busy but to operate at less-than MAXIMUM HORSEPOWER. The challenge, today and tomorrow, will be managing time and tools so that *you* are managing them and they aren't managing you.

> TEACH YOUR PEOPLE TO CONTROL THEIR MIND SPACE AND BEHAVIORS, AND THEY WILL HAVE A BIG EDGE WHEN COMPETING AGAINST OTHERS WHO DON'T.

Salespeople will only improve their results if they work harder or smarter, so instant or easy access to endless information becomes either a helper or a hindrance. In sales, working harder means longer days, more calls, more stress, and more (sometimes electronic) paperwork. For managers, working harder means more hours, more activity tracking, more inspection, and less patience, which can create more stress for everyone in their quota-bearing vortex. Working harder can drive short-term results, but long-term activity tracking usually drives talented performers right out the door. Every time you run a good salesperson off, you have to go find another one and help him or her up the efficiency curve. Depending on your business model that may or may not be a trade you're anxious to make.

The ideal, of course, is to enable your sales organization to work smarter. Smarter means many things: working with a heightened sense of urgency, increased sales call effectiveness, more effective value generation, better decisions tied to time investments and divestitures, increased hit rates [wins/attempts as a percentage], better margins, improved account control, bid avoidance, customer retention.

Tools, then, either help or hinder the "working smarter" behaviors. Scrutinize your internal processes. How do your tools influence the behaviors of your revenue generators? How do your top performers use those tools in contrast with your low performers? What speeds things up? What bogs things down?

MAXIMUM HORSEPOWER requires strengthening the influential effectiveness of our revenue generators. Doing so means removing unnecessary crutches of digital dependency, policing bad habits, and becoming a student of behaviors both good and bad.

Scrupulously guard your people against over-dependence, since over-reliance stifles creative thinking. Remind your people to value their brains more than their BlackBerries. There's a great life in the mind, one that travels way beyond where Google and PowerPoint stop. In the world of complex dealmaking, it's vital to challenge your people to thrive by using their tools to support deeper, creative thought.

CUSTOMERS HIDE, TOO

Customers, of course, abuse and hide behind technology, too. They are susceptible to reshaped behaviors and the generation of bad habits, just like we are. The customer having access to more information than ever might seem imposing to a sales rep, but access doesn't mean the customer knows what it all means. Do not allow your reps to let their customers disappear down the rabbit hole of digital isolation. Selling is a dialogue sport, in-person and on the telephone. Protect those means of communication at all costs.

Use multiple communication channels if necessary, but it's vital to stay in touch with your customer base. If you don't, trust me: competitors will.

If your customers submerge in their digital submarines and you do too, the communication problem is doubled. It's tough to sell digitally. Very tough.

Tool use, of course, is habit-forming. Habits are made and can be broken. Police what's going on with your people, and with their key accounts.

> IT'S TOUGH TO SELL DIGITALLY.
>
> VERY TOUGH.

IMPACT FACTOR #4: IMMIGRATION AND THE CHANGING FACE OF SALES PERSONNEL

America used to be a melting pot. No longer. Now it's a sizzling wok and fajita grill, culturally diverse workers tossed together like stir fry. Thanks to relentless immigration, social demographics are changing.

Mixing the traditional majority white American sales force with relentless infusions of millions of ethnic workers continues to reshape the landscape of America's sales force. In America, Hispanic-owned businesses are up thirty-one percent in the past five years, a number expected to continually trend northward.

> AMERICA USED TO BE A MELTING POT. NO LONGER. NOW IT'S A SIZZLING WOK AND FAJITA GRILL.

Changing demographics provide immediate opportunities to cultivate a new source of eager-to-learn sales professionals. The impact of changing demographics also extends to the flip side of selling, because ethnic leaders are playing increasingly large roles in customer decision-making.

First-generation immigrants usually arrive in America seeking opportunity, not a retirement home on a golf course. Second-generation immigrants are eager to learn and armed with better command of both the language and social nuances of the society they've grown up in, so they gain quicker business traction.

On the professional selling side, the immigrant sales pool doesn't have the benefit of growing up in an environment of built-in familial coaching similar to what Baby Boomers and their offspring have enjoyed. Most immigrants arrive from impoverished nations where price is king and pennies matter. Teaching second-generation immigrants how to succeed in the value-driven marketplace requires sales talent development and reinforcement coaching that must come externally, on the job rather than in the home.

Smart businesses embrace cultural diversity. They recognize the opportunity to tap into this exciting pool of new, eager-to-learn talent. Western Union is a great example. While many companies talk about diversity, modestly reconfigure, and/or offer diversity awareness training sessions, the legendary financial services company was at the forefront of bear-hugging multicultural selling. Under the leadership of President Christina Gold and Senior Vice President Royal Cole, in 2003 the company moved swiftly to ethnically reshape its sales force to mirror its consumer base.

Royal Cole was straightforward in explaining why. "People want to do business with people like themselves," he said at the time. "We all do."

Western Union's payback was swift. Revenues boomed to record levels, profits grew despite an increasingly competitive global money-moving marketplace, and agent attrition (a key gauge of customer loyalty) decreased. Sales turnover now hovers at barely 10 percent. The go-to-market efficiency of the organization's vision and execution is a textbook example of how forward-thinking multicultural investment, smart hiring, talent development, and teamwork improves a good business.

LIKE FATHER, LIKE SON (OR DAUGHTER)

Aside from immigration, a second difference between this sales generation and previous ones is that the children of the post-war Baby Boomers are in the workforce. On the heels of World War II, America was a manufacturing country, domestically producing goods bought and sold from coast-to-coast. We bought from each other, not China. The husband was the breadwinner, the wife stayed home with the kids, cigarettes were the norm and cocktails were at five. Selling was a popular, well-respected head-of-household profession.

The post-war children, the Baby Boomers, were raised in the economic surge that followed the nation's expanding manufacturing boom. Sons were raised appreciating the role of the salesman in society and learned from their fathers, often within a dual-parent familial structure. Much like doctors beget doctors, lawyers beget lawyers, and children of good athletes often become good athletes, children of good salespeople grew up learning how to influence others and how to sell. Women began being accepted as sales professionals, too. So were African-Americans, whose talent had been suppressed by a nation divided.

Thanks to imprinting and osmosis, successful post-war salesmen begat the next generation of salesmen and saleswomen and it was this second generation who learned the growing importance of differentiation and value. As market alternatives multiplied, a premium was placed on a higher level of professional selling. Techniques evolved from the hard sell to a softer one. Selling styles become customer-focused, more subtle and sophisticated. The older-school hammering style of the "hard close" sale that typified the product-centric style of the 1960s and 1970s stopped working and gradually faded away.

In addition to changing selling styles, also changing were employee attitudes toward loyalty. Post-World War II workers were lifers, loyal to the company. Boomers learned the hard way that company loyalty isn't always reciprocal. So while the profession of selling passed on from one generation to the next, the loyalty factor wasn't.

Employment loyalty in the U.S. will continue to be worker-centric. The dramatic exodus of manufacturing across oceans means that things that used to be made in America now will arrive in sea cargo containers, the mystical offspring of invisible creation. Product life cycles are shorter, coming and going quicker and cheaper than ever before. A sales pro's allegiance is to him or herself, since products, jobs, and companies that are here today might not be here tomorrow. The king of global business, Bill Gates, admitted as much nearly a decade ago during an interview with the BBC: "Eventually," he said, "all companies are replaced."

EMPLOYMENT LOYALTY IN THE U.S. WILL CONTINUE TO BE WORKER-CENTRIC.

Family dynamics have changed, too. Post-Boomer America reflects its own social and familial structure. Families split up, trading the traditional two-parent household for the changed dynamic of a single parent arrangement or nuclear remix formulated by remarriages. Gone, as a result, is much of the uninterrupted parental imprinting and daily coaching that was part of the "like father, like son" continuity of family stability.

A third change dynamic in the sales workforce pool is that now both female and minority sales professionals, who were *persona non grata* during the post-war boom, are earning their way to better careers, and progressing up the executive escalator. They are reaching new goals—along the way earning money, power, responsibility, and a personal fulfillment that comes with a better life.

Whereas the Boomers' sons are the third generation of modern American salesmen, women and minorities are now beginning their second generation of salespeople. Showcasing millions of talented female and minority salespeople is something the sales landscape didn't have a generation ago. Two of the toughest recruitment job requisitions a headhunter has to fill are for a female sales superstar and a high-potential minority talent. The diamonds of the recruiting business, they are preciously scarce. There are not near enough to go around.

WHEREAS THE BOOMERS' SONS ARE THE THIRD GENERATION OF MODERN AMERICAN SALESMEN, WOMEN AND MINORITIES ARE NOW BEGINNING THEIR SECOND GENERATION OF SALESPEOPLE.

THE GREATEST PROFESSION

Selling is the purest of all professions: colorblind, gender-blind, and age-blind. Above all it is fair, which is all a motivated person asks. When seeking to carve out a good living, any good salesperson—male or female—is quite happy to compete.

Consequently, the selling profession benefits tremendously from having an expanding number of women and minorities enter its force. The challenge will be holding that growth model steady in view of declining birth rate; population data dictates that the future pool of potential legacy sales pros will statistically diminish. The innovative sourcing and recruiting of available talent will increase in difficulty, heighten in importance, and rise in cost.

While much of the American sales landscape is watching its first generation of great female and minority salespeople in action, the second generation is on its way.

The second generation will be significantly more powerful, having benefited from the role models, mentors, and peers who shape and inspire their careers. The marketplace will change. Forward-thinking companies will flourish. Slow-reactors will wither and die. Which will your company be?

For these four reasons—a changing market, corporate repositioning, evolving technology, and a changing demographic—the time is *now* to strategically strengthen your salespeople. Do so and they'll sell more. Probably stick around longer, too.

But if you opt not to, but your competitors do, who will checkmate who?

CHAPTER

THE FOUR BARRIERS TO SALES PERFORMANCE

WHY SOME REPS DON'T SUCCEED

Sales is a rollercoaster livelihood, blessed and cursed, with adrenaline highs that flood dungeons of rejection. Nothing in business feels quite as good as winning, but the reality of the sales profession is that nobody smiles all the time. When you're winning, you wish the day would never end. When you're losing, sundown can't come quickly enough.

In any sales environment, there are four main barriers to sales performance: can't do it, won't do it, prevented from doing it, and skill shrink (the erosion of effectiveness over time). When the ill winds blow and performance tanks, one of these is the culprit. The first two have internal remedies. The third often comes from factors that are external and uncontrollable. Listed below are thumbnail dissections of the first three barriers to performance, followed by a discussion on *skill shrink*.

CAN'T DO IT

Since knowledge can be taught and skills can be developed, *Can't Do Its* are remedied by education and skill practice. Every rep is accountable for his or her proficiency development. Don't blame dead weight if you've contributed zilch to helping the rep gain the necessary knowledge or to better his or her skills. If knowledge transfer and skill practice have not increased proficiency, neither foster nor tolerate relentless futility. In sales we are all accountable for our bottom-line results; the customer's money casts the deciding vote on sales competency—for the rep, or against him or her. If your person loses the election, have a heart-to-heart. If necessary, make a change.

Focus: Internal. These are competency problems. The solutions rest with the reps, the hiring and onboarding managers, and the sales leadership team.

Likely causes:

- Knowledge gaps
- Skill gaps
- Unbridgeable gaps

KNOWLEDGE GAPS

When a motivated talent is giving effort but struggles to succeed, the first question to ask is whether he or she has command of the job's essential body of knowledge. Common causes of knowledge gaps include:

- *No proof of knowledge prior to hire.* Never mistake experience for knowledge. Knowledge correlates directly to absolute results, and people either have enough to sell consistently or they don't. If you assume someone possesses astute industry insight, then find out they don't, whose fault is it? Trust but verify. Test if you can. A lot of empty suits are professional interviewers who B.S. a whole lot better than they sell.

NEVER MISTAKE EXPERIENCE FOR KNOWLEDGE. A LOT OF EMPTY SUITS ARE PROFESSIONAL INTERVIEWERS WHO B.S. A WHOLE LOT BETTER THAN THEY SELL.

- *Substandard onboarding process.* Too often companies hire people and toss them into the field without adequate preparation. No one can sell products if they don't know the specs, strengths, limitations, competitors, differentiators, pricing boundaries, job empowerments, etc. This is doubly true for products or services that don't dominate their competitive space. Customers can smell incompetence, hate it—and won't buy it.

CUSTOMERS CAN SMELL INCOMPETENCE, HATE IT—AND WON'T BUY IT.

- *Lack of hiring manager ownership and accountability for success.* A sound base provides a stable platform upon which to build. So, just as the rep is accountable for his or her results, so is the hiring manager. The manager must make sure that the required knowledge transfer is swift, thorough, and tested.

  Strong managerial commitment creates an allegiance factor, too. When a rep sees his or her manager committed to success, that rep reciprocates. If the rep feels abandoned or cheated, he or she won't emotionally commit.

  Accountable managers gain four advantages over other managers: a more loyal team, a more motivated team, a better-performing team, and lower, less disruptive turnover.

- *Inadequate ongoing knowledge investments.* Complacency rots potential.

Knowledge comes to salespeople in one of two ways: sought or forced. People who proactively seek and eagerly absorb knowledge can't help but sell better. On the flip side, learning-minimalists wait until business information is forced upon them. If they struggle, it should come as no surprise.

Contrast these two competing workforces: One proactively has knowledge cascading throughout; the other reactively is learning only when something is forced down through the organization. Over time, which one will eat the other's lunch? The former, of course.

Inspire a learning environment and knowledge gaps will diminish. Online learning, both mandatory and voluntary, is a tool that offers an easy way to bridge gaps while assuring informational consistency in the field. Completion of the modules is easy to monitor, although retention of the content is tougher because expediency trumps reflection; also, salespeople often view mandatory online learning as something to be memorized and a speed race against the clock. The quicker they click through, the sooner they're done. To beef up your ongoing knowledge investments, test repeatedly for retention.

SKILL GAPS

Four-thousand students on four continents have taught me that the general competence of the global sales force is a left-heavy bell curve. This curve skews left because the median performer is closer to the worst than the best. Overall, professional selling skills competing in the value-added space are mediocre, so the upside opportunity to improve individually and organizationally remains tremendous. The rewards for doing so are astronomical.

Skills assessment is subjective, so pinning a performance shortfall to a specific skill deficiency is best determined through sales-call observation and client insight. Map every skill problem you detect to a positive developmental opportunity. Do not expect help on skills to come from online training modules. Skills do not radiate out of a computer;

they're strengthened by practice, in context. Unless your company offers a robust portfolio of professionally coached skill-development programs, the quickest remedy might be found externally.

PROFESSIONAL SELLING SKILLS COMPETING IN THE VALUE-ADDED SPACE ARE MEDIOCRE, SO THE UPSIDE OPPORTUNITY TO IMPROVE INDIVIDUALLY AND ORGANIZATIONALLY REMAINS TREMENDOUS.

Because skills must be developed, the work involved with closing skill gaps should always be packaged and presented up and down the organization as a positive growth investment. Don't harp on the cost as an angst-ridden expense. Investing in people fosters loyalty—while helping to boost performance. Motivated attendees who sacrifice field time in skill development sessions are fully aware that they owe the company a return on that investment. Great sessions are uplifting and invest emotional equity in workers. Reps will recommit and repay the company by enthusiastically applying their new skills to drive better results.

Skill development is an investment, not an expense, and provides both tangible and intangible benefits. How big those benefits become often depends upon the coaching and reinforcement environment to which the reps return. When coaching is strong, skills strengthen. Stronger skills drive and deliver better and consistent, absolute results.

The danger in misdiagnosing a *Can't Do It* skill problem isn't guessing wrong about which skill needs to be improved. The danger is in not knowing that a definable, coachable skill deficiency exists. Way too many managers attack performance shortfalls by inspecting activities and intimidating someone to work harder—as if working harder solves the problem. Berating an unskilled performer solves nothing. Better techniques yield *results* that solve problems.

If you've got motivated employees who are trying hard but just can't reach the effectiveness stage, invest the time to observe them in action. Talk to the people they deal with internally and externally. What do those reps do well? What *don't* they do well?

Map what you witness against the role-model skills of others in the organization. Where there's a gap, act aggressively to bridge it. Since not all managers are superb salespeople, make sure that whoever owns the rep's critique (manager or mentor) knows what he or she is looking for. Decisions drawn from observation are only as credible as the observer.

UNBRIDGEABLE GAPS

The hard calls come when you've got someone trying his or her best who keeps failing regardless of what you invest in knowledge and skills. Managers and organizations owe employees a fair chance to succeed if a job matches their knowledge, skills, and attributes (KSAs) or they can bridge to them. If neither is the case, everyone's emotions will grow increasingly strained. A stressed rep can't sell; and a stressed manager can't coach, lead, or inspire.

If change is inevitable, cut the cord and move on, sooner rather than later. Superstar selling is hard for the same reason medical school is hard: not everyone is cut out for it. Having desire is nice, but desire is an attribute and the MAXIMUM HORSEPOWER success formula relies on knowledge and skills just as much as the *want to*.

> **SUPERSTAR SELLING IS HARD FOR THE SAME REASON MEDICAL SCHOOL IS HARD: NOT EVERYONE IS CUT OUT FOR IT.**

Moral of the *Can't Do It* story: When it comes to sales performance, every member of the team is either a part of the problem or part of the solution. Futility is deflating. If someone can't do the job, counsel him or her toward a better career fit, even if that fit is outside the organization.

DEALING WITH "CAN'T DO IT" PERFORMANCE ISSUES

This is a "move them up" or "move them out" process, because it deals head-on with knowledge and skill issues, both of which can be improved.

Isolate the problem into a knowledge, skill, or attribute issue. If it's a knowledge shortfall, work with the rep to determine what body of information needs to be gained, how to transfer that knowledge, and how to measure it against the yardstick of expectation. Knowledge progress should always be measured. Celebrate substantive gain and do not tolerate a slacker. The onus is on the manager and company to help pinpoint the gaps. It's up to the reps to do the work.

If the *Can't Do It* issue isn't knowledge related, chances are it's due to a soft skill set. Skill development is less precise to measure than knowledge, so get a fair assessment on what needs to be strengthened and agree on how it will be worked.

Always use a stair-step approach when developing skills. Work on one element at a time. Most adults are repetitious learners, meaning they've got to repeat a behavior over and over before it sticks. Trying to accomplish too much too quickly doesn't work. Prioritize the skills, develop your interactive in-context learning plan, and practice the heck out of whatever is at the top of your list.

Drill the salespeople until they're sick of it, then drill them some more. When it looks like they've finally got it, make them teach it to someone else. Tattoo them with skill practice—*disciplined effort smartly executed* (DESE). As you coach them through their development, follow the four-step teaching process coined by Cal Ripken, Sr.:

1. *Keep it simple*

2. *Make it fun*

3. *Celebrate the individual*

4. *Explain why.*

AS YOU COACH THEM THROUGH THEIR DEVELOPMENT, FOLLOW THE FOUR-STEP TEACHING PROCESS COINED BY CAL RIPKEN, SR.:
1. KEEP IT SIMPLE
2. MAKE IT FUN
3. CELEBRATE THE INDIVIDUAL
4. EXPLAIN WHY

THE "NET/NET"

Since a *Can't Do It* performance issue results from a person who is trying to succeed but failing, *Can't Do It* performance problems are *not* attribute related. They will be knowledge or skill related. Teach the knowledge, develop the skills, and coach to higher expectations. If, after all of that, the person still can't step up, then move him or her out of that specific role. Sometimes what is frustrating for a person in one role disappears when redeployed to another area of the business.

Skill development should be positive, not punitive. When you take the time to explain *why*, the reps are able to put the foundational learning into context, which enables them to embrace and retain the key learnings.

Solving a *Can't Do It* performance problem involves caring and coaching. Every person on your team is an existing investment. Like other investments, some are more valuable than others. Concerned coaching and smart teaching boost individual and collective performance, which increases the value of your "portfolio." By creating a nurturing environment that coaches to higher expectations, you'll soon be able to wipe out most of your *Can't Do Its*.

If you've earnestly invested in someone who just isn't making the grade, counsel him or her out of the job. Failing at a sales job doesn't make anyone a failure. For example, people who are great at strategic selling are often frustrated by activity-based commodity sales and vice-versa.

For many top performers, high performance and professional fulfillment come after trying (and sometimes failing at) different things. The search for what comes easily and is fulfilling—something someone can love and do well—rarely comes in a straight line. Helping to steer a person in destiny's direction is a noble, rewarding purpose.

"CAN'T DO IT"

DEALING WITH REPS WHO CAN'T GET THE JOB DONE

(Read the plan from the top down. Execute the plan from the bottom up.)
Note: A detailed explanation of how to build these plans is covered in Chapter 6.)

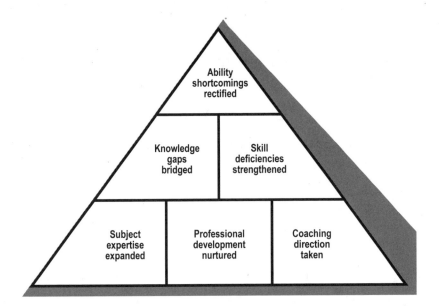

IF IT'S A KNOWLEDGE OR SKILL PROBLEM, YOU CAN FIX IT
BUT IF IT'S AN ATTRIBUTE PROBLEM, YOU'VE GOT TROUBLE.

Willing reps who try hard but just can't do the job often suffer from either knowledge or skill gaps. The want to is there; the ammo to win isn't. Close knowledge gaps and develop relevant skills.

While low performance is frustrating for a manager, it is doubly so for a caring rep. Failure in cases like this usually comes from a mismatched set of Knowledge, Skills, and Attributes (KSAs). The KSAs of the person do not match the KSAs of the job; nor can they be bridged quickly enough to assure ongoing success.

If you've done all you can to correctly diagnose and fix the performance issue, but the desired results remain below standard, make the hard call: Move the employee out.

Nobody benefits from a lingering failure. If necessary, redeploy the person into a role with a better KSA match. If none exists, let him or her go.

WON'T DO IT

These problems are frustrating, because they occur when a rep is quite capable of doing what is expected but chooses not to. *Won't Do It* nonperformance issues are solved in one of three ways:

- *Institute fair rewards, if rewards are lacking but deserved.* Lousy comp plans drive disinterest. Tighten up the pay plan and aggressively award overachievement. Watch what happens. Incentives drive actions. Pay fairly for what's fair, pay big for big things. Avoid a slow wallet when it comes to rewarding earned incentives. After all, the payoffs are funded from the customer's money and the reps know it.

- *Install and follow up with suitable penalties for nonperformance.* If slacking off creates no punitive action, what's the incentive to knuckle down and perform? Private sector people consider the slacker environment "the government worker syndrome." Lifers with no incentive to overachieve and no fear of losing their jobs have no incentive to work at MAXIMUM HORSEPOWER efficiency. The penalty should fit the crime. If introduced, follow up. Toothless tigers that have no bite scare no one. When you want to send a strong message to the team or organization, select the right underperformer for the right reason, and make them pay the price. Word will spread quickly.

- *Double-check to make sure that your rep isn't being taken advantage of by "performance punishment."* With this negative emotional experience, people feel they are being penalized for being good at what they do. When the reward for good work is extra work, human nature eventually will push back. Too often talents are called upon to do extra work because of their proficiency. Once a rep starts thinking, *"The better I am, the more I have to do,"* the more vulnerable he or she becomes to emotional rebellion. The rebelling response is behaviorally predictable: People who feel taken advantage of shut down.

PEOPLE WHO FEEL TAKEN ADVANTAGE OF SHUT DOWN.

Focus: Typically, *Won't Do Its* are people who have the knowledge and skills to do what's required but for some reason choose not to do it. These are internal issues, the fix for which rests primarily with the management team. *Won't Do Its* are aggravating to deal with, because they have what it takes to succeed but choose not to do the work. Erratic and situationally bad performance drives managers batty, because the reps involved are capable. When results sink because their motivational train has slowed, remember the three likely causes:

- Perceived lack of a suitable reward for performing as desired
- Lack of (or lack of enforcing of) a penalty for nonperformance
- Performance punishment ("The more I do, the more I have to do.")

PERCEIVED LACK OF A SUITABLE REWARD

Every parent knows that dangling a trip to Dairy Queen spurs the child to clean his or her room a lot faster than asking pretty please. The kid wants the reward. When a capable rep suddenly shuts down performance-wise, often it's because he or she does not see a suitable correlation between the amount of work effort needed and the reward payoff. In selling, often the reward is money; sometimes it's not. Carrots to a salesperson are the comp plan and recognition. Both drive behavior.

During my career at Xerox, each January the field sales network relied on a handful of high-performance sales vets to act as "compologists." As soon as the company's Rochester headquarters compensation team released the annual incentive pay plan to the field, it was the compologists' responsibility to tear it apart. They looked for leverage, accelerators, and loopholes. Once money drivers were found, word spread. Coast-to-coast comp discussions were as much a part of February as Valentine's Day. As a result, the collective efforts of Xerox's national sales force rode on whatever opinions the compologists offered.

The symptoms of a lack-of-reward shutdown can be obvious or invisible. Performance trends are a good indicator, because a field sales force typically develops an almost militaristic camaraderie. A one-person meltdown is not indicative of a comp plan problem; but if a whole team or region wallows, it very well may be.

Sales comp is a labyrinth unto itself, and tweaks and spiffs typically create one of two pay structures:

One: If you sell a lot you make a lot. If you don't, you don't. Disjoint causes behavioral shutdowns. So incentives should map to things the sales rep controls. When incentives map to uncontrollable things, the sales rep sees it as a tease.

Two: Sales is put in such a narrow comp range that there's no leverage. Overachievers don't like plans without leverage because such plans are, by design, inherently unfair; they target mediocrity and reward sub-par performance. Without leverage, sales comp is a merchandized salary that neither incents, nor rewards, overachievement.

> **OVERACHIEVERS DON'T LIKE PLANS WITHOUT LEVERAGE BECAUSE SUCH PLANS ARE, BY DESIGN, INHERENTLY UNFAIR; THEY TARGET MEDIOCRITY AND REWARD SUB-PAR PERFORMANCE.**

Performance slowdowns can also result from an appropriate lack of recognition, both formal and informal. Smart sales leaders recognize good work both publicly and privately. Salespeople thrive on recognition. When it's earned, give it.

LACK OF—OR LACK OF ENFORCING—A PENALTY

If Dairy Queen doesn't inspire the kid to clean his or her room, unplugging the television will. Just as rewards break nonperformance logjams, so do penalties. Less-than-stellar sales organizations often tolerate lax performance. MAXIMUM HORSEPOWER sales teams work with a discipline that expects each team member to deliver, because sales leadership governs with an expectation of results accountability. Everyone—from the top down—signs up for and role-models a *Can Do, Let's Win* behavior.

Good sales reps are competitive by nature. Foster a *need to win* environment and you'll get better results. When immersed in a winning culture, reps who step out of line or fail to perform should expect to pay a commensurate price.

Soft or inconsistent leadership has the opposite effect. In underperforming sales organizations, the reps usually behave like adult kids. They test you. However much slack they get today, they try for more tomorrow. When nonperformance yields no punitive accountability, where's the need to perform? The need does not exist and, because it does not exist, the results don't come either. Organizational excellence comes via cohesive execution. There is no room for a talent who performs only when he or she feels like it.

In selling, we are all accountable for our results. Never let your people duck that responsibility.

IN UNDERPERFORMING SALES ORGANIZATIONS, THE REPS USUALLY BEHAVE LIKE ADULT KIDS. THEY TEST YOU. HOWEVER MUCH SLACK THEY GET TODAY, THEY TRY FOR MORE TOMORROW.

PERFORMANCE PUNISHMENT

I grew up outside Annapolis, Maryland near the Chesapeake Bay. As a kid I made money by trapping furbearing animals and selling their pelts to furriers who made coats. I loved the outdoors, fishing, and crabbing when the weather was warm; hunting and trapping when frost hit the ground. I left home to attend college and worked my way through school as a meat cutter in a grocery store. I was a tradesman at eighteen, able to cut up anything that moved. For a college kid, it was a great job. I made good money, stayed physically fit, and ate like an emperor.

A few years after college, I was working for Xerox and got invited by a co-worker to hunt deer in middle Georgia. He belonged to a hunting club that leased 400 acres. The acorn-rich land was overrun with whitetails, so the guys I joined easily harvested quite a few.

When it came to cleaning the animals back at the camp, speed mattered because the club abided by a strict rule that no animal was to be wasted. Every deer had to be completely processed and its meat carefully packed in the cooler before anyone was permitted to drive to town to eat. Some of the guys were what the locals referred to as "soft paws," city slickers who drove desks for a living and were clueless about skinning knives.

Watching a soft paw fumble around in slow motion made time stand still. Rather than deal with such delay, I stepped in, grabbed the knife, and swiftly finished the work. I was, by far, the fastest in camp at dressing a deer; my butcher days had taught me how animals are put together.

Eager to be accepted, at first I was happy to volunteer. I cleaned a lot of whitetails in succession, voluntarily at first, reluctantly after a while. By my seventh deer, my enthusiasm waned. After cleaning ten in a row, I finally pushed back. The others stood around waiting for me to disappear inside their dirty work and I flatly declined to take the knife for an eleventh.

"I'll teach *you* how," I said, "but I'm not doing it."

This behavioral rebellion—a conscious shutdown—is very common when people feel they're being taken advantage of. Their reactions are universal: *The better I am at this, the more I have to do it. Phooey! The heck with this. I've had enough. Let somebody else do it for a change.*

When a good player suddenly quits performing, find out why. If it's due to the lack of a suitable reward, offer one. If it's due to the absence of an appropriate punishment, instill one. If it's due to a performance-punishment issue, wise up, back off, and spread the work around. Never let one of your people remain burdened by the yoke of extra work just because he or she is better at it than someone else.

This managerial temptation is often perceived as punitive by the salesperson, whose typical backlash is, "This isn't fair! Make someone else do it for a change!"

Guard against performance punishment, both on your team and in your organization. It's tempting, because most managers come to rely on their "horses" to deliver results. When those horses keep delivering, they keep going back to them, rather than holding others who are slighting to a higher performance standard.

NEVER LET ONE OF YOUR PEOPLE REMAIN BURDENED BY THE YOKE OF EXTRA WORK JUST BECAUSE HE OR SHE IS BETTER AT IT THAN SOMEONE ELSE.

Eventually, overt managerial reliance builds inside the mind of the rep the perception that "performance punishment" is taking place. When this happens, the result is a behavioral rebellion. The aggrieved reaches an emotional conclusion that he or she is being taken advantage of, that what he or she is expected to contribute is out of skew compared to others—that the extra work is a penalty for being good.

The beneficiaries of that person's extra work aren't just the manager and organization, but also the slackers who are allowed to slide by with inferior results. The slackers enjoy lower expectations and, consequently, less pressure. The pressure to deliver stellar performance is greatest on the high performer, because the organization has come to rely on the star to sell enough to carry the others.

DEALING WITH "WON'T DO IT" PERFORMANCE ISSUES

Won't Do Its are the bane of every manager who ever signed an expense report. Few things in business are more frustrating than relying on adequate talent to whom winning doesn't matter, underperformance is acceptable, and getting better is something they don't think about. To these people, the company owes them a living . . . and they don't owe it a return on the investment. These are people who *could* get the job done, but for any one of a number of reasons choose not to.

This problem stems from a lack of energized motivation. Remedies for nonperformance come quickest from whichever is appropriate: the institution of a reward, or the installation and disciplined follow-up of a punishment. Sugar works sometimes;

fear works other times. Sugar is addictive, but after a while what used to be special isn't anymore; rewards become expected and bad habits—slacker habits—return. Fear works in the short term, but in the long term is demoralizing and causes attrition. Regardless of the fix strategy, managers have to juggle brains and resist the occasional urge to drop one on the floor to see if it bounces or toss one against a wall to see if it sticks.

FEW THINGS IN BUSINESS ARE MORE FRUSTRATING THAN RELYING ON ADEQUATE TALENT TO WHOM WINNING DOESN'T MATTER, UNDERPERFORMANCE IS ACCEPTABLE, AND GETTING BETTER IS SOMETHING THEY DON'T THINK ABOUT.

Won't Do It performance remedies work best in a climate of realistic expectations, where the desired behavior is clearly communicated and fairly rewarded. Achievement kudos should be commensurate with the achievement. Negative performance behavior should not be tolerated, especially when it's attitudinal. Curing these problems involves more "between-the-ear management" than what's required to fix knowledge or skill shortfalls. Let nothing go unspoken; confront the performance issue head-on and focus on the work, not the person. These are part of the behavioral ups and downs of a sales career, so keep in mind that personal attacks inspire no one. Derisive comments and negative shots will often spark acrimony and unplanned attrition.

When someone is skilled enough to do a job well and has a proven track record of solid performance, results suddenly turning south are often a symptom of a solvable problem. Once you see the signs, step in and seek to understand why the performance downturn is occurring. Too many ineffective managers address the issue by yelling at their people to sell more. That's not a coach, that's a fan in the stands.

Won't Do Its arise in every sales organization, the exasperating bane of every sales manager, but their solution remedies comes when you solve for the *why*. If you diagnose that a reward is deserved but missing, provide one. If a penalty is missing, install a fair one. If you opt to utilize either of these things—a reward or punishment—always follow through. But if you step back, study the situation, and conclude that you've rewarded your overachievers by dumping more work on them, redistribute the burden.

How many *Won't Do Its* there are in a sales organization can, to some extent, be dictated by a company's culture. Great teams have very few. Weak ones have many. For anyone running a team or organization, it is unrealistic to expect *Won't Do Its* not to pop up from time to time. They will.

The key to maintaining a MAXIMUM HORSEPOWER sales environment is to make sure they don't happen too often or linger too long. Create a culture where *Won't Do Its* are weeded out quickly. Focus on a "How can we" high-performance sales culture. Squelch fixable performance dips as they arise.

When inspired, ordinary people can do extraordinary things—individually and collectively. Challenge your people to prove it.

WHEN INSPIRED, ORDINARY PEOPLE CAN DO EXTRAORDINARY THINGS—INDIVIDUALLY AND COLLECTIVELY. CHALLENGE YOUR PEOPLE TO PROVE IT.

"WON'T DO IT"

DEALING WITH SALESPEOPLE WHO CAN DO THE JOB BUT CHOOSE NOT TO

(Read the plan from the top down. Execute the plan from the bottom up.)

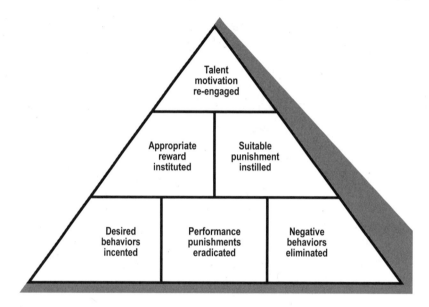

Talent
motivation
re-engaged

Appropriate
reward
instituted

Suitable
punishment
instilled

Desired
behaviors
incented

Performance
punishments
eradicated

Negative
behaviors
eliminated

NIP THESE IN THE BUD, QUICKLY

Nobody who has ever sold has escaped the situational malaise that life's curveballs can toss. When good people who have sold well before start slumping, chances are one of three things is happening:

1. *No perceived reward.* If a reward is merited, grant it. If you grant it, pay it. Never renege.

2. *No perceived punishment.* If a penalty for non-performance is warranted, instill one. Don't overdo it; make sure it fits the crime. If you instill it, follow up on it. Leaders lead, and no good leader tolerates capable people slacking off.

3. *Feels victimized by "performance punishment."* If the reward for good work is more work, a rep will feel taken advantage of. He or she will behaviorally rebel by shutting down.

Remember the motto of American patriot George Simmons, who died on *9/11* inside the plane that was skyjacked into the Pentagon: "No stinkin' thinkin'." If you worked for George, you were a positive leader. If you weren't, you didn't work for George.

Won't Do Its pollute a MAXIMUM HORSEPOWER sales culture. Since non-performance stems from a series of behavioral choices, your job as a sales leader is to identify these scenarios quickly and prevent them from perpetuating. Once you recognize them—deal with them swiftly.

PREVENTED FROM DOING IT

"I have seen the enemy . . . and it is us."

—Pogo

The third barrier to performance comes when motivated talent exert the willingness to do good work but get derailed by roadblocks that are beyond the sales rep's control.

Whenever third-party interference (internal or external) creates a performance impediment, the sales leader's job is to identify the barrier and help to remove it. If it can't be removed, a smart sales leader focuses immediately on a workaround. If there is no way around the barrier, work with a heightened sense of urgency to think up a new plan. If stalemated—without other options—teach your people to have the courage to walk away and shift their focus to the next winnable deal. Too many reps cling far too long to pipe dreams and lost causes . . . *because the manager lets them!*

Dawdling over *Prevented From* sales slowdowns can waste tremendous amounts of time. To minimize that wasted time, aggressively increase the pace of developing and executing the workaround strategy. Because reps are eternal optimists, sales managers and leaders need to help ferret out the true winnability of the deal.

Prevented From problems can arise from barriers that are external or internal, due to: reorganizations, company policies or procedures, traditions, empowerment levels, approvals or protocols. When barriers pop up that are internal—our own creation—every solution must have an aggressive champion. That might be you.

The ramifications of change sometimes straddle organizations, yours and the customer's. Customer reorgs, for example, grind all sales cycles to a halt. Change is disruptive—especially when impacting customer coverage models—and fewer people know how to manage change smartly than those who do. This is discouraging, because changing sales strategies and alignments is common in today's dynamic market. Changing players implodes a lot of sales cycles, too, regardless who is the instigator: the customer or you.

All good troubleshooters dive in and smoke out a *Prevented From* performance problem as soon as they sense one. What is the barrier's root cause? Is the derailment a perception or a genuine, immovable showstopper?

Seek to understand, clarify, and manage by fact. Inspire your reps not to roll over and give up if someone internally gives them a "Can't Because" excuse. Often reps face a barrier and stop because they don't have the perspective that comes from multiple workarounds. They take what they hear at face value, rather than as a starting point for a Plan B workaround. In other words: "They don't know what they don't know."

Never tolerate a "Can't Because" environment, and don't permit a non-supportive internal attitude that throttles your people. Teach your team to live in a world of *"How can we?"* Smart leaders seek to dissect roadblocks and to brainstorm workarounds. Every company features its own political navigation maze, with channels that either dead-end you or usher you to where things will get done. Don't let your people get stymied by frustrating internal barriers. Broker smart remedies.

Customers create both real and perceived barriers. Real might be budget constraints, merger and acquisition logistics. To deal with these, get creative and innovate; Plan B can often sell just as much as Plan A. Help your team think through the upsides and downsides of multiple alternative solutions. Remind them that motivated clients often help find a way to get what they need. When a rep senses sincere customer interest and summons the courage to ask the customer how best the two sides might circumvent the problem, often a motivated customer will figure out the solution.

Many *Prevented Froms* are political by nature, and too many reps operate in a total vacuum of political awareness. They misread political agendas and the true decision-making factors. This, of course, is where instructional coaching pays dividends.

USE CONTRARIAN THINKING

For a great example of creative problem-solving, look no further than under one particular roof in suburban Washington, D.C. where a few of your tax dollars are spent. The CIA uses several techniques to train its agents how to solve troubling challenges, one of which involves contrarian thinking:

If you take everything you believe to be true about a situation, flip-flop it and assume it is false, what will you see differently?

Many times you gain new insight that is key to a winning strategy. Following are some quick examples of contrarian thinking:

CONVENTIONAL VIEW	CONTRARIAN VIEW
We're winning.	We're losing.
We have the necessary political sponsorship.	We don't have the right political sponsor.
They like our value proposition.	They don't like (or don't see) our value proposition.
We understand the decision-making process.	We do not understand the true decision-making process.
We know everything we need to know in order to win.	What don't we know?

Often *Prevented Froms* stem from the evolution of a sale, which makes contrarian thinking so helpful. In major account, big deal selling, it's rarely what we know that derails us. More likely, it's what we *don't* know. So, always be ready to flip around conventional wisdom, challenge it, and problem-solve to circumvent a sales cycle blockade.

IN MAJOR ACCOUNT, BIG DEAL SELLING, IT'S RARELY WHAT WE KNOW THAT DERAILS US. MORE LIKELY, IT'S WHAT WE DON'T KNOW.

WHEN CHANGE CREATES THE IMPEDIMENT

Every time we change sales assignments or coverage models, we also implode the dynamics of customer relationships. Sometimes the relationship disappears. When customers have had their own reorgs to deal with, the resulting emotional and political upheaval can cause sales-cycle paralysis until things settle down. While the aftershocks of customer change may be invisible to your people as they to sell into the customer's organization, these aftershocks exist in a very real and stressful form. A customer's typical reaction to internal change is that their decision-making process grinds to a halt.

Dealing with change smartly can provide a competitive edge, because people tend to respond to disruptions in very predictable emotional and behavioral patterns. Reps typically do not deal with customer change very well. Help them. Coach them though the answers they need to uncover to get to the facts. Sometimes it is easier for managers and sales leaders to ask the tough questions than it is a general line rep.

Teaching change dynamics will help your reps learn how to deal with *Prevented Froms* and eventually lead to better results. In-depth coaching tips dealing with change management are shared in Chapter 10, "Managing the Noise."

DEALING WITH "PREVENTED FROM" PERFORMANCE ISSUES

Prevented Froms cause progress derailment, so the goal is to get a motivated worker with sufficient knowledge and skills back on track and advancing as quickly as possible through his or her sales cycles.

The manager's role is to quickly engage and decipher precisely what the barrier issue truly is (visible or invisible, real or perceived), then offer strategic counsel on how to remove that barrier or skirt around it.

Many reps, especially young ones, fear asking hard questions because the killer question might produce an answer the rep does not want to hear. Good managers never fear asking the hard questions. The remedy begins with ferreting out the truth that is stopping a sales cycle due to an unexpected issue that's arisen outside the norm.

Once a problem is specifically defined, the next question is whether the problem can be removed or worked around. If not, shift focus to Plan B. Time, energy, money—none can be wasted. Problems do not remove themselves; people remove or circumvent them. Do neither and nothing will change; the deal will remain in limbo.

Since creativity sells, a clever alternative adds to Plan B effectiveness, because true creativity in sales is so rare. Mediocre organizations sell by repetitive predictability. Great ones sell creatively. So, a huge differentiator when presenting an alternative to a client is the ability to uniquely *repackage* with an innovative alternative solution.

If you have access to creative problem solving, use it. If you don't have it, seek it. If you can't find it, keep looking. Whatever you do, don't just sit there waiting for *Prevented From* barriers to remove themselves. They won't.

Creative thought involves innovative assessment, like the CIA's contrarian thinking model in which all that's held to be true is flipped around and assumed to be false. This structured methodology creates a kaleidoscopic view of a singular challenge. With this methodical study of multiple viewpoints come new ideas.

If a deal has been worth investing time, it's usually worth winning. When an internal or external barrier impedes progress, engage the resources you need to remove it. Figure out a workaround or innovate a new Plan B.

Whatever you do, don't sit on your hands. Make something happen. Sales cycles that sit tend to be sales cycles that die. Sales cycles that keep moving tend to be sales cycles that close. Keep them moving!

SALES CYCLES THAT SIT TEND TO BE SALES CYCLES THAT DIE. SALES CYCLES THAT KEEP MOVING TEND TO BE SALES CYCLES THAT CLOSE.

"PREVENTED FROM DOING IT"

JUMPSTARTING STALLED SALES CYCLES

(Read the plan from the top down. Execute the plan from the bottom up.)

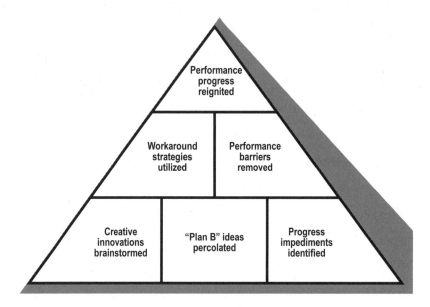

Performance progress reignited

Workaround strategies utilized

Performance barriers removed

Creative innovations brainstormed

"Plan B" ideas percolated

Progress impediments identified

WHEN A DEAL BOGS DOWN, FIND OUT WHY

When a skilled and motivated talent gets stuck, sometimes what throttles him or her are other forces getting in the way. These impediments can be internal or external. When you diagnose a Prevented From issue, there are four actions to take:

1. *Remove the barrier(s).* Many times, managers can fight battles that reps can't.

2. *Figure out a workaround.* If fighting is pointless, accept it and work around it. Politics work nicely here. Study all angles of political ramifications tied to what is at stake.

3. *Scrap the plan that led to the roadblock.* Create a new Plan B and get moving.

4. *Abandon the opportunity and walk away.* Part of smart selling is knowing when to invest time and resources and when not to. One of the hardest things to teach a developing rep is when to walk away. When derailments cannot be circumvented, coach your people to move on to the next prospect. Don't let them cling to false hopes.

Roadblocks are best solved with multiple minds. MAXIMUM HORSEPOWER sales teams pool ideas. They do whatever it takes to help each other win.

SHRINKING SKILLS...& NOWHERE TO HIDE

Without a process of strategic skill development, quality coaching, and ongoing reinforcement, skill erosion is common. As blue-chip developmental sales rep factories have diminished and mediocrity has increased, signs in the sales classroom and marketplace ominously point to "skill shrink" as a growing problem.

Skill shrink is the decreasing effectiveness an individual demonstrates when trying to influence major account selling cycles. Rather than getting *more* effective over time, he or she is becoming *less* effective. When a rep becomes a stale creature of habit, he or she will fall competitively behind. This is a growing problem, because the market is moving so quickly. In many cases, the market moves faster than people are able to adapt.

Bad habits that fester in a vacuum of unawareness will always produce substandard results. Following are nine points why skill shrink occurs. The *why* explanations offer remedy suggestions.

BAD HABITS THAT FESTER IN A VACUUM OF UNAWARENESS WILL ALWAYS PRODUCE SUBSTANDARD RESULTS.

Why Skill Shrink Happens

1. *A computer screen is not a coach.* One-dimensional video screens are supplanting the human fundamentals that used to shape, strengthen, and reinforce improvement in sales talent. For example, an online learning module can't teach someone how to listen; and someone who can't listen will never sell as much as a sales pro who has mastered a cognitive process to archive the content and emotion of what a customer has to say. Weak listening, coupled with a societal movement toward interruptive speaking, weakens a salesperson's impact on a customer during a call. Customers, of

course, are moving the other way. They expect to be heard. If your people can't do it, customers will find suppliers who can.

2. *In a dynamic market of rising customer expectations, someone who cannot craft a strategic plan has less value than someone who can.* Computers don't fix this, either. Coaches do. Value-driven customers want to know where you're taking them and how they'll get there. If your people can't paint the macro picture and back it up with micro necessities, they will lose an increasing number of deals. Customers want smart, relevant advice that quantifies the upside and pinpoints the risks. They have zero tolerance for what Neil Rackham calls "talking brochures."

3. *Fewer opportunities to develop.* Shrunken expenditures result from companies that view talent development as an expense rather than an investment. Without reinforcement intervention, most sales reps don't evolve, and those who don't evolve quickly fall behind. The market is moving, so complacency is a loser's strategy.

4. *Virtual teams, fewer touches.* More managers are driving desks than cars. When desk drivers do get out, they tend to inspect, not coach. Desk drivers shuffle papers; they don't teach. More hours of desk-driving translates into fewer hours in the field, which means even fewer hours of quality coaching. Desk drivers also tend to hire *compliants*, reps who are uncomplicated to manage, never question what they're told, are easy to task manage, are followers rather than leaders. There's an adage in the recruiting business: "A players hire B players, B players hire C players, and C players hire D players." A roster like this, of course, creates a freight train of dead weight.

THERE'S AN ADAGE IN THE RECRUITING BUSINESS: "A PLAYERS HIRE B PLAYERS, B PLAYERS HIRE C PLAYERS, AND C PLAYERS HIRE D PLAYERS."

5. *Less coaching means fewer skilled coaches, creating a dwindling number of **new** coaches.* As the traditional American blue-chip farm system for grooming strategic sales talent shrinks, the need for good coaches grows. Unfortunately, the coaching supply is shrinking, too, a casualty of the strategic selling shortage. Fewer developing coaches mean fewer coaches overall, and fewer coaches translates to fewer coaching opportunities.

6. *Declining sales leadership.* Coaching leaders are on the decline. Task managers are on the rise. Of the two, coaching leaders are the likeliest motivators. Task managers are the likeliest de-motivators. *More task managers = fewer coaching leaders who are able to add and teach strategic value.* There is a big difference between telling someone *what* to do and teaching them *how* to do it better than the competition. The sales profession is growing long on the former and short on the latter.

THERE IS A BIG DIFFERENCE BETWEEN TELLING SOMEONE WHAT TO DO AND TEACHING THEM HOW TO DO IT BETTER THAN THE COMPETITION.

7. *Fewer value-adding contributors.* A decline in skilled coaches means more deadwood in the field, leading to sub-par performance and a competitive disadvantage. Deadwood doesn't grow; it rots. *More dead wood + a competitive disadvantage = Big Trouble.*

8. *Big Trouble = exodus of talent.* When your top talent leaves, you're choked off from sourcing referral hires from where you most want those hires to come—the upper-echelon. Since a skilled sales organization develops by osmosis and cross-pollination, referral hires from low-performing slugs generally aren't worth two bags of dirt. A weak organization hampered by revolving-door talent never improves. Mediocrity leads to clone referrals, none of whom move the performance needle.

A WEAK ORGANIZATION HAMPERED BY REVOLVING-DOOR TALENT NEVER IMPROVES.

9.   *Talent exodus = less time at the effectiveness stage of performance.* Customer attrition, declining revenues, open territories, increased cost-per-hire, etc., are a bad vortex in which to be trapped. Few ambitious talents seek to swan dive into swirling quagmires.

The GOOD News

Sales talent development techniques work for both genders and all cultures. When you invest in strengthening and reinforcing a diverse team by teaching and coaching the proper skill techniques, you help to protect your organization's strength regardless of the changing demographic of the field sales force.

> SALES TALENT DEVELOPMENT TECHNIQUES WORK FOR BOTH GENDERS AND ALL CULTURES.

The BAD News

Inflexible new-school task management doesn't work with a changing field sales populace to whom the competitive edge must be taught. Patience and smart coaching are vital.

The *Watch Out* in all of this is how to strengthen the middle of your bell curve while protecting against the exodus of your top performers. Some companies try to do this by promoting top individual contributors to sales management positions, a traditional reward that is fraught with pitfalls.

The jump from salesperson to sales leader, based on a record of individualized success, often does not work. Gunslingers rarely make good range instructors. Managing generates an entirely different set of positive and negative emotional experiences than solo selling.

Also, for a star salesperson, often a kick upstairs means more responsibility, hours going up—but income heading down. All too soon he or she learns they can't cash a job title. Sometimes this new set of circumstances and group pressures causes the emotional wires of a new sales manager to arc, spark, and pop into a behavioral short-circuit. As a sole contributor, the star controlled his or her own destiny. As a manager, that's no longer true.

Their success is now gauged by the collective results of all the team members, including the weakest link. No longer can the star shine alone. According to a survey by the Sales Executive Council in Washington, D.C., 70 percent of promoted high-performing individual contributors fail to perform at a similar level after being handed a team. Stars can't relate to mediocrity and struggle because of it. They aren't used to relying on less-skilled people. Nor do they have the time, patience, or finesse to teach. When a deal presents itself, they can't resist butting in and taking over sales calls. Such behaviors are dispiriting to the general line sales force and deaden their motivation.

People who feel they aren't growing professionally tend to vote with their feet. In another study, the Sales Executive Council identified stunted professional growth as the number one cause of sales talent attrition. Manager problems ranked second. Money rated third.

> **PEOPLE WHO FEEL THEY AREN'T GROWING PROFESSIONALLY TEND TO VOTE WITH THEIR FEET.**

Well-coached sales talent development, thriving in a MAXIMUM HORSEPOWER environment, positively impacts all three.

Help helps, if you'll pardon the pun. Proactive transitional assistance can decrease the odds that this implosion won't happen in your organization. Statistically speaking, most great sales managers were middle-of-the-pack salespeople, not superstars. Their attributes are the success traits of good leaders, because mid-level salespeople tend to relate well to both underachievers and overachievers.

Nowhere to Hide

Coupled with *skill shrink*, also dwindling in this changing sales marketplace are the opportunities to hide weak sales people behind powerhouse products and brands. Expecting proficiency to radiate from a brand name on a business card is fool's gold. It might get you in the door but it will not earn a second meeting.

Brand differentiations are blurring. Managers must learn how to polish their talent to consistently win in an increasingly difficult selling environment. Helping to *create* proficiency is the new name of the managerial game.

HELPING TO CREATE PROFICIENCY IS THE NEW NAME OF THE MANAGERIAL GAME.

With all of these erosion factors going on, what should you do? If you operate in a problem-solving, value-added, or explanation-oriented sales environment, how can you quickly build for long-term strength?

Raise expectations. Don't sit on your hands. Drive a stronger sales culture. Don't mess around. Here is how to start immediately:

- *Create new hiring opportunities.* If you keep doing what you're doing, you'll keep getting what you're getting. If you're hiding weak talent, cull it. A fresh sourcing approach with multiple innovative prospecting avenues will help drive better talent into your pipeline. Have a fine-tuned process that will enable you to swiftly close talented prospects. Profile precisely what you're looking for and expand where you're searching. Do both and you'll find talent. When you find talent, treat them like gold. Grab them.

- *Foster a coaching and talent development climate.* Great sales coaching is a fading art. Managers must know where to invest their time and where not to waste it. They must know who, what, how, when, and how much to coach. They also need to know who *not* to coach. *(note: This topic is covered in-depth later).*

- *Inspire a positive, retention-oriented environment.* Happy, growing, well-managed sales talents tend to stick around. Creating that environment is the best way to protect against torpedoes mid-ship (revenue-generator attrition).

  Remember, the number one reason salespeople leave is that they are not growing. Number two is the boss. Teaching and coaching positively impact both. A rep who continually learns from a concerned, committed boss will develop loyalty. Loyal people stick around.

- *Maximize customer loyalty via competence, teamwork, and workforce stability.* Upheaval is expensive. Turnover and realignments are annoying to customers and disrupt sales cycles. In a relationship management business, once you change the players, you erase the relationship. Skilled, motivated talent thriving in a stable environment do great work over the long haul. The smartest defenders against competitive inroads use their ears more than their mouths and spend the customers' money as if it's their own. Invest emotional equity in your sales force whenever you can. Integrated teamwork pays the greatest return.

IN A RELATIONSHIP MANAGEMENT BUSINESS, ONCE YOU CHANGE THE PLAYERS, YOU ERASE THE RELATIONSHIP.

- *Insist that everyone is creating, selling, and reaffirming value.* Companies are just like people. They evolve through four distinct life stages: birth, growth, maturation, and post-maturation.

COMPANIES ARE JUST LIKE PEOPLE. THEY EVOLVE THROUGH FOUR DISTINCT LIFE STAGES: BIRTH, GROWTH, MATURATION, AND POST-MATURATION.

Each salesperson's ability to create client value is essential, regardless of which of the four corporate life stages your company is in. External client companies go through exactly the same maturation. Because all corporations continually evolve, what matters to them—their perception of value—will change, also. Being able to send to market a maximum impact sales force, which is relevant to customers in any of the four life stages, is vital.

All four barriers to performance—can't do it, won't do it, prevented from doing it, and skill shrink—are fixable, assuming your sales leaders know how. If they don't, teach them. Business opportunities are too hard to find to let them slip away.

Armed with this knowledge about what derails sales success, on the following pages is a comprehensive list of fifty common sales execution problems. Study it and score your sales organization's current weaknesses. We'll build solutions to these problems throughout the course of the book.

FIFTY COMMON SALES EXECUTION PROBLEMS

Listed below are fifty common problems tied to various stages of the selling cycle. In the column to the right, circle how you rate your team. Seek multiple respected opinions. Your findings will help shape the focus your MAXIMUM HORSEPOWER strategic plan.

	PROBLEM	RATING		
Stage 1:	EFFECTIVE PROSPECTING	Weak	Average	Excellent
1	Can't assemble comprehensive, relevant data.	Weak	Average	Excellent
2	Struggles to build a legitimate prospect list.	Weak	Average	Excellent
3	Prospect list is consistently thin.	Weak	Average	Excellent
4	Lacks prospecting creativity.	Weak	Average	Excellent
Stage 2:	PRE-CALL PLANNING	Weak	Average	Excellent
5	Struggles to formulate a good preliminary value proposition.	Weak	Average	Excellent
6	Weak on framing a good value strategy.	Weak	Average	Excellent
7	Not good at drawing good statistical conclusions.	Weak	Average	Excellent
8	Inefficient at researching and identifying the right level and person to approach.	Weak	Average	Excellent
Stage 3:	APPROACH & VALIDATION	Weak	Average	Excellent
9	Not good with elevator speeches. Struggles to gain interest quickly.	Weak	Average	Excellent
10	Not strong enough. Soft first impression. Struggles to control the approach call.	Weak	Average	Excellent
11	Chronically low-impact. Can't keep the customer actively engaged.	Weak	Average	Excellent
12	Slow to validate the right level(s) of contact.	Weak	Average	Excellent
13	Weak at pinpointing the true decision-making process and stakeholders by name, title, and role in the process.	Weak	Average	Excellent
14	Talks more than listens.	Weak	Average	Excellent
15	Suspect-to-prospect advancement rates are very low.	Weak	Average	Excellent
Stage 4:	DEVELOPING ACTIONABLE INTEREST	Weak	Average	Excellent
16	Struggles to identify value-driven customer problems and improvement opportunity areas.	Weak	Average	Excellent

	PROBLEM	RATING		
17	Not good at building a sense of client urgency.	Weak	Average	Excellent
18	Weak at developing problems via implication questions.	Weak	Average	Excellent
19	Can't create and/or sustain a compelling value proposition.	Weak	Average	Excellent
20	Unsure about when to lead, follow, or get out of the way by engaging the right resources.	Weak	Average	Excellent
21	Doesn't listen well. Interrupts rather than wait to clarify or test understanding.	Weak	Average	Excellent
22	Haphazard unfocused questioning techniques. Struggles to gain meaty info.	Weak	Average	Excellent
23	Not good at differentiating between our offerings and those of competitors.	Weak	Average	Excellent
24	Timid about asking the tough questions.	Weak	Average	Excellent
Stage 5:	**RESOLVING POLITICAL RAMIFICATIONS**	Weak	Average	Excellent
25	Struggles to understand political barriers and enablers.	Weak	Average	Excellent
26	Blind to political winners and losers.	Weak	Average	Excellent
27	Not adept at selling through the political realities of each stage of the selling cycle.	Weak	Average	Excellent
28	Unskilled at gaining political sponsorship.	Weak	Average	Excellent
29	Struggles to stay politically neutral.	Weak	Average	Excellent
Stage 6:	**PROPOSAL CREATION & DELIVERY**	Weak	Average	Excellent
30	Creation ability is unimpressive. Lives and dies by boilerplates.	Weak	Average	Excellent
31	Content creation, messaging, customization, and relevance are weak.	Weak	Average	Excellent
32	Proposal presentation skills are boring.	Weak	Average	Excellent
33	Not good at managing group dynamics.	Weak	Average	Excellent
34	Struggles to gain group consensus.	Weak	Average	Excellent
35	Not relevant to all in the room.	Weak	Average	Excellent
36	Multiple channel mastery is missing.	Weak	Average	Excellent
37	Not nimble on his or her feet.	Weak	Average	Excellent

	PROBLEM	RATING		
Stage 7:	CLOSING	Weak	Average	Excellent
38	Struggles to handle objections and/or is unwilling to push back on tough issues. Often hears clarification and request-for-info questions as objections.	Weak	Average	Excellent
39	Not strong enough at asking for the order and getting it.	Weak	Average	Excellent
40	Not a polished closing style. Too brusque, too meek.	Weak	Average	Excellent
41	Lacks confidence.	Weak	Average	Excellent
42	Caves quickly to price objections, rather than reselling value.	Weak	Average	Excellent
43	Susceptible to being intimidated at crunch time.	Weak	Average	Excellent
44	Not good at knowing when to push the deal, when to wait, when to cut the cord.	Weak	Average	Excellent
45	Unable to match his/her closing style to the preferred buying style of the client.	Weak	Average	Excellent
Stage 8:	POST-SALE OPPORTUNITIES	Weak	Average	Excellent
46	Tends to overcommit by setting "perfect world" expectations.	Weak	Average	Excellent
47	Scared to deliver bad news.	Weak	Average	Excellent
48	Underperforms at unearthing expansion and revenue growth opportunities.	Weak	Average	Excellent
49	Not good at engaging resources to tackle complex opportunities outside their comfort zone (i.e., doesn't proactively ask for help).	Weak	Average	Excellent
50	Weak at matrix contact management.. Ineffective at developing new contacts vertically and horizontally throughout the account.	Weak	Average	Excellent

WHERE ARE YOUR WEAKNESSES?

MAP EACH "WEAK" RATING INTO THE SELLING CYCLE

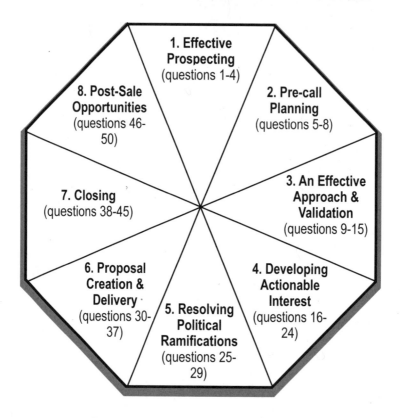

MAP YOUR CHALLENGES

Review the previous list of fifty common sales problems. Transcribe the number of each "weak" rating to the appropriate stage of the selling cycle.

This scattergram lets you quickly dissect the shortfall behaviors of your organization, see where your team is most vulnerable, and pinpoint which stage(s) of the sales cycle must be strengthened. Bringing smart focus to strategic talent development will help to create maximum impact with minimum investments in time and money.

Competitors will repeatedly attack wherever you are weakest. If you noted a weakness, they already know it. Strengthen those areas and you will improve your customer impact and competitive positioning, while boosting the confidence of your salespeople.

By taking the time to map your team's limitations, you will be able to bring strategic focus to what sales-cycle priorities matter most. This quick tool helps maximize your human and financial ROI.

CHAPTER

THE HUNT FOR THE PURPLE SQUIRREL

HALLMARK SUCCESS TRAITS OF GREAT SALESPEOPLE AND TEAMS

"Eagles don't flock. You have to find them one at a time."
– H. Ross Perot, American executive and philanthropist

A friend of mine, Greg Garrison, is a staffing expert in Austin, Texas. We frequently bounce ideas off each other, because he makes his living by matching clients with talent and I make mine by evaluating and developing talent already hired. Greg works the mouth of the pipeline; I'm farther back, mid-pipe so to speak.

While his business involves sourcing a much broader range of talent than my world of sales, the reality of the staffing life is that everybody is selling all the time. Greg has to sell senior execs on the merits of his firm's services, staffing leaders on his company's competencies, candidates on an opportunity, hiring managers on the candidate, etc. Greg's is a tough industry because his products are human: flawed creatures with strengths and weaknesses, track records in place but their promise unfulfilled.

Finding great talent can be a maddening game, because there's a lot that goes into it. Seeking and selecting the right person to slide into the right slot at the right time to do the right thing—better than anyone else in that competitive space—is sometimes a Herculean challenge. Securing major players is a team sport and a lot of people are involved, even after the talent is located.

Once identified, the real game of candidate-chess begins. Gaining hiring agreement must come quickly enough to lock down the right candidate. No talented player sits idle. He or she is a product unto him or herself, and skilled revenue generators can quickly create multiple options for themselves in an increasingly competitive job market.

Not only does the offer have to be right, the chemistry between the courted and the suitor needs to mix, not combust. Metaphorically speaking, the strategic staffing business is a series of human horse races. Candidates are sourced and lined up next to each other as if in a starting gate. Each contestant loads in with anxious anticipation, hopeful to be the one from the group who will surpass all the others and will get to pose with a smile in the winner's circle.

However, as all of these eager candidates collectively poise to run, each is standing alone. Each will race with a varying talent level, a different experience history, and unequal preparation. The candidates also offer a full spectrum of differing potential. All will run this race, as well as future races, with fluctuating degrees of competitive success.

Once the bell rings and the race begins, the contestants will run their personal best in their own unique style. Lacking an experienced jockey to steer every step, not every candidate will run in a straight line; some will veer erratically, maybe even crash and not finish.

In theory, the winner—the best candidate—is awarded the job. In reality, that doesn't happen. Shockingly often, the hiring manager rebuffs the top candidate. There are several reasons the winner of this human race is disqualified.

IN THEORY, THE WINNER—THE BEST CANDIDATE—IS AWARDED THE JOB. IN REALITY, THAT DOESN'T HAPPEN.

Many hiring managers are intimidated by great talent and prefer to manage someone with a lower profile who will be easy to manage; precocious stars are threatening. Managers often pass on the best candidate and settle for someone further down the line: a compromise candidate. On the flip side, sometimes a terrific candidate gets tired of waiting for a series of interviews and pulls out of being considered.

The reason these searches often end in frustration, Greg explained, is that the corporate hiring managers are looking for "purple squirrels."

"You bring them a close-to-perfect candidate," he said, "one who matches the criteria and interviews great but isn't a purple squirrel. They're a gray squirrel, just like everyone else on the team. It's a team of gray squirrels, but suddenly the manager needs a purple one. You finally find one, but the purple squirrel has needs of its own that are different from gray squirrels. Those differences don't match the comfort level of the hiring manager. The hiring manager can look forever, as long as he or she wants, but there aren't a lot of purple squirrels out there. Even if you find one, they're different animals. To a lot of people, purple squirrels are very threatening."

Purple squirrels command a hefty premium in terms of time, energy, and money. If a company clamoring for a purple squirrel balks with sticker shock at forking over that premium, usually because they're concerned that their comp plan will become skewed, the hunt has been a colossal waste of time for everyone involved.

Greg Garrison's message, of course, is that recruiting a high-performance sales team from the outside is wishful thinking unless the sales leadership organization is committed, talented enough, confident enough of its own corporate standing, and willing to pay.

Buying a high-performance sales team comes at a multiple premium ante in terms of money, leadership, and political digestibility.

Rather than stare out the window waiting for a herd of purple squirrels to stand on their hind legs and knock at the door, Greg believes it's smarter to take a fast gray squirrel who has a great work ethic and is committed to finding acorns, than it is to watch the acorns fall and get stolen by the squirrels next door.

Every revenue-generating sales organization wants purple squirrels; and not just one, but as many as they can talk onto the team. In a dream world, they'd like the office overrun with them. The reason few companies pull it off is that finding, and hiring, an entire team of purple squirrels only works when you've got the revenue stream, checkbook, and spending culture of the New York Yankees. It's smarter and cheaper to develop your sales talent than to pay full retail plus bennies and perks for migratory mercenaries who come in the front door pursuing a sweet deal, then leave out the back when sweet-talked toward a sweeter deal.

> **IT'S SMARTER AND CHEAPER TO DEVELOP YOUR SALES TALENT THAN TO PAY FULL RETAIL PLUS BENNIES AND PERKS FOR MIGRATORY MERCENARIES.**

The challenge, then, is building a powerhouse team while investing emotional equity. Doing so as the players grow in skill fosters a culture of loyalty and performance. Organizational success also fuels quality referral hires, strengthens teamwork, and aids in strategic retention.

Traits of the greats vary, but high-performance sales teams have many common characteristics. Here is a robust list of sixteen reasons MAXIMUM HORSEPOWER teams consistently outsell the others.

- *All great sales teams honor the profession.* Every team member relishes the belief that selling is not a job, but a marvelous profession that rewards overachievers. It's hard but fair and that's the way they like it.

- *Top-notch teams do not fear competition.* They believe winning matters. Each opportunity is like a beauty pageant with no consolation trophy for congeniality. Coming in second is as worthless as ninth or forty-third. Great teams chase wins and encourage their teammates to win also. Winning is an attitudinal trademark, a single-mindedness that fuels self-motivation. They despise losing and never get used to it, so fear of defeat fuels harder, better work. In the competitive world of pro selling, hard-workers create a whole lot of luck.

- *Great teams work together.* They realize it's not what they know that will lose a deal as much as what they *don't* know. High-performance team members park their egos, collaborate, willingly seek help, coaching, and multiple points of view. Smart wins.

- *Great teams operate without hidden agendas in environments of open and honest communication.* The better a sales organization communicates, the higher its "hit rate" [the number of successes divided by the number of attempts]. The higher the hit rate, the more efficient the performance.

- *Each team member is self-motivated.* Individually and collectively everyone works hard for personal, team, and organizational success.

- *To high-performance sales teams, being average stinks.* Each team member works with a heightened sense of urgency for success because mediocrity is unacceptable. Top performers realize that when someone is average, he or she is just as close to the bottom as to the top—and where is the joy in that? Who can be happy wallowing in mediocrity?

> **TOP PERFORMERS REALIZE THAT WHEN SOMEONE IS AVERAGE, HE OR SHE IS JUST AS CLOSE TO THE BOTTOM AS TO THE TOP—AND WHERE IS THE JOY IN THAT?**

- *Because of higher aspirations and expectations, great salespeople on high-performance teams don't make big deals out of little things.* Little things are expected. So are medium things. Big things are the pursuit. Small and medium achievements are nice, but they are merely mile markers along the road to grander things. In selling, as in life, you find what you are looking for. Too many mediocre salespeople think too small.

IN SELLING, AS IN LIFE, YOU FIND WHAT YOU ARE LOOKING FOR. TOO MANY MEDIOCRE SALESPEOPLE THINK TOO SMALL.

- *MAXIMUM HORSEPOWER teams are formed, not born.* Team members are proud to be a part of something great, and each is quick to protect that collective greatness with pride and energy. They lead by example, and they consistently perform. They are accountable for their behaviors and results. Their will to succeed fuels every day into the next. On high-performance teams, everyone feels a sense of duty to encourage each other.

- *Team ego drives success and never hinders learning and development.* Sales stars who continually sell more than others are very well aware of their personal success formula: Whenever they see something that might aid success, they grab it and add it to their arsenal. Great talents evolve relentlessly. Ego drives the need to succeed. Heart drives the need to get better. Guile steers it.

- *Great teams maintain a disciplined focus on being productive.* Nearly 2,500 years ago, Aristotle sold wisdom to the Greeks. He wrote, *"We are what we repeatedly do; excellence is therefore not an act but a habit."*

  MAXIMUM HORSEPOWER performers know the world is crowded with busy people yet scarce of productive ones. Great producers clearly see the difference. They know precisely what activities will make them and their team productive. They know what impedes results and will drag the team down. Once a star has honed his or her effectiveness formula, he or she fiercely protects that success chemistry, especially the demands on time. Sales stars hold themselves and their teammates to a higher productivity standard.

- *Members of great teams waste less time—and invest more time—than other salespeople*. Over the long haul, their time-use formulae for positive results adds up dramatically. Time is too precious to waste, so they calculate strategies and choices. Their choices dictate their behaviors—upon which they relentlessly focus on their big payoff sales cycles. The increased sales that MAXIMUM HORSEPOWER teams deliver ties directly back to better time utilization, which stems from better decisions shaped by priorities. Payoffs drive priorities, which come directly from the formula that the performers know works best: Time decisions are calculated and disciplined. Actions are never random, never haphazard.

  The sum total of smarter decisions is, over time, is a huge reason why stars consistently separate from and outperform mediocre talent. Simply put, star professionals make smarter choices . . . and star teams make accumulations of them. Is strategic decision-making a knowledge, skill, or attribute? You could argue it's all three. Can it be taught? Mentored, certainly.

- *Top-notch sales teams use support tools with efficiency and precision*. They log on, find what they need, then log off. They batch and manage email and telephone calls for quantity, content, and time. They keep up with technology and make the time to gain proficiency to maximize command of better methods. They manage their tools without becoming enslaved. They know the difference between using gizmos and maximizing their utility.

- MAXIMUM HORSEPOWER *teams live, work, and inspire each other with a relentless sense of urgency*. Success is infectious. When people live with a sense of urgency, working with urgency is easy. When salespeople don't live with urgency, flipping a switch and working with one is hard. People who live and work with passion produce more than those who don't. The reason is simple: To motivated people, accomplishments are yardsticks of self-worth. MAXIMUM HORSEPOWER sales teams thrive on productivity.

PEOPLE WHO LIVE AND WORK WITH PASSION PRODUCE MORE THAN THOSE WHO DON'T.

- *MAXIMUM HORSEPOWER performers and teams strive to add value, at home, to the company, and to their customers.* Whether at home, work or in the community, members of strong sales teams know that accumulated relevance drives importance, and being important leads to being valued. Neil Rackham's succinct definition of value is the best I've heard: *"Value = Benefits minus Cost."*

Benefits take two forms: tangible and intangible. Cost takes two forms: direct and indirect. Positive impact in any of these four categories increases value, which drives increased relevance, and relevance shapes influence. Working to shape all of these impact factors is part of the *modus operandi* of terrific sales performers. All high-performance teams know this and work this way. Every team member strives to add value to every project with which he or she is involved. They *want* to be integral.

- *Great teams capitalize on market reality: There has never been a better time to be a skilled, value-adding sales professional.* It's never been easier to differentiate skill in the sales marketplace, nor to impact positive change upon a team and organization. Great teams realize that across-the-board mediocrity permeates the prevailing selling landscape, so they help each other get stronger (anticipating that most competitors' skills will stay flatlined).

GREAT TEAMS CAPITALIZE ON MARKET REALITY: THERE HAS NEVER BEEN BETTER TIME TO BE A SKILLED, VALUE-ADDING SALES PROFESSIONAL.

MAXIMUM HORSEPOWER teams understand that the far-ranging domino effect of the Wal-Mart factor has lowered service levels and dumbed-down customer expectations. With negative emotional experiences all around, smart sales pros realize that creating positive emotional experiences for customers gives them a decisive edge for competing in this marketplace of expanding choices.

- *Above all, great salespeople and sales teams believe in themselves.* They believe in their teammates, their managers, their leadership team, their products and services, their support infrastructure, and the organization they represent. They remain positive, believe there is greatness in everyone, and encourage their teammates to pursue big things. Cheering is easy, as is sharing success. Star teams understand that the sum total of the inspired whole far outweighs the talent of any individual.

Great performers rise each day with a defined sense of purpose, a mission, and it's the ongoing pursuit of that mission that drives sustained success. Every day is show time. There are opportunities to cultivate, proposals to present, problems to solve, and deals to close. What fuels these great performers to do these things, day after day, month after month, year after year? Belief. They believe that what they do is important, that their team is competent and ethical and above reproach, and that every customer they do business with is better off because of the relationship.

How Purple Squirrels Manage Their Time

MAXIMUM HORSEPOWER teams are comprised of motivated, result-oriented purple squirrels who live and work with a heightened sense of urgency. This work style permeates the team, from the top down, and the teammates inspire each other to do good work. Each is aware that efficiency is a cornerstone of success.

Time management, therefore, is a lynchpin of efficiency. Typically, everyone on the team lives and works with a heightened sense of urgency, matrixing against two different time utilization grids. One is a "time quality" grid that presents choices based on how they decide to utilize every waking minute. Time use choices present four options: every waking moment being either Wasted, Spent, Invested, or Cherished. The cumulative effect of these time-use decisions profiles how the performer's life goes. High achievers invest more and waste less than others.

TIME USE CHOICES PRESENT FOUR OPTIONS: EVERY WAKING MOMENT BEING EITHER WASTED, SPENT, INVESTED, OR CHERISHED. THE CUMULATIVE EFFECT OF THESE TIME-USE DECISIONS PROFILES HOW THE PERFORMER'S LIFE GOES. HIGH ACHIEVERS INVEST MORE AND WASTE LESS THAN OTHERS.

The second matrix that teams of purple squirrels use when making their behavioral decisions is an activity grid that contrasts payoffs with priorities. With so many choices available to preoccupy their time, high performing teams assess time utilization according to which of the four quadrants in which the activity falls. If it's got a big payoff and is a high priority, they invest time in it. If it's a low priority with a low payoff, they try to avoid wasting so much as a nanosecond on it.

Maximum time utilization requires clever choices. Better performers make better choices, and they make them methodically with discipline. Living and working with a sense of urgency feeds both prioritization and decision-making, so the tight circle of what makes someone more productive each day is the direct byproduct of orchestrated behaviors.

THE 25ᵀᴴ HOUR

When I worked for Xerox during its sales heyday, Bill McDermott was named divisional president of our outsourcing group. Bill's meteoric career ascension had been swift but well earned. His first job involved cold calling for copier sales in New York City. By age twenty-four, he was running a sales team. No matter what Bill did, he did it well and his results spoke for themselves. He could sell, manage, and inspire. He could also lead, which not all managers can do.

Bill was a high-profile leader, energetic, showy, and passionate. More importantly, he knew what he was doing. He lived and worked with passion and urgency. Added together, these great traits made him a lot of fun to work for.

Bill McDermott implored his salespeople to work like "Ivy League streetfighters," a phrase he lifted from Jim Holden's 1990 book *Power Base Selling*. By inspiring his people to great personal and collective achievement, Bill methodically nurtured two things that perpetuated his success: loyalty, and the desire of other top performers to come work for him. Because of his style and charismatic leadership, Bill was a talent magnet.

While at Xerox, Bill urged us to find, and live, what he called "The 25th Hour." Bill was so passionate when he spoke about the 25th hour, that years later I still keep a small card printed with that advice in my office.

To *find* the 25th hour, Bill advised:

- Set high standards
- Get organized
- Do your homework
- Execute flawlessly
- Stay in shape.

To *live* the 25th hour, he coached:

- Take care of home base
- Perpetual optimism
- Change minds, champion the cause
- Lead and teach
- Have an unbreakable spirit.

Bill McDermott's dream was to run a great company. When he was recruited away from Xerox at the age of thirty-seven, he left as the youngest president in the legendary company's history. Soon after he exited, a lot of great talent followed him out one door and through another.

Now President and CEO of the $7 billion software giant SAP Americas, little in Bill's world has changed. He role-models what he speaks about—as purple squirrels always do—and he has quickly spearheaded a great transformation by championing necessary change.

SAP has morphed from a dormant giant into a global force, the world's largest, most powerful business software company. They enjoy greater competitive success, double-digit organic revenue growth, and increased profits with healthier margins. Charts of the company's key metrics over the past five years look like upward escalators.

How Purple Squirrels Make Smart Time Decisions

MAXIMUM HORSEPOWER performers realize that time passes in one of four ways: They can either *Waste* it, *Spend* it, *Invest* it, or *Cherish* it. If our waking hours are a pie, everyone's pie is cut into four slices. The size of each slice depends on the decisions we make. To illustrate, if our sixteen waking hours are divided into four equal time-use segments, each slice represents four hours. With four equal slices, our time utilization pie looks like this:

THE MEDIOCRE PERFORMER EQUAL-DISTRIBUTION MODEL

16 DAILY WAKING HOURS ARE SPLIT EQUALLY AMONG THE FOUR CATEGORIES

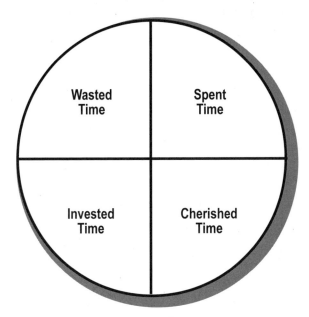

For the sake of simple illustration, the pie is cut into four equal slices. In reality, few people have four hours of "cherish" time per day, although their lives would be greatly enriched if they did.

Waste time is just that; Spend time covers unavoidable time decisions like commuting and getting ready for work. Invest time involves the activities a person to does that will eventually help pay off in positive ways, whether it's personally or professionally. Cherish time catalogs the wonderful moments of life that make life most worth living.

If every waking day is spent the way this diagram details, the accumulated average of the life this person lives is reflected with these four equal slices of pie. In that vein, the pie is really a "quality of life" map. Salespeople who are non-productive or whose lives are out of balance could figure out why simply by tracking how their time goes by each day.

All of us are given the exact same amount of time to work with: 168 hours per week. Subtract 56 for sleep (7 nights at 8 hours) and a person's achievements in life must come during the remaining 112 waking hours. How those 112 hours are spent involve personal choice.

People who get things done in life make better time decisions than people who don't. Results won't change unless time decisions do, too.

THE MAXIMUM HORSEPOWER TIME-DISTRIBUTION MODEL

PURPLE SQUIRRELS MAKE BETTER CHOICES
(THEY KNOW THE DIFFERENCE BETWEEN BEING BUSY AND BEING PRODUCTIVE)

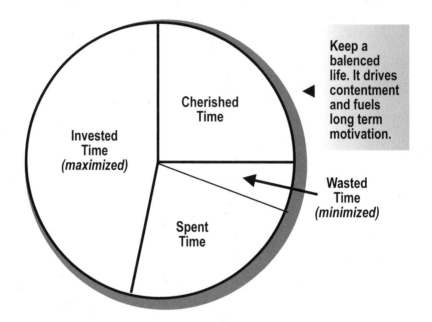

Purple squirrels aggressively minimize *Wasted* time in order to increase Invested time, which always pays off—dramatically over the long haul. A little bit better every day builds a powerhouse over time, and whether we're talking about business, music, sports, or show business, all the greats have paid the price over time.

Conscious decisions trigger what high performers consider vital behavioral choices. By investing in themselves, their organization, and their profession, top performers relentlessly grow stronger. Maximizing Invested time is a key component of how stars attain the highest level, and a huge reason why they remain there.

What Aristotle said—that success is a habit—remains true. Times have changed since he said it, but the formula hasn't. Smarter time decisions drive better results.

TIME MANAGEMENT PRIORITY GRID

WHERE DO YOUR TIME DECISIONS FALL?

(PURPLE SQUIRRELS INVEST THE MOST TIME IN Q1 & Q2)

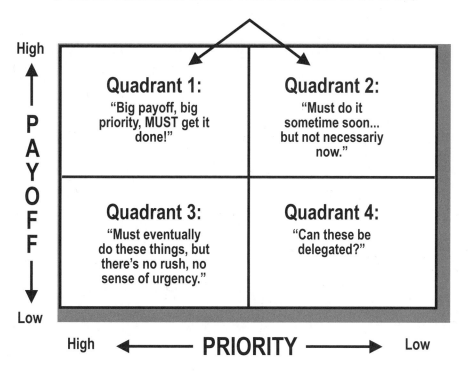

Beware of the Three Priority Traps!

1. *What hits first.* These could keep you busy but not necessarily productive.

2. *Easy street.* The path of least resistance rarely leads to the big payoff.

3. *Pseudo-crisis and pseudo-emergency.* Don't confuse false importance for the real thing.

TIME MANAGEMENT PRIORITY GRID

WHERE DO YOUR TIME DECISIONS FALL?

Quadrant 1 Activities

"Do it now!" Production. Crises and emergencies. Meeting deadlines. Immediate need. Delays are no longer possible.

HIGH payoff & HIGH priority

Quadrant 2 Activities

Delayable projects. Longer-range goals. Preventive maintenance. Crises prevention. Recharge time. Self-development.

HIGH payoff but LOW priority

Quadrant 3 Activities

Sense of urgency challenges. Pressing items. Routine tasks. Interruptions/phone. Paperwork. Boring meetings, droning conference calls. Time gets "stolen."

LOW payoff but HIGH priority

Quadrant 4 Activities

Time wasters. Pleasant distractions. Procrastination. Escape reading. "Mindless" TV. Gossip. Busy work. Couch-potato living.

LOW payoff & LOW priority

WORKFORCE STABILITY

How Developing Purple Squirrels Helps

Too many companies languish over the first question below. The power comes from trusting the second and third:

1. What if you train and they leave?

2. What if you train and they stay?

3. What if you train and they stay, and then they recruit others who learn and stay, too?

Typical Workforce Stability Without an Investment in KSAs *

(* KSAs = Knowledge, Skills, and Attributes)

Disengaged	Somewhat Disengaged	Somewhat Engaged	Engaged
25%	25%	25%	25%

Every Sales Organization Includes These Four Types of Reps:

• Disengaged: Reps who are actively looking for a new job

• Somewhat Disengaged: Open to leaving, but not actively looking

• Somewhat Engaged: Reasonably satisfied, but not actively engaged

• Engaged: Actively committed to the job and the organization.

WORKFORCE STABILITY

HOW DEVELOPING PURPLE SQUIRRELS HELPS

Typical Workforce Stability <u>with</u> an Investment in KSAs *

(* KSAs = Knowledge, Skills, and Attributes)

Disengaged	Somewhat Disengaged	Somewhat Engaged	Engaged
15%	22%	30%	35%

Attrition Drops as Loyalty and Commitment Increase

- Disengaged DECREASES

- Somewhat Disengaged DECREASES

- Somewhat Engaged INCREASES

- Engaged (actively committed) INCREASES.

BUILDING A TEAM OF "PURPLE SQUIRRELS"

(Read the plan from the top down. Execute the plan from the bottom up.)

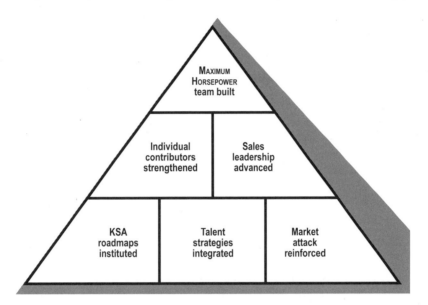

MAXIMUM HORSEPOWER
SALES ORGANIZATION ARE BUILT BY DESIGN

Strong teams don't just happen. They are the byproduct of motivated talent who are well-matched to the work at hand and are relentlessly developing toward professional excellence.

The commitment to excellence starts at the top. It is role-modeled by the leadership team and permeates the culture of the organization.

Central to success are developmental action plans for every stakeholder. The plans are built upon a three-legged platform: Knowledge, Skills, and Attributes. Improvement areas are mapped out and prioritized by a team of subject matter experts who build to the future needs of the business.

Every plan is customized to the specific performance enhancement areas of each participant. Progress is monitored by the sales leadership team.

When completed the result is fabulous: The professional talent level rises, individually and collectively. Roadblocks are best solved with multiple minds. MAXIMUM HORSEPOWER sales teams pool ideas. They do whatever it takes to help each other win.

4

CHAPTER

HOW TO FIGURE OUT WHAT YOU NEED

ANALYZING KSAS: KNOWLEDGE, SKILLS, AND ATTRIBUTES

As chapter two detailed, three of the four things that prevent salespeople from operating at MAXIMUM HORSEPOWER are either: they *can't* do the job, *won't* do it, or are *prevented* from doing it. Having covered the fourth, Skill Shrink, this chapter teaches how to build high-performance profiles that will eliminate the *Can't Do Its*.

High performance talent modeling requires the impartial evaluation of three vital components: Knowledge, Skills, and Attributes (KSAs). The end goal is to define the KSAs of a terrific rep who still will be flourishing two or more years into the future.

Since strengthening a sales force works best when the change strategy capitalizes on the collective wisdom of recipient stakeholders, engage the resources of the people who lead, support, or depend on the output of each sales role. Have these points of view represented during the profile customization of the "ideal rep." Separately dissect each different sales role, because what's needed to succeed varies. For example, the KSAs of sustained excellence in hunting new business are dramatically different from what it takes to be a superb relationship manager; and since these two ideal talent sets are quite different, many people who flourish in one would bust in the other.

Knowledge—What a person knows relative to what he or she needs to know in order to be successful; the body of information learned through past experience and personal initiative. Knowledge assessments involve every angle that matters: product, company, marketplace, competition, vertical industry, client specifics, etc.

Factor into the Knowledge profile whatever a high performer must know (internal knowledge and external) in order to sell with great velocity. Regardless of how a body of information comes to a salesperson, he or she either knows enough about the business or doesn't. Knowledge can be easily and objectively measured. The simplest way is to test for it.

Skills—The demonstrated ability to consistently deliver the desired results over time. Skills are performance enablers, shaped by discipline, proper technique, and repetition. This is where hiring managers sometimes mess up, confusing experience with skills. Just because someone has sold before doesn't mean he or she has the skills to sell consistently well.

Coaching, critique, and the need to get better all drive stronger skills. Measuring these—a common clamoring in metric-centered companies—is an imprecise science. Aside from using sales performance results as an objective yardstick, skill assessment is largely subjective. While knowledge can be taught and measurably tested, skills must be developed and judged.

Attributes—Character traits, personality DNA. These differences are why every salesperson is intrinsically unique. Attributes are the intangibles that enable us to react well or poorly under pressure, that make us quick or slow on our feet, a fast or repetitious learner, concept or detail-oriented, positive or skeptical, outgoing or introverted, careful or a risk-taker.

There is no magic set of attributes; nor does a set that's perfect for one job automatically transfer to another. For example, great individual contributors are often promoted to sales manager, then fail to perform, causing organizational frustration both above them and below. It's a very negative influence on a sales force to watch a peer superstar get promoted, stumble, then fall. The bounce creates a loud echo throughout the organization.

Thrust into a different job, the nuances and finesse talents of a great sales manager include patience and willingness to coach—traits that are typically in short supply for a short-fused superstar who is used to going it alone. What is easy for the star to do is hard for a less-talented rep. Too often the new manager impatiently tells the struggling rep what to do . . . but doesn't teach *how* to do it. When this happens, how likely are positive change and rep development? Not very. Often you will get the opposite: discouragement and frustration.

While Knowledge can be taught, and Skills can be strengthened, Attributes need to be identified, nurtured, and inspired. It's fruitless to expect a sales force to be drones with matching traits. MAXIMUM HORSEPOWER comes from motivated people doing great work over time. Fostering an inspiring, motivating climate is the manager's organizational responsibility; contributing to the organization is the rep's. Attitude can be a factor, but attitude is a subset data point, just one attribute of many.

Orchestrating the strengthening of a sales organization depends upon embracing, harnessing, and steering the power of inspired attributes. Few companies do this, which is why few companies are able to harvest the true potential of their sales organizations while also minimizing attrition. Attributes are one-third of the sales-talent wheel, and a full partner to Knowledge and Skills. Attributes and *abilities* are two different things. Many Human Resource organizations refer to job descriptions using the lingo of "Knowledge, Skills, and *Abilities*," which is somewhat redundant and imprecise. *Ability* is a generic synonym for skill. *Attributes* encompass the non-skill intangibles that define the uniqueness of an individual. Be specific and define what you want, which is specific focus on the *Attributes* of your candidates and salespeople.

Attributes are often latent in adults and dormant until inspired by either a significant life event or a person of influence pushing the right buttons to motivate someone to hike up his or her socks and chase greatness rather than plod along on the treadmill of mediocrity.

The methodical inspiration of your sales force *must* be factored into your improvement plan. Doing so is very smart business, because Attributes contribute to both sides of the P&L. On the revenue side, they impact attitude and motivation, which drive performance and absolute results. On the expense side, they positively impact retention and referral hires, helping to minimize the cost of labor. To a strong sales organization, all of these are important.

People who feel really good about where they are and what they're doing are much more likely to be self-motivated and vigorously pursuing goals than workers who don't. Nurturing goes way beyond firing up salespeople twice a year with motivational speeches. If that's all you do to recharge the troops, those events are little more than warm showers that make everyone feel good at the moment. What's needed is a strategically more robust and comprehensive environment where your people are firing themselves up every single day in pursuit of great results.

PEOPLE WHO FEEL REALLY GOOD ABOUT WHERE THEY ARE AND WHAT THEY'RE DOING ARE MUCH MORE LIKELY TO BE SELF-MOTIVATED AND VIGOROUSLY PURSUING GOALS THAN WORKERS WHO DON'T.

High performance profiles, therefore, involve all three categories equally: Knowledge, Skills, and Attributes (KSAs). When the KSAs of the people match the necessary KSAs of the job, the net result is sustained high performance over time. When there's a mismatch: lower performance and all the bad things that come with it.

BUILDING THE HIGH PERFORMANCE PROFILE: WHO GETS INVOLVED?

The best internal opinions to assess your talent come from the recipients and beneficiaries of the work output. Cross-sectional collaboration and brainstorming of vested stakeholders build the best profiles, because multiple stakeholders offer different points of view, which enables a sales organization to blend different perspectives into a vision reflecting the best of everybody.

Western Union did this with great success. During their drive to expanded field sales multi-ethnicity, nine highly respected panelists from five job areas defined a vision of future high performers for two forward-thinking sales roles. Invitees were carefully chosen based on their internal credibility, candor, and expressed willingness to proactively get involved in spearheading positive changes.

Your choice is similar: Build for today, or build for the future. Change takes time. If you build for today, by the time your net improvement time has passed, the market will have moved and you'll be behind again. Instead, build for the future. Focus your discussions on where you want your salespeople to be one, two, three years out—in the competitive space that will exist then, rather than now.

Smart collaboration involves pulling people in for a day or two of roundtable discussions. Sit in a semi-circle, block out distractions, and stay focused on creating great output. Do this in person, not over the telephone. Conference calls do not work; far too many distractions dilute the quality of collaboration.

The group objective is to discuss, then build, a high-performance sales talent who is customized to one specific job responsibility. Separately discuss each of the three success components: Knowledge, Skills, and Attributes. Don't let the team build Superman, Frankenstein, Spiderman or Wonder Woman. You are looking to define a replicable role model—findable for recruiters, moldable for sales talent developers, dependable for sales leaders. Detailed below is a tight four-step process to build these profiles.

STEP ONE: KNOWLEDGE DISCUSSION

What to do. Divide Knowledge into two categories: internal and external. Then subdivide each according to its business complexity. Brainstorm every topic someone needs to master in order to produce results at a consistently high level.

The goal. Agree upon a robust, prioritized list of what a high-performing sales star must know in order to be successful.

How to do it. Discuss internal knowledge categories first, and laundry list every topic the team offers. Do the same with external knowledge topics. The only idea policing at this stage is whether the subjects offered are "need to know" or "nice to know." The team should stay focused on the *Need To Knows*. During this initial brainstorming session, don't debate the relative merit of each offered subject. Build a list of all volunteered ideas. Defining the subtexts of what matters within each topic will come later.

What to watch out for. Avoid conversational rabbit holes. Keep a disciplined discussion focused only on the critical topics that top talent really need to know. Police the whiteboard with that challenge: "Is that a *need* to know, or a *nice* to know?" The facilitator asks the question, but leaves the answer for the assemblage. Even if only one person decides the subject is a "need to know," write it on the board. Do not allow "nice to know" topics to bog down the discussion; they will spin the team dizzy to infinity if you fall into the trap of debating them.

When to summarize. Once the contributors' brain-drain slows progress to an obvious pause, the facilitator non-judgmentally reviews, in order, everything the team listed on the board. The objective is to put definition, clarity, and boundaries around each topic. As each topic is discussed, *test understanding* so that each member of the group interprets the topic in the same way.

Once the team shares a common understanding of the boundaries on each topic, discuss it in as much depth as the subject requires. Finishing this step is not a race. It is an exercise in strategically pinpointing the key Knowledge planks that create a competitive edge for the sales force.

People tend to defend and sell their nominations, so give them every opportunity to explain what they think and why. Police their input, since no one should dominate the meeting. The shared goal is equal involvement, so it's important to respect all contributions. Clarify what you hear, so you know you understand it clearly. Listen carefully for two things: content and emotion. Don't interrupt or pre-judge. If you need to better understand what you heard, aggressively ask questions. Questions should do one of three things:

1. Seek additional information
2. Clarify what you've heard, especially with broad, general topics (*"Company knowledge,"* for example—what exactly does that mean?)
3. Test your understanding.

Once all topics have been discussed, the next step in the process permits each participant to vote, based upon his or her conclusions.

THE FIVE STEPS TO MEASURE THE GROUP'S OPINIONS

1. Once the subject list is complete, everyone votes privately, giving each participant ample time to prioritize in numerical order every topic on the board. All listed ideas should be ranked in the order of most important ("1") to least important. For example, if the team identifies 22 things they think a high-performer should know a lot about, the most important of those is rated "1". The fifth most important is rated "5". The least important in this case would be "22". Each scorer should rate the entire list.

2. Voter by voter, the facilitator records the ratings on a scoreboard, correlating each

Knowledge topic with its corresponding numerical ranking, as given by each panel member. [*note:* a sample scorecard is shown below]

3. Once the panel has shared its rankings and the entire scorecard is filled in, tally the raw scores of each Knowledge topic.

4. When the summarized numerical opinions of all topics have been determined, rank them from lowest team score to highest. The results are like golf: *The lowest score wins and is the subject that the group collectively has deemed most important.* The highest total is what the group collectively felt is least important.

5. To protect against bias, throw out the highest and lowest score on each topic and re-add. This protects against singular weighting when someone is adamant that his or her view is right regardless how the group thinks. Recalibrating the adjusted totals crosschecks the group's consensus. Usually, this step reaffirms what the group decided the first time. Rarely will it cause a material change.

The following table shows the four essential elements of this exercise. At the end of this chapter are lists of Knowledge, Skill, and Attribute considerations the group may want to use as thought starters. These lists are designed to spur discussions and are not, by any means, all-inclusive. Typically, strategic KSA lists can be quite comprehensive, far more robust than this simplified example.

STEP ONE: THE KNOWLEDGE DISCUSSION SCORECARD

Objective: To construct a KSA profile, using input from eight respected professionals, each offering a different point of view.

Sales Position: Territory Manager, geographic assignment, low and mid-volume accounts, calling on small business owners.

"KNOWLEDGE"

*Voters for this particular discussion**

TOPIC	S	L	A	B	M	T	J	W	Raw Total	RANK	Adj. Total **	Adj. RANK ***
Compensation	6	5	1	7	1	4	1	2	27	3	19	3
Products	1	1	2	1	2	1	2	1	11	1	8	1
Legal Ts & Cs	7	6	5	6	5	7	7	6	49	7	37	7
Competition	2	7	6	3	7	2	3	4	34	4	25	4
Pricing	4	2	3	2	3	3	4	3	24	2	18	2
Contracts	3	3	4	5	6	6	5	7	39	5	30	6
Credit process	5	4	7	4	4	5	6	5	40	6	29	5

* *S is Susan, L is Liz, A is Andrea, B is Betty, M is Myron, T is Tim, J is Jim, W is Walt.*
and * -- *Adjusted Total and Adjusted Rank are after the High/Low for each topic are tossed.*

According to this four-women, four-men panel of experts, Products, Pricing, and Compensation are the three most important *Knowledge* topics. This held true before *and* after the voting totals were adjusted. Legal Ts & Cs were deemed the least important, because access to legal support minimizes the need of a rep to argue a deal's legal merits.

The Knowledge priorities against which company recruiters and hiring managers should map have now clearly been pinned down. Because Knowledge is easily measured, a test to gauge proficiency can easily be crafted, administered, and scored.

STEP TWO: SKILLS DISCUSSION

What to do. Knowledge is easy to measure objectively. Skills aren't. The Skills discussion repeats the same team idea nomination process. Focus on identifying the *Skill* traits of superstar performers.

The goal. Pinpoint the top five skill characteristics that the sales force should be able to demonstrate flawlessly, specific skills you want to be hallmark traits to identify your sales force. As you proceed, remember the Skill definition—the demonstrated ability to deliver the desired results over time.

How to do it. As before, brainstorm and laundry-list the collective thoughts of the panel. Follow the same voting and ranking process.

What to watch out for. Know what a skill is and isn't. For example, regarding computer proficiency: Is it a knowledge topic or a skill proficiency? When a topic lends itself to multiple interpretations, discuss in-depth until reaching group clarity and consensus.

When to summarize. When the group runs out of ideas or starts repeating itself, it's time to summarize. Rank each nominated skill via personal voting. Tally the scores and rank accordingly.

How to verify your priorities. Throw out the high/low and recalibrate the consensus.

STEP THREE: THE ATTRIBUTE DISCUSSION

What to do. Attributes are invisible; however each job has certain intangible traits that seem to propel high-achievers. After mapping out the desired Knowledge and Skills, shift the team focus to pinning down and prioritizing key superstar *Attributes*. Staffing and hiring managers will have a strategic focus if the interviewers zero in on the success intangibles that matter the most.

How to do it. Volunteer ideas and list them on the board. Don't judge, just list. The Attribute topic is the most subjective, so take plenty of time to thoroughly discuss the *whats* and *whys* of each idea. This is vitally important for in-depth dissection and discussion, because the Attributes of your people are the invisible motors that propel their work.

What to watch out for. Guard against defensive opinions (plus knowledge and skill creep). Attributes are personality traits, so it's easy to harbor bias and *very important* to clearly explain each offered term. Nothing should be lost in translation or misinterpreted. "Good worker," for example, is vague. Discuss the concept and redefine it in more universally understood terms. *Persistent* and *diligent* are more specific. When it comes to discussing Attributes, even more than Knowledge and Skills, *semantics do matter!* Hash things out until the team agrees on the perfect descriptor.

How to summarize. Follow the additive math process as before.

How to verify your priorities. Throw out the high/low and recalibrate the consensus.

STEP FOUR: PUTTING IT ALL TOGETHER

What to do. Build the success predictability profile of the position you just defined.

How to do it. Summarize, in order, the top five KSA traits (Knowledge, Skills, and Attributes). With fifteen key high-performance components strategically pinpointed, now you can map sales talent against a blueprint of high-performance desirability.

What to watch out for. Team buy-in is critical—because what you profiled is how you'll benchmark talent moving forward. Before selling your project results internally, you must *buy* them first. The exercise was important enough to invest the time. A solid process led to creating this important collaborative output. The work product is certainly important enough for all on the team to embrace it as their own. Support the profile, even if it differs from your own personal opinion. Stay true to the profile moving forward, too. Communicate your work loudly, and make certain that hiring managers are well informed and accountable to strategy allegiance.

How to summarize. Document your findings. Educate your salespeople and departmental support teams. Recruiters should shape their behavioral interviewing questions toward these specific Knowledge, Skill, and Attribute areas. Interview scoresheets should also objectively map to them.

Utility. Whether sourcing candidates externally or interviewing promotables internally, you now have a blueprint of exactly what you're looking for. You are building for the future—so a candidate doesn't need to map perfectly today. *Knowledge gaps can be closed. Skill deficiencies can be strengthened. Attributes can be inspired.*

Sometimes a shove toward greatness is all it takes to turn potential to stardom, a good talent into a superstar. All great sales organizations create a climate of education and an expectation of sharpening skills. But MAXIMUM HORSEPOWER overachievement comes from the inspiration of the people. Challenge them, individually and collectively, to chase individual and organizational greatness.

In closing, *trust the process.* If you do, it will steer your organization toward becoming a MAXIMUM HORSEPOWER sales team quickly and economically—a team that is vital to your business and your customers'—and certainly one that will drive MAXIMUM HORSEPOWER results.

KSA THOUGHT STARTERS

Where does the creation of job definitions belong? Who owns these things, Human Resources or Organizational Development?

When it comes to making strategic sales personnel decisions, the responsibility for defining the right combination of Knowledge, Skills and Attributes for revenue-generating sales roles must remain in *sales.* This shaping model should never transfer into the domain of Human Resources or Organizational Development, because only those closest to the customer know what it takes to drive the business. Sales owes the staffing team strategic direction—with staffing integrated into the end result execution of the vision.

For the best chance at quick results and maximum impact, the sales faculty should spend a considerable amount of time delving inside each of the three KSA categories. A disciplined front-end search pays off with high-upside talent, all of whom arrive with a strong probability for success. When the KSAs of the people match or can bridge to the KSAs of the job, you get excellent performance. When they mismatch and can't be gap-closed, you don't. You will be repetitively beaten by competitors whose players better match the success traits of the job.

Organizations that accelerate to MAXIMUM HORSEPOWER start with smart hiring. Smart talent acquisition benefits everyone and fires the furnace of vibrant, successful organizations. Focus on pinpointing and prioritizing the best possible KSA list for each specific sales assignment. Manage that list to, and through, the hiring process. For some hiring managers, this may be uncomfortable. Stars are leaders by performance and they're harder to manage than grunts—so make sure to police the execution on the hiring side.

The suggestions on the following pages will help you begin to identify traits of the person you're looking for. These lists are designed to help get you going, they are not comprehensive.

Trust the process! The power of this methodology is its effectiveness when customized smartly to the intrinsic needs of your unique environment. Take the time to think through and discuss, without bias, the future course of your sales organization. Build by priority, endorse the results, and forge full steam ahead. Follow the process and it will lead you where you need to go.

"I not only use all the brains I have—but all I can borrow."
—Woodrow Wilson (1856-1924), 28th U.S. President

POTENTIAL KNOWLEDGE TOPICS

KNOWLEDGE: *What you know, relative to what you need to know, in order succeed.*

Look for quick learners and people with a demonstrated curiosity for learning. Once your list is finished and your top five are prioritized, focus on them from top down during the behavioral interview. Multiple sets of questions are required. Without them, the hiring team hears canned, rehearsed answers.

Internal Topics	External Topics
Knowledge of the sales profession	Industry knowledge
General business knowledge	Market familiarity
Computer knowledge	Vertical market trends
Software knowledge	Target client familiarity
English language proficiency (written)	Direct target client experience
Math knowledge (algebra, stats, trend analysis)	Corporate politics
Product knowledge	Org chart understanding
Class of trade differences	Business finance
Brand awareness	Market history
Bilingual capability	Components of presentations
P & L proficiency	Powerhouse proposal elements
Company history	Wall Street
Company familiarity (culture & people)	Professional relationship management
Company marketplace niches	Closing techniques

POTENTIAL SKILL TOPICS

SKILLS: *The demonstrated ability to sustain desired performance over time.*

Skills can be developed. Skill development often feeds off attributes like ego, ambition, competitiveness, discipline, and pride. Troll for these skill development triggers during the attribute portion of the interview process. Seek people who have demonstrated self-propelled improvement.

Discussion Starters

Communication skills (verbal)	Presentation skills
Selling skills	Negotiating skills
People skills	Speechwriting skills
Listening skills	Public speaking skills
Problem-solving (approach, option evaluation process, remedy selection)	Great closing skills
Calculated risk-taking (risk/reward evaluation and decision-making process)	Rapport-building skills
Communication skills (written)	Demonstrated ability to create actionable interest
Time management & prioritization process	*"Busy vs. Productive"* Which skills make them productive?
Organizational skills	Demonstrated computer proficiency
Analytical skills	Strategic thinking

POTENTIAL ATTRIBUTE TOPICS

ATTRIBUTES: *Personal intangibles*

Of the three KSAs, Attributes are the hardest to measure and project. Since past history is a good predictor of future behavior, avoid "gut instinct." Find patterns and proof through demonstrated past achievements. Nobody turns on a dime. Also, don't always hire in your own image. Build a diverse organization. Different skill sets, points of view, and opinions are all good.

Self-motivated	Business maturity
Self-confident or cocky	Pressure-tested
Competitive	Resilient
Mental toughness	Likeability (charisma)
Team player (collaborative)	Positive and optimistic
Trustworthy/Integrity	Introverted or extroverted
Adaptability	Concept or detail-oriented
Work ethic	Steady or urgent work style
Relentless positive attitude (*vs. attitudinal volatility*)	Emotion management
Leader or follower	Problem-solver
Self-discipline	Initiative
Creative	Appearance
Goal-oriented with proven success	First impression
Maturity (personal)	Listens or interrupts

HOW TO FIGURE OUT WHAT YOU NEED

(Read the plan from the top down. Execute the plan from the bottom up.)

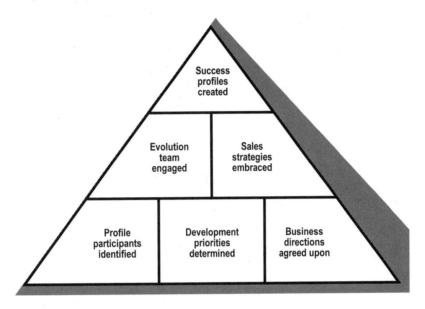

SEEK MULTIPLE POINTS OF VIEW

Analyze where the business is headed, followed by an in-depth discussion on the talents it will take to flourish in that future sales space. A team of work-output recipients should identify these ideal traits, profiling what's necessary in three categories: Knowledge, Skills, and Attributes. During each topic discussion, stack-rank the agreed-upon high-performance components in order of importance.

Align talent modeling with the future direction of the business. The better the contributions of a strong, visionary leadership team during this formulation stage, the better results you'll get. Build for two, three, or five years out (skip today since permanent change is not instantaneous).

For best results, the strategy developers should come from a cross-section of positions that contribute different points of view. Each should be the direct or indirect recipient of the job's work output. Profile each sales position separately, because many roles have job-specific KSAs that differ from other sales roles in the organization.

DIFFERING SALES SUCCESS FORMULAE

Different businesses require different KSA combinations in order to succeed. Which typifies what's needed to move more of what your company offers? Compare the needs of business excellence with the existing KSAs of your people. Do they align? If not, will gap closure drive revenue? Better margins? Higher customer retention?

If your business requires this: **Consider this:**

#	Knowledge	Skills	Attributes	Comments
1	*High*	*Medium*	*Low*	You'd better be a sole source. Drill your people on expertise and differentiation.
2	*Medium*	*Low*	*High*	Stay positive, inspire attributes, and spoon-feed ongoing knowledge.
3	*Low*	*High*	*Medium*	Interview hard for a proven behavioral track record of absolute performance.
4	*High*	*Low*	*Medium*	Subject matter expertise is paramount. Need a strong product in a field of limited options. Anytime soft skills are okay, you enjoy a seller's market.
5	*Medium*	*High*	*Low*	Challenge your talent to compete. Nurture and inspire attributes. This is often a veteran force satisfied to reach plan but lacking the drive to overachieve. Guard against turnover.
6	*Low*	*Medium*	*High*	A hungry business dominated by call activity. Inspire attributes. Invest in skills. Maximize retention. Encourage personal knowledge growth.
7	*High*	*High*	*High*	*A den of purple squirrels!* Inspire the emotional experience. Stay close and keep development accessible.
8	*Medium*	*Medium*	*Medium*	Order takers or order creators? How much impact could improvement have on moving the revenue needle?
9	*Low*	*Low*	*Low*	A commodity sale. Worry about staffing, not development.

5

CHAPTER

WHAT YOU'VE GOT VS. WHAT YOU NEED

ADAPT TO YOUR CORPORATE LIFE CYCLE

Many managers find it tough to fairly and accurately assess the strengths and weaknesses of their salespeople. Familiarity tempts them to turn a blind eye to existing strengths that could grow stronger or downplay a weakness. Thriving sales organizations work through personal bias inhibitors, because it is the relentless pursuit of positive improvement that drives peak performance.

The cycle of developing a new hire into a solidly contributing veteran can be fast or slow depending on the company's business—but talent *evaluation* should be relentless. The market stays in perpetual motion and never sleeps. What a salesperson brought to the organization when he or she joined might not be what is needed now. Many loyal employees cannot adapt new behaviors as fast as the market demands, so the net result is slumped performance.

The improvement culture enables a company to keep pace with the changing market. What elements are changing and how must your sales teams change, too? The cure starts with the awareness that relentless change is mandatory.

Earlier we built the KSAs of the ideal rep. The next step requires an assessment team to yardstick your existing sales force against those identified KSAs. Clarity comes from unbiased distance, which usually involves assessment teams similar to those that built the desired KSA model. Direct managers are often too close to fairly assess. They bring so many unintentional biases—good and bad—that you're better off using other evaluators.

The *Watch Out* here is to avoid familiarity. Daily coworkers operate on a "reflexive loop" of very predictable assumptions and behaviors and tend to have formulated opinions that don't change. To avoid bias, avoid familiarity.

The assessment map is what you've already built—the desired state. The assessment panel should behaviorally rate each existing sales rep against that desired state. Advance information (e.g., performance history) is only helpful when it's treated for what it is: a data point. Data should not provide conclusions. The *panel* will provide the conclusions.

Excellent assessment demands that the interview team clearly understand what they are there to assess. The yardstick is not for the business today—but the business tomorrow. Assess each category (Knowledge, Skills, Attributes) against the future vision.

For example, if the business trend is toward increased technical complexity, how fluidly does each rep understand that future world? If traditional success in the business has not relied upon technical expertise, there is a very real possibility that some of your top performers may not have the body of Knowledge it will take to succeed in the *evolving* marketplace. The panel, then, has to decide whether or not historically that rep has demonstrated a proclivity for learning. Is he or she an innovative learner or a reluctant learner? What is his or her preferred learning style: audio, visual, or kinesthetic?

Is there a proven track record throughout his or her career of Knowledge accumulation and adaptability?

For the health of future business, the challenge is creating and transferring a body of Knowledge successfully. How hard or easy is that likely to be? Will the rep show the initiative, or will the burden be on the company to assemble, polish, teach, test, and archive that Knowledge?

This same inspection applies to the required Skills of the next generation of top performers. The Skills needed might not change. Then again, as buyer behavior keeps evolving, they could change drastically.

THE FOUR STAGES

Companies, like people, go through life cycles. Where your company is in its life-cycle continuum has a big impact on how you gap-close your talent. From a selling point of view, there are four basic company life stages: Infancy, Growth, Maturation, and Post-peak. Selling is different at each stage, so part of your planning needs to factor in where your company sits now in its life cycle.

COMPANIES, LIKE PEOPLE, GO THROUGH LIFE CYCLES. WHERE YOUR COMPANY IS IN ITS LIFE-CYCLE CONTINUUM HAS A BIG IMPACT ON HOW YOU GAP-CLOSE YOUR TALENT.

THE INFANCY STAGE

Revenue generators fuel the emergence of a fledgling company or division. Innovators spy a niche, stick out their necks, and enter the marketplace. The sales role is simple: Power the revenue arrow from a startup blip to ongoing legitimacy. During the startup stage, sales success validates the vision. Salespeople dance to the music of the revenue gods. Unshackled by rules and bolstered by positive energy, a company's infancy stage is all about birthing and nurturing the fledgling business, hoping to build a big enough client base to achieve sustainability. Typical strategies are differentiation, price, and flexible terms.

UNSHACKLED BY RULES AND BOLSTERED BY POSITIVE ENERGY, A COMPANY'S INFANCY STAGE IS ALL ABOUT BIRTHING AND NURTURING THE FLEDGLING BUSINESS, HOPING TO BUILD A BIG ENOUGH CLIENT BASE TO ACHIEVE SUSTAINABILITY.

THE GROWTH STAGE

Companies that survive Infancy incubation focus on growth. Salespeople have one role: Swarm the marketplace and maximize revenues. Sell as much as you can as fast as you can and toss the orders over the wall to Accounting—then go out and sell some more. It's a simple message, loudly shouted, and easy to echo. The growth engine is nimble and proactive, enabled, and empowered. A *How Can We* attitude permeates the culture. This is a great energy, an inspiring and infectious vibe.

COMPANIES THAT SURVIVE INFANCY INCUBATION FOCUS ON GROWTH. SALESPEOPLE HAVE ONE ROLE: SWARM THE MARKETPLACE AND MAXIMIZE REVENUES.

THE MATURATION STAGE

As the company or division matures to the peak of its lifecycle rollercoaster, the salespeople try to protect the cresting revenue line because doing so assures stability. However, companies don't grow forever. Like a rollercoaster, every business slows as it chugs up toward its peak. From that lofty precipice, the company faces a savvy, knowledgeable marketplace that is ripe with aggressive competitors; as well as commoditization, cannibalization, inflexibility, or a combined myriad of stress factors that cause retention problems and client attrition. Customer abandonment means declining revenue. Competitors smell blood and step up their attacks. It's a vicious cycle, often more defensive in nature than offensive. The focus shifts to customer retention more so than new business. Stress rises accordingly. Attrition increases as previously engaged salespeople become disillusioned and disengaged. Once disengaged, they are wide open to quitting.

Mature companies are very predictable and often slow to respond to change. Growth companies tend to be aggressively proactive; mature companies are passively reactive. The *How Can We* growth culture gives way to a bureaucratic *Can't Because*. For every special tactic that Sales wants to try, they're told there's a policy that prevents it. Deals shift from relationship-based to P&L-based. Sales success hinges on past relationships and traditional business history. If these historic customer milkings lack customer value, losses increase. Maturation Stage companies often become "sitting ducks." As such, they are increasingly easy to compete against.

MATURE COMPANIES ARE VERY PREDICTABLE AND OFTEN SLOW TO RESPOND TO CHANGE. GROWTH COMPANIES TEND TO BE AGGRESSIVELY PROACTIVE; MATURE COMPANIES ARE PASSIVELY REACTIVE.

THE POST-PEAK RETENTION STAGE

Once a business has peaked and its revenues have begun to decline, the salespeople face a really tough challenge. They must reaffirm value, renew contracts, and for as long as possible protect against the accelerated erosion of their customer base and revenue line. If the customer base is under siege, saving customers by slashing price and margin points can snowball a drop in revenues. *Companies that have not continually demonstrated ongoing value throughout the life of a multi-year relationship typically cannot fashion a profitable renewal strategy out of thin air.* Instead, they panic, hinging customer retention hopes on desperate price slashing. Win or lose, these companies are doomed to a precipitous fall.

The only way a value-based retention strategy succeeds is by maintaining it throughout a previous contract's multi-year life. Even if pressured for price concessions, value retention diminishes the amount of the necessary decrease—buying time for fresh ideas, innovative strategies, new products, and strategic acquisitions.

The key is for your salespeople not to pin their hopes to a delusion of reestablishing value when under siege at contract time. Selling, reaffirming, and trumpeting value must be a corporate mantra threaded through the days, weeks, months, and life of *every* agreement. You can win when you *reaffirm* lifecycle relationship value in its *totality* at renewal time. You will lose if you wait until then to try and reestablish it.

SELLING, REAFFIRMING, AND TRUMPETING VALUE MUST BE A CORPORATE MANTRA THREADED THROUGH THE DAYS, WEEKS, MONTHS, AND LIFE OF EVERY AGREEMENT. YOU CAN WIN WHEN YOU REAFFIRM LIFECYCLE RELATIONSHIP VALUE IN ITS TOTALITY AT RENEWAL TIME. YOU WILL LOSE IF YOU WAIT UNTIL THEN TO TRY AND REESTABLISH IT.

If your team operates with a relentless value message, value renewals have an excellent chance of succeeding. If your team does not operate this way, it has commoditized itself and will pay an ugly price. Commoditized suppliers live in a cesspool of reverse auctions where price is king, margin is the court jester, and the customer is the auctioneer. It's a gooey and muddy moat to snorkel.

The following graphic depicts this business lifecycle reality. Money is mapped on the vertical left axis against the horizontal axis of time. *Value creators are vital for significantly different reasons throughout each of the four business stages.* A professional salesperson's contributory value is always big, regardless of the company's lifecycle stage. Value creators are *always* integral to a business—no matter which lifecycle stage the company resides.

COMPANY GROWTH AND LIFE CYCLES

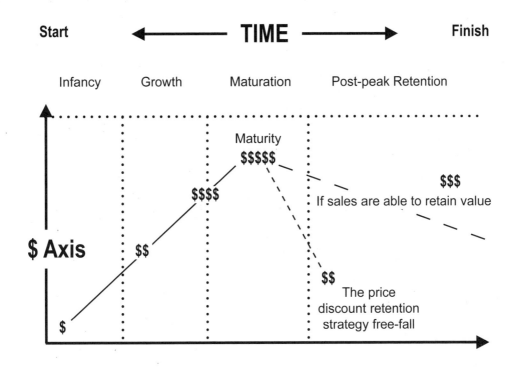

Value is Essential at Every Stage

All sales operations, regardless of scale, find themselves somewhere on this maturity continuum. A business is either: starting up, growing, reaching a marketplace peak, or faced with the grim challenge of hanging on post-maturity. *Regardless where in the lifecycle the company resides, value creators are vital!*

In a positive, supportive environment, develop your sales talent to skillfully create, maintain, reaffirm, and *sell* value. This MAXIMUM HORSEPOWER approach is the smartest route to sustained profitability.

EXTERNAL HIRING VS. INTERNAL DEVELOPING
WHICH BEST GETS YOU WHERE YOU NEED TO GO?

HIRING WHAT YOU NEED   VS.   *DEVELOPING* WHAT YOU NEED

	If you import experienced talent from the outside	*If you develop your talent internally*
1.	Costs a premium to source and on-board, both in direct and indirect expense.	Cheaper startup per employee.
2.	Theoretically cheaper to develop (skills assumed). Validations depend on the quality of the hire.	Requires an investment in KSAs (Knowledge, Skills, and Attributes) to reach the effectiveness stage.
3.	More likely to leave due to nature of how they arrived. Did they arrive running *from* something or running *to* something?	Flourishes in a coaching/mentoring and people-centric culture. Deeper roots due to accumulated emotional equity.
4.	Nomadic job history tempers loyalty.	Better retention due to deeper emotional loyalty. If the company invests in them, *they* invest in the company.
5.	All arrive with different backgrounds. No common culture, language or process. No continuity of execution.	Common language and process provide better organizational synergy.
6.	Creates an "eagle" and independent culture.	Creates a "flock" culture. Better for teamwork-dependent environments.
7.	Less mentoring.	The teamwork climate makes it more likely that people will seek help, or will coach and mentor others.
8.	Group dynamics susceptible to frequent reformulations.	Family atmosphere helps teamwork.
9.	Company culture acquired.	Company culture ingrained.
10.	Skills assumed.	Skills developed.
11.	Attributes inherited.	Attributes inspired.
12.	What if they leave?	What if they don't?

THE SALES TALENT DEVELOPMENT ELLIPSE

1. Pre-school Prep

Strategic Hiring to Specific KSAs	Field Ownership for Hiring & Prep	HQ Expectations

2. Basic Sales Development	3. Advanced Talent Development
Guest presenters, their content, and delivery methods are tightly managed.	Mining the sales force for knowledge gaps, skill gaps, and future leaders.
Builds on KNOWLEDGE. Emphasizes SKILLS. Nurtures key ATTRIBUTES.	By invitation only. Additional Strategic Knowledge. Continued emphasis on critical Skills. Nurtures Attributes.
Curriculum emphasizes interactive skill development.	Strategic programs with heightened opportunities focus on major and large customers.

4. Changes Over TIme

Changes to the Basic School	Changes to the Advanced Schools

Internal Resources
- SME's (subject matter experts)
- Field sales
- Existing best practices
- All others we can find

External Resources
- Industry Information
- Consultants
- Competitors
- All Others

EMBRACING THE SALES TALENT DEVELOPMENT ELLIPSE

Having assessed your company's life-cycle position and future vision, overlay those findings against what you've already got in place. Study your current strengths and weaknesses from these four vantage points:

- *New hire recruitment, onboarding, and pre-school prep*
- *Basic assimilation and sales training*
- *Advanced sales talent development*
- *Changes over time.*

You will want to strengthen each of these four categories differently. MAXIMUM HORSEPOWER sales cultures blanket the needs of all four of these career development scenarios over top of their clearly understood market position. Take the time to analyze and meet the needs of each.

NEW-HIRE RECRUITMENT, ONBOARDING, AND PRE-SCHOOL PREP

Development starts at the point of entry. Once you've made the hiring decision, make sure the focus immediately shifts to effective onboarding. At this point, every new hire is a revenue drain, so immediately prep him or her for swift assimilation. This should be process-driven by the hiring manager and/or onboarding team, who must be accountable for expedient onboarding success.

> ONCE YOU'VE MADE THE HIRING DECISION, MAKE SURE THE FOCUS IMMEDIATELY SHIFTS TO EFFECTIVE ONBOARDING.

BASIC ASSIMILATION AND SALES TRAINING

Pre-course prep assumes that all class participants will acquire the same knowledge base. This is vital because class time is expensive and when people aren't prepared, the facilitator must teach to the least common denominator. Dumbing-down wastes time and fails to maximize the learning opportunities for those who have properly prepared.

It's important that the basic program emphasize interactive learning. This matters for two reasons: Skills improve with practice, and assessing talent is best done during interactive evaluations.

Every program should incorporate some attribute nurturing. The emotional experiences of your new hires combine to create either an energized, fatalistic, or somewhere-in-between feeling with each new member of the team. Strive to make sure that all experiences to this point consciously create a positive emotional impact on the recipients.

ADVANCED SALES TALENT DEVELOPMENT

Nurture the next generation by investing KSA development in those who will provide a suitable return in both the short and long run. These programs should prioritize earned entrance. Study the 80/20 rule of revenue and accounts: In many companies, eighty percent of revenue typically comes from twenty percent of accounts. If your business portfolio is somewhat similar, develop talent who are responsible for moving the revenue needle of the company. When doing so, never miss an opportunity to inspire the attributes of those key people.

CHANGES OVER TIME

Build the modularity of change into your programs. Every module must have an owner, who must stay on top of the field realities well enough to proactively modify whatever is required to keep each program current. Expect this to be done annually at the very least; business demands might force quicker adaptations.

Tweaking programs is much like yard work. Knowledge updates are like cutting the grass. Skill emphasis is like edging and weeding. Attribute nurturing is like pruning and fertilizing the bushes to keep them healthy and strong.

Building real-time modularity into programs you teach your people will help you avoid the risk of wasting money due to obsolescence or irrelevance. By assigning ownership of the key modules, you can easily incorporate ongoing modifications. Doing so is much smarter, faster, easier, and cheaper than wholesale rewrites and overhauls.

Closing the gap between what you've got and what you need is a process-driven discipline. Keep the process tight, and execute it methodically. When you do, each rep will benefit from real-time professional development.

GAP CLOSURE

"WHAT YOU'VE GOT" VS. "WHAT YOU NEED"

(Read the plan from the top down. Execute the plan from the bottom up.)

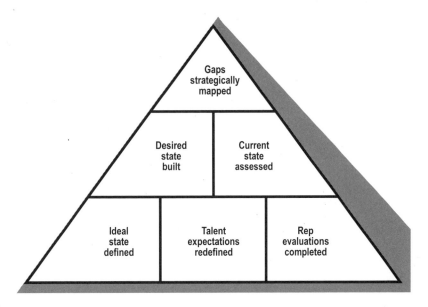

SEE THE END AND WORK BACKWARD

Knowing where you're headed beats the heck out of scratching your head and guessing, so mapping the future vision of your sales organization is imperative. So, too, is accurately assessing your current state, both individually and collectively.

Raising the level of what is expected internally can be inspiring or painful, depending on how you do it. Gain consensus from subject-matter experts to help define the ideal state. Talent expectations to reach that state should be whiteboarded, then judged against the competencies that achieving the future vision will demand.

Since you are dealing with people's careers, this is a "tough love" exercise. What qualifies as good today might not be good enough tomorrow. What it takes to be great tomorrow might be a collective weakness in today's sales force. Build the desired state first, then map your current talent against it. Be firm and fair when assessing.

Resist the urge to compromise or cut yourself short. Aim high—but aim at a target. Since most sales reps overestimate their talent, you must rely on the recipients of the rep's work output to accurately define future high-performance needs. Trust their opinions.

IMPROVEMENT POSITIONING:

PINNING DOWN SPECIFIC GAPS

(Read the plan from the top down. Execute the plan from the bottom up.)

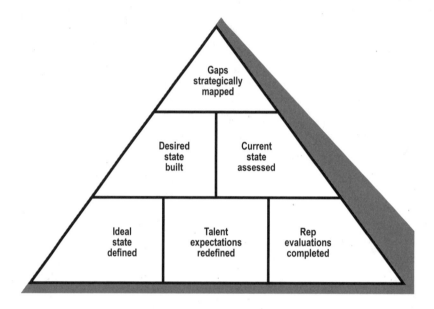

IDENTIFY & PRIORITIZE SPECIFIC KSAs TO STRENGTHEN

This granular, drill-down step comes after you have identified your gaps.

Compartmentalize those gaps into categories. Define Knowledge gaps with topics, bodies of work, learning transfer plans, etc. Identify Skill shortfalls organization-wide (macro) and by the individual reps (micro). Mechanically break down developmental components into specific categories and topics. The goal is to position these areas so a tight, executable strategic plan has a high probability of flawless execution.

Above all, stay relevant to the rep, the company, the customer, and the marketplace. Invest in relevance—what's needed, not nice. Focus on the strategic few that truly matter. Your team is better off being great at specific things than mediocre at several. Invest the time to define what those strategic few need to be.

(KSA=Knowledge, Skills, and Attributes)

STRENGTHENING THE EXISTING SALES FORCE

PART ONE: "THE EVALUATION"

(Read the plan from the top down. Execute the plan from the bottom up.)

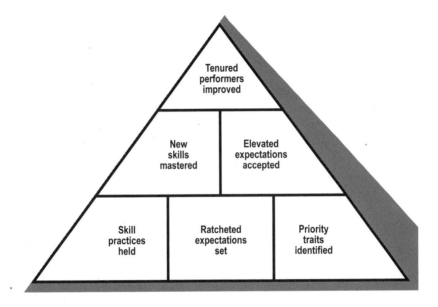

DON'T SIT STILL

Since the market is moving, maintaining the status quo means you are falling behind. So, develop your veterans with just as much urgency as your new people.

Any salesperson worth his or her incentive check wants to get better because better means more money. Tenured reps tend to have habits and predictable behaviors. Some habits are great, some aren't. Keep the good ones and jettison the bad ones!

Raise what is expected and manage through the awkward moments of behavioral change. Most tenured reps are repetitious learners, comfortable in their styles and habits. Repetitious learners need to practice or nothing changes. Direct that practice, inspect that practice, and raise your level of expectation.

Get the vets to buy-in to what you're doing. Teach the why. Tenured reps push back when told what to do without understanding the why. Explain the why and you'll have a better shot at getting your vets to embrace new techniques.

Stay positive during reinforcements, too. You'll get faster change from sugar than a bullwhip.

HIRING BETTER PLAYERS

(Read the plan from the top down. Execute the plan from the bottom up.)

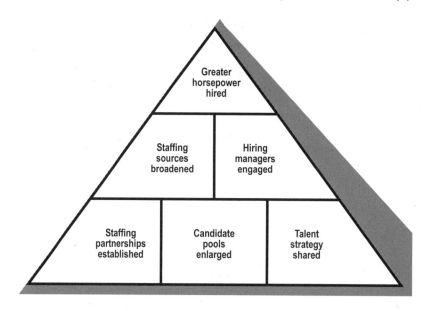

MAKE TALENT ATTRACTION AN ONGOING STRATEGY, NOT A SITUATIONAL TACTIC.

Strategic hiring builds great organizations. Reactionary hiring creates vulnerable ones. Great sales talent is in shorter supply than demand. So, smart hiring is essential if you have any hope of building a MAXIMUM HORSEPOWER organization.

Because of high demand, great talent has a short window of availability. Treat the talent like customers (which they are) and make a strong impression. Wait too long to interview or make an offer and you'll lose them. Snooze and lose. Talent has options.

Integrate your staffing team into the strategy process. Seek their advice on the realities of the job market. Stay open to new ideas. "Keep doing what you're doing and you'll keep getting what you're getting." Change the rules of the hunt and you'll change what you find.

Finally, the hiring managers must remain engaged. When they don't source talent with a prioritized sense of urgency from attraction through commitment, they'll lose that talent to companies that do.

NEW HIRE SALES SUCCESS

(Read the plan from the top down. Execute the plan from the bottom up.)

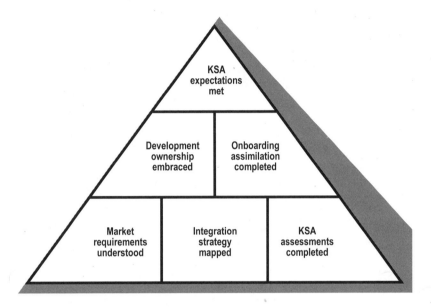

SMART ONBOARDING ACCELERATES PERFORMANCE.

Only hire people who match, or can bridge to, the KSA priorities of the position they would assume. Knowledge can be taught and Skills developed. Attributes can be inspired, though the person better have some good ones or you're in for a root canal of assimilation.

Never tolerate "dump and run" onboarding. No one who joins an organization in good faith should be left on his or her own to learn the ropes. Just as recruiting is a team sport, so is onboarding. The manager, rep, and surrounding team all share joint responsibility to help the new hire quickly ramp up the effectiveness curve.

Realistic expectations are key. The new rep should have a customized action plan that clearly delineates the developmental priorities. He or she also must have access to the ways and means needed in order to quickly progress. New reps want mile markers of progress. Make sure they have them.

Ongoing, scheduled coaching helps sales leaders gauge progress and to assure speedy ascension up the effectiveness curve

THE DEVELOPMENT CONTINUUM

(Read the plan from the top down. Execute the plan from the bottom up.)

MANAGE ALL FOUR QUADRANTS OF MAXIMUM HORSEPOWER IMPROVEMENT

There are four segments to the relentless process of making sales people better: onboarding, new hire development, tenured rep development, and changes over time. Each step requires remaining relevant to the customer, the rep, and the ever-changing needs of the business.

Development starts the instant you extend an offer letter. Every new hire joins with the expectation that he or she will strengthen the organization. To make that a reality, you need to strategically onboard and develop their KSAs.

Experienced reps must grow, too. Developing talent is like climbing a mountain. It takes work. Nobody gets to the summit without taking all the steps and putting in disciplined effort. However, the view changes for the better—marvelously so—the higher you go.

Changes over time must be factored into the development of both new reps and tenured. Building programs that serve these planks—sourcing, developing new talent, strengthening veteran talent, incorporating changes over time—all serve to create your strategic continuum.

ADAPTING TO CHANGES OVER TIME

(Read the plan from the top down. Execute the plan from the bottom up.)

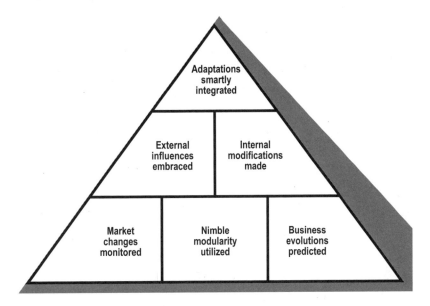

THE MARKET RELENTLESSLY MOVES. SO MUST YOU.

Speed of change impacting wins and losses is faster than ever before, so it's smart to assume the pace will continue. Build all strategies with modular flexibility. Compartmentalize all Knowledge and Skill traits. How you inspire the Attributes of your people may evolve, too.

Be proactive. Scrutinize the surrounding business climate, both externally and internally. Externally, stay a step ahead of those against whom you compete. Continually take a pulse-reading on the marketplace, your customers, and your competitors. Look for trends, macro and micro. Be relentless in bird-dogging where the business is headed, and proactively adapt your development modules to enable your people to win.

The same holds true internally. As the company's strategies, priorities, and directions change, so too must the people who are chartered with delivering the promise. Insist that your sales force stays forward thinking. Be the company against whom the others benchmark.

COACHING MAKES WINNERS

(Read the plan from the top down. Execute the plan from the bottom up.)

COACHING IS TEACHING, NOT TELLING.

Coaches teach. Managers tell. Teachers outperform tellers over time; because teachers mobilize armies of improving talent while tellers oversee armies of stagnant mediocrity.

Coach at the *strategy formation* stage and during the *actionable interest* stage. Leave the rep alone during the middle of the selling cycle.

Develop your mid-level performers, and stay in touch with your A players. Don't waste a lot of time with low performers. Make them earn the right to receive coaching support.

When you coach, follow the Cal Ripken Sr. credo: "Keep it simple, make it fun, celebrate the individual, and explain why." Be stern; hard but fair. Relentlessly drill your people with one skill at a time—until they are "unconsciously competent" and can demonstrate that skill flawlessly.

Reps like coming to a coach, because the coach teaches them things. On the other hand, they will duck a manager, since managers don't teach. They just tell people what to do.

MAXIMUM HORSEPOWER ACHIEVED

(Read the plan from the top down. Execute the plan from the bottom up.)

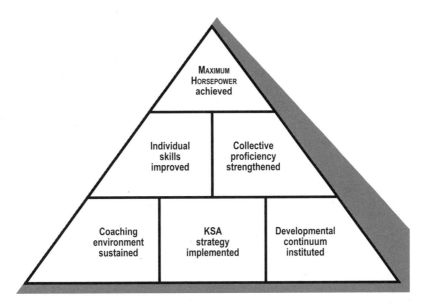

"A RISING TIDE LIFTS ALL BOATS."

When everyone gets better, success rates skyrocket. Winning is infectious and a high-performance sales organization does two things in parallel very well: It develops its people individually and it consistently exceeds plan.

Creating a MAXIMUM HORSEPOWER brand that defines the reputation of your people in the marketplace will not happen by accident. Define what you want that brand to be. Then, individually and collectively, develop the people in that brand's image.

Expect to coach often. Continually develop new programs and curriculum. Learning is relentless but so are opportunities. Whoever is best prepared will win the business. Selling rewards good work, so coach your people to greater proficiency and you will reap the benefits.

6

CHAPTER

IN THIS CHAPTER

- **Planning smartly to gain actionable interest**

- **Step by step "how to" guide for building quick strategic sales plans**

- **The five success principles of all solid plans**

- **How to test your plans for complete-ness and winnability**

Motivated talent wants to develop. They want to play Carnegie Hall and are willing to pay the price—to *practice, practice, practice* to get there. Ego-driven sales competitors relish the opportunity to advance through their chosen profession . . . because they hunger to win and are frustrated by defeat. Winning is joyous, exponentially so when it involves earning the authorization signature on a big money deal they were expected to lose. Losing—and having to recount all the wasted time, money, effort, energy, and emotion that go with it—is miserable.

No rule says a company must spend a lot of money recalibrating its talent development strategy. Throwing money at shortfalls does not make anyone better, nor does teaching people to parrot tactics: "Do this," "Say this." Improvement comes from teaching the how *and* the why. A smart strategy, well executed, is what drives results. A smart strategy is free to build, and need not be expensive to execute.

How customers receive the sales talent who call on them—process what they see and hear, formulate an opinion, act or not act—hinges on the behaviors and messages the salespeople transfer throughout the selling cycle.

Focus your strategic plan on maximizing customer receptivity. Key success factors include mastery in four categories: account relevance, call control, gaining actionable interest, and demonstrating competent confidence (without arrogance).

ACCOUNT RELEVANCE

Time pressure, info access, and increasing marketplace alternatives combine to make *relevance* more important than ever. If your reps are irrelevant to a customer's business, they'll never be perceived as *value creators* and they'll never succeed at selling competitively for a premium. Relevance demands knowledge and insight, for which there are no substitutes. The hierarchy of relevant knowledge and insight, the usual suspects in major account selling, is all customer-focused. Reps must know:

- *The hierarchy and priorities.* What matters to them? What causes meetings?
- *The customer's internal workings.* Who gets things done?
- *The customer's external reality.* What's their current competitive climate?
- *The customer's industry.* Industry dynamics: growing, contracting, evolving?
- *The customer's competitive threats.* Who, what, when, where, why, and how?

All of this information is fundamental to building a winnable plan. Hold your people accountable for knowing it.

Call Control

A great sales professional leads with his or her ears, not the mouth, because the person who talks the most in sales usually loses. Controlling a sales call is the trademark of a pro and comes from orchestrating a very specific set of mastered skills. *Listening* is foremost among them. Your strategic development plan must drill your people on these critical behaviors:

Message management. High-impact messaging is carefully designed and smartly scripted, never left to chance. Development of this talent requires teaching the critical *do's and don'ts* of what works, what doesn't, and why.

Effective channel management. A channel is whatever communication vehicle is chosen to deliver a specific message. Death by PowerPoint (or similar abuses of mismatched media channels combined with low-impact delivery) can wash weeks, months, even years of hard work down futility's drain. Skilled reps know the pluses and minuses of every potential delivery channel, and shrewdly select the one(s) most likely to land with maximum impact on the audience. [*note:* Channels are discussed in detail in Chapter 9.]

Professional delivery. Mediocrity is boring. *Pizzazz* is good. Excellence wins.

Attainment of specific pre-call objectives. Success in the complex sale environment is a stairway toward a desired result. Every sales call must have an objective, and one that can be measurably judged afterward as being completed or not. The same holds true with every presentation. Every great deal starts with an impactful initial approach, then sequences toward the close. Great strategists bite big challenges off in chewable, digestible pieces. They usher the client through the cycle in methodical progression by attaining their call objectives time after time. Flawless sequential execution closes deals.

GAINING ACTIONABLE INTEREST

Relationships are wonderful. Slick talking is clever. Fancy presentations are flashy. But in selling, what truly matters is gaining actionable interest—influencing someone to take action and actually *do* something to champion the deal and move it toward closing. Without actionable interest, a salesperson is a public relations rep in disguise.

IN SELLING, WHAT TRULY MATTERS IS GAINING ACTIONABLE INTEREST—INFLUENCING SOMEONE TO TAKE ACTION AND ACTUALLY DO SOMETHING.

One day during the infancy of my Xerox career, I telephoned my sales manager Jim Graham from my rural assignment in Ocala, Florida, to report the results of the day.

"How'd you do?" he asked gruffly. "Sell anything?"

"No," I replied, "but I built a lot of rapport. I had several excellent conversations and met some really nice people. None need a new copier, but they were all very nice about it."

"YOU AREN'T PAID TO BUILD RAPPORT!" Jim bellowed. "You are *PAID* to collect ink [get signed contracts]! Tomorrow you worry *more* about getting ink and *less* about rapport!"

Welcome to the world of absolute results. Rapport is nice. Collecting ink is what matters. Without actionable interest, the ink stays in the customer's pen, not on a contract. Sales is all about moving people toward the close. Without any deals in the hopper, there are no results, no bonuses, and no justification for the money the company invests in field personnel. It was a rude lesson, abruptly delivered, but I needed to learn it sooner or later. Jim Graham chose that day to officially end the honeymoon phase of my fledgling career. Welcome to the ocean, little fish. Eat or be eaten. Watch out for the sharks and have a nice day.

DEMONSTRATING COMPETENT CONFIDENCE, WITHOUT ARROGANCE

Arrogance takes two forms: corporate and personal. Neither works. Confidence grows from preparation. Arrogance comes from ego. *Customers buy preparation.* They shun ego.

When Neil Rackham summarized necessary behaviors, he was blunt: "At the end of your sales call, would the customer pull out the checkbook and write you a check for what he or she just learned? Was your sales call that valuable? Every call should be."

CONSIDERATIONS

As you prepare to build your talent development strategy, keep in mind:

Organizationally

- ❑ *Is your leadership team committed to the necessary changes?*
- ❑ *Will your company culture absorb the pain that goes with change?* Maintaining the status quo is easy. Changing expectations and people is hard. Is what you are contemplating synergistic with the way things historically evolve?
- ❑ *Do you have the internal resources to pull off your plan, or will you need external help?* If you need external help, do you have the internal political support and access to capital to get the right resources? Shortcuts are convenient but generally only band-aid a situation. Be wise with where your money goes.

Your Sales Environment and Culture

☐ *Does your sales organization traditionally* embrace *or* resist *change?*

☐ *Are the demands you'll put on your people a big stretch or an easy fit?*

☐ *Do you need tools?* Could technology be an enabler to increase efficiency, or is it a distraction that keeps your reps busy but not productive? Know whether or not your sales deficiencies are human problems or possibly tool problems.

Customer Relationship Management (CRM) systems, for example, can be very expensive and don't always work, largely because salespeople don't want them to. They add busywork to the rep's day but not value. Companies too often aspire to do everything a tool is capable of doing, rather than having the discipline to only use slivers of capability in order to execute flawlessly.

Getting better need not require spending *more*. Often, "bad" money can be redirected. Look to channel "failure cash" down smarter avenues. Positive change often results from simply spending *differently.*

☐ *Discovery comes individually before it shapes an organization collectively.* Keep that in the forefront of your strategy construction when building your bridge from its current to its desired state.

☐ *You can't (and won't) improve everybody.* Don't worry about people who won't "get it." Some won't. Don't let that interfere with bridging what you need.

☐ *When the time comes to execute, don't coddle anyone.* Leave the stragglers behind. Your message must be consistent: It's their job to catch up. If they don't, purge as necessary.

Your Change Process

❑ *Strive for a methodical dissection.* When you carefully analyze your current state, do so thoroughly and methodically. Every plank of the new bridge you want to build should be carefully crafted by strategic design.

❑ *Are your subject-matter experts (SMEs) engaged?* Lean on every SME you can find, to close the gap between where you are and where you need to be. Brainstorming sessions always help (referred to as "thought showers" in Northern Ireland as a concession to political correctness—*go figure*). Never fail to maximize the use of your human resources. Multiple points of view generate additional data points. More viewpoints are better than fewer when it comes to smart planning.

❑ *Don't dwell on or bemoan a problem.* Live in pursuit of solutions.

❑ *When it's time to tighten the screws and step-up expectations, be fair, not harsh.* Don't get angry with someone because he or she can't demonstrate new proficiencies right away. Maybe that person was never taught enough to make the leap in one step.

Your Customers

❑ *Ponder customer tolerance.* Customers don't like change any more than reps do. Many companies aspire to cross-sell their major accounts; their go-to-market strategy includes multiple reps calling on the same person or people, each carrying his or her individual quotas. Tugging independently on different parts of Goliath's jacket generally makes Goliath more aggravated than motivated.

The Talent Marketplace

❑ Will the talent pool in the marketplace make it hard or easy for you to change? Is talent plentiful or scarce? Is that talent hard or easy to keep?

❑ Do you pay well or not? If not, what's your "allegiance" plan? Where will the emotional equity come from to offset the hard-dollar pay differential in order to retain the valuable talent you need?

❑ Half the time your gut is right. Half the time your gut is wrong. When it comes to judging sales talent, those two things are precisely why sales leaders should never make decisions based on a reactionary "gut instinct." Judge talent based on its track record. Always put more credence in what someone has done than in what he or she promises to do.

BUILDING THE PLAN

The Good News

This section teaches how to quickly build a smart plan to strengthen your sales force.

The Bad News

The American Management Association estimates that 70 percent of strategic plans fail. There are dozens of reasons why . . . and a zillion excuses, to boot.

More Good News

This is the simplest, most effective strategic planning process you'll ever see.

A Little More Bad News

I begin with a gentle caution: This is the hardest section in the book. While much of MAXIMUM HORSEPOWER is an easy-to-read conversational text, this unit takes a different approach. Some readers will grasp this technique instantly, while others might struggle for a very predictable reason: While everyone processes information and thinks in one of two ways—*detail-to-concept* or *concept-to-detail*—this is a "concept-to-detail" learning exercise.

Detail people use accumulated data to draw a logical conclusion. They converse easily with other detail people. Their discussions with concept people are more difficult.

Concept people need to see the big picture first, then worry about the details later. When concept people get together, their idea processing is similar, so talk comes easy. When a concept person interacts with a detail person, good communication can get tricky.

This section blends *both* thought processes. Hence, the warning. It will make you think. Strategies are *built* "concept-to-detail." Strategies are *executed* "detail-to-concept."

The Best News of All

If you invest the time to learn, practice, and master this process, you will gain command of a tremendously powerful tool that will help you succeed with plans that matter to you—in both your personal and business lives. The strategic planning process explains *what to do* and *how to do it*. Use this process to bring clarity and order to talent development, and facilitate smooth execution.

WHAT TO DO

You need a smart plan, or positive change won't happen. To strengthen your team with minimal wasted time, money, and motion, you must build a customized plan that *blueprints* the route to take.

We begin by *seeing the end and working backward*. Visualize the desired result; after your plan is finished, what will have happened? You must see that end vision clearly enough so that it is easily explainable to others. Once that end goal is clearly defined, you will work backward, step-by-step, to where you are today. Doing so makes sure that when you execute—from today forward—your progress will methodically lead precisely to where you want to end up.

*For this exercise, you must **think** differently.* This process requires a little "thought re-engineering," because people tend to think forward chronologically ("What do I do next?") rather than backward ("What must happen in order for that to occur?").

Once you become "unconsciously competent" at thinking in this way, and working with this simple process, the ability to "see the end and work backward" will become an effective part of your consultative arsenal. In consultative selling, customers want to know two things: (1) Where are we going, and (2) How are you going to get us there? This process teaches both.

The Five Fundamental Principles of an Executable Strategic Plan

1. Goals need to be realistically attainable.

The goal should be objectively doable. Think big. Life's greatest accomplishments often result from being broken into smaller, achievable pieces.

2. Utilize a disciplined, repetitive completion process.

Building a good strategic plan requires a rigid structure that is easy to learn but vital to respect. Master the process and use it whenever a personal or business challenge looms. This is a nimble tool, instantly adaptable for spontaneous "on the fly" use. The plans you build are easy to modify and building them is process-driven, so make sure you take the time to learn to construct them properly.

3. Build with flawless execution in mind.

Smart strategic planning enables you to work quickly in a straight line, which helps you to become less "busy" and more productive. When planning saves you twenty minutes a day, you save 120 waking hours each year, the equivalent of eight waking days. Multiply those eight days by the number of people in your sales organization. Then multiply those "people days" by their average sales output per day. The upside reward of smart planning becomes both obvious and enormous. Great plans, flawlessly executed, drive results.

People spend an average of 267 hours a year—nearly seventeen waking days—waiting on someone or something. Invest those waits at every opportunity. When those waits are forced upon you, having a quick, smart planning process to map opportunities turns *down* time into *your* time. Airtight plans are always easier to execute than half-baked ones, so build with execution in mind. In the words of Dave Chappelle, "Keep it real."

4. Words matter.

People talk between 120 and 180 words per minute. They *think* four to five times that fast—which is why attention wanders during endless PowerPoint parades and rudderless business meetings. Senior-level executives and high-achievers want to hear *strategic* ideas without excessive rhetoric. They want to know where your sales vision will take them and how you plan to get them there.

This strategic planning process challenges you to summarize your ideas in writing with succinct brevity. *Plans are built with as few as eighteen words, so every word is vital!* So does word sequence and verb tense. The words you choose are vital, because they serve the purpose of cue cards, capturing the essence of your vision and eliminating irrelevant rambling. Precise word selection and accurate sequencing display smartly organized, prioritized thoughts that are cleanly laid out in a simple presentation format. A scarcity of verbiage allows the delivery focus to stay on *you*, precisely where you want it.

5. Practice pays off.

Mastering the planning technique will help to drive better results faster. Although you build each plan from your end-vision backward, you *execute* your plan from today forward. Practice is critically important. Gain a fluid mastery building and testing your plans in both directions—from the strategically envisioned result backward, and from the current state forward. Build properly and your strategic plan will be rock solid in both directions. Test to eliminate flaws and loopholes. Flawed plans go *kaput*. A solid plan, smartly executed, delivers MAXIMUM HORSEPOWER results. Practice the process, test your logic, and rehearse the plan's delivery. Plans are explained beginning with the end vision.

Mastery demands a Carnegie Hall commitment: practice, practice, practice!

HOW TO DO IT

General Overview

There are three phases to the strategic plan construction process: *Build, Test,* and *Flawlessly Execute*. Below are synopses. Detailed explanations follow.

Build

The most important step is visualizing the future vision of what you want to achieve. If everything goes right and things work precisely the way you want, what will have occurred? This is your *end vision*. Your plan starts here: at the end. From there, you will methodically build *backward* toward where you are today.

Test

Once the plan is built, it must be tested and it must be airtight from both perspectives: from the end-vision back to today, and from today forward through each progressive step to the end vision.

The testing step challenges whether or not what is required can be executed efficiently. Never bank on a strategy component that has a flawed probability of success. If the plan does not test flawlessly, it isn't ready. If each step cannot be successfully completed with a very high degree of probability, reconfigure the plan until it *can*. If the pieces do not interlock perfectly or a key element is missing, success will not follow. Avoid logic loopholes.

If your goal *is* attainable and the pieces *do* interlock, your strategy is achievable.

Flawlessly Execute

In a good plan, every step is integral to the success of the strategy. Each step, in turn, must be executed flawlessly. Expeditious efficiency drives progress, which saves you time and money.

OVERVIEW SUMMARY

For some, thinking from the end backward will be a learned skill, not a natural one. It takes practice, the amount varying dramatically from person to person. "Concept people" typically grab hold of an idea big-picture first and tend to master the strategic planning process more quickly than "detail people." Detail people tend to think in an orderly, almost binary, fashion; for them, high concept strategies are tougher to grasp than logical conclusions.

Learning the process well enough for it to become automatic—one that stands up under the stress of a high-pressure sales situation—requires a personal commitment that some people make and others don't. A commitment to good practice eventually will make this way of thinking automatic, your default thought process when the need arises to solve problems, develop strategies, and share consultative visions. Because this process focuses on desired results and works backward to where you are today, it is also a marvelous coaching and counseling tool.

The "See the End" process is next detailed step-by-step. Take the time to work through it. Mastering the methodology does take practice, but the *process* is easy to learn. In some ways, it's similar to riding a bike. You might wobble a bit while learning but, with practice, both techniques–sequencing and construction–will become virtually automatic.

This strategic planning process is interchangeably helpful in both business and daily living. Commit to its mastery and it will come in handy for the rest of your life.

PART ONE: BUILDING THE PLAN

PART 1: DEFINE YOUR ULTIMATE GOAL

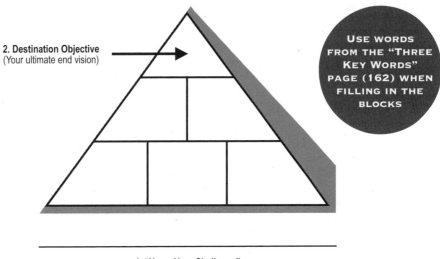

2. **Destination Objective**
(Your ultimate end vision)

USE WORDS FROM THE "THREE KEY WORDS" PAGE (162) WHEN FILLING IN THE BLOCKS

1. "Name Your Challenge"

1. Name Your Challenge

Beneath the base of your pyramid, identify your plan. If you build a plan for a customer, quote that person's strategic objective precisely the way he or she described it, using his or her words in quotation marks. If not, the title should include a perfect description that clearly defines *exactly* what you want to achieve.

2. Describe the End Vision

After you've named the action plan, at the top of the pyramid describe your *End Vision* in *three* words, in this specific order: adjective, noun, verb *(past tense)*.

Verb tense is vital! Verbs are action words. Past tense demonstrates your vision of *assumed* completion: You clearly see the strategy successfully attained already. Jumbled tense (past, present, future) creates confusion during the presentation stage. For clarity's sake, stay true to the process: adjective, noun, verb *(past tense)*.

At the end of this section, on page 162, there is a chart with sample columns of adjectives, nouns, and verbs *(past tense)* to help you develop a feeling for the right completion rhythm for your plan.

This planning strategy is a *process*. Once you gain a feeling for the proper rhythm of the words—adjective, noun, verb *(past tense)*—with that rhythm will come increased confidence and greater efficiency when working with the format.

This three-word description (adjective, noun, verb) is your ***Destination Objective.*** Write it inside the mini-triangle at the top the pyramid. This is your *end goal*—your ultimate objective.

After this first step (naming your strategy and defining your Destination Objective) you will advance your plan by building backward from your end goal to your current state. The next step defines what is required to position you for success.

The pyramid's middle row is sectioned into halves. These are the two **Empowerment Objectives**. *Empowerments* are the two (2) things that *must* happen for your final goal to result.

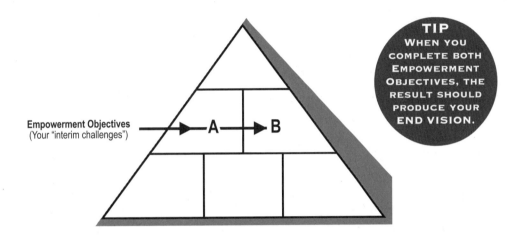

Empowerment Objectives
(Your "interim challenges")

A → B

> **TIP**
> WHEN YOU COMPLETE BOTH EMPOWERMENT OBJECTIVES, THE RESULT SHOULD PRODUCE YOUR END VISION.

Since you have a clearly defined end vision, **A** and **B** are the two things that *must* occur in order to make that vision a reality. When both *Empowerments* are accomplished, will they produce the desired result? The key is to make sure that **A + B** deliver your *Destination Objective*. The two *Empowerment Objectives* can't help you simply get halfway to your goal; they must *combine* to produce your end vision.

The Watch Out: Don't get bogged down by overcomplicating your plan. This is a big-picture strategy. Keep it simple.

If you achieve one empowerment objective (**A**), then the other (**B**), will the two combine to produce the end result you want? Solving these two mid-level challenges are your keys to success.

After you have identified both critical success factors, test what you've got: *"If I complete **this** (A) and **this** (B), will the combined results produce my destination objective?"*

If the answer is YES, you are halfway home and all that remains is identifying the three initial steps along the triangle base.

If the mid-level answer is "no, maybe, or not necessarily," tighten your *Empowerment Objectives*. A sophisticated sale has milestones of progress. What you are building with this plan is the *sequence* in which these milestones must occur.

POSITIONING SUMMARY

At first glance, the triangle looks simple; however, filling it out properly is far more complex than the image's visual innocence portends. Building a great sales plan, with all its necessary milestones identified and sequenced, is a problem-solving jigsaw puzzle. Like every jigsaw puzzle, its successful completion relies on all the pieces interlocking. The bigger and more complex the deal, the more puzzle pieces you need to lay out and put together. Some puzzles are harder to solve than others. Capturing those necessary strategies in the smartest sequence, described in the right words—adjective, noun, verb (*past tense*)—can seem elusive. Trust the process and stick with it.

THE COMPLEXITY FACTOR

Since this technique is process-driven, once you learn the process, building airtight strategic plans is replicable and scaleable. For complex strategies, such as your success plan, build the big-picture first. Then expect to "subdivide" that big-picture plan into smaller, separate ones.

Peeling back complex challenges this way (subdividing to where every block of the big-picture plan becomes a standalone pyramid unto itself) helps to dissect and simplify even the most complicated, multi-layered sales challenges you will face.

Building *achievable* plans hinges on smart mid-row positioning. Get too grandiose or vague with your mid-row strategies, and you'll flounder.

With that in mind, be careful to pinpoint and define your two necessary *Empowerment Objectives* properly, so your goal will be attainable.

"Imagination is more important than knowledge."

—Albert Einstein (1879-1955), German physicist

PART ONE: BUILDING THE PLAN

STEP 3: STRATEGIZING THE BASE

Once the top two-thirds of the pyramid is complete, focus on the base. The following three baseline activities (C, D, E) are your *Action Steps.* Strategic plans are built from the top-down (executed from the bottom up), so these action steps are the first things to accomplish en route to a flawless execution.

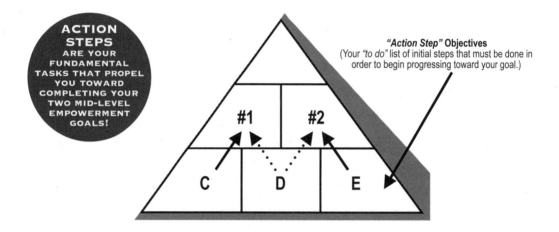

ACTION STEPS ARE YOUR FUNDAMENTAL TASKS THAT PROPEL YOU TOWARD COMPLETING YOUR TWO MID-LEVEL EMPOWERMENT GOALS!

"Action Step" Objectives
(Your *"to do"* list of initial steps that must be done in order to begin progressing toward your goal.)

To identify the first Action Step C, study your mid-level *Empowerment Objective #1* and ask, *"What must be accomplished to successfully reach my Empowerment Objective?"*

Building your plan's foundation requires pinning down which specific tasks must be completed in order to position yourself to succeed. Describe Action Step C in three words (adjective, noun, verb—*past tense*) and write it in the lower left box. It should tie to the attainment of your left mid-row *Empowerment Objective #1*.

After you've finished, leave the middle box temporarily empty, switch over to the right side, and replicate the process. Action Step E should feed up and help deliver right-hand Empowerment #2. Once you have defined Action Step E, fill in its box.

To complete the strategic pyramid, focus on the middle box, Action Step D, and solve for your final Action Step D. For maximum impact, especially during external client presentations, strive to identify something that ties Action Step E to both middle-row empowerments straddling above it. If you can identify a solution that makes this piece of the plan relevant to solving *both* #1 and #2, you will tightly tie the strategic plan together.

When built smartly, an airtight plan, practiced and professionally presented to a customer, dramatically increases your consultative effectiveness and enhances your chances of winning. The top of the pyramid is your end-vision (your final destination). The middle of the pyramid consists of the two major achievements that produce your end result. The base of the pyramid details the accomplishments you need in order to position yourself to succeed.

Since consultative selling must show the customer *where* you're taking them and *how* you plan on taking them, this format perfectly explains both. For conceptual thinkers, seeing the end, then working backward toward the present, suits their preferred style of processing ideas. For detail people, explaining the plan in reverse—step by step from the bottom up—helps them understand the sequential logic of your idea. ("This leads to this, which helps achieve this, which positions us to reach the goal.")

Therefore, this presentation format works very well in a group setting, because it appeals to both concept and detail thinkers. It will be *relevant* to all.

PART TWO: TESTING THE PLAN

Bulletproofing your plan is every bit as important as building it. Testing validates your sales strategy, so never assume a plan is airtight until you've assumed it isn't, challenged it from every angle, and tried to find a gap.

Challenge the sequential logic from top to bottom. Then test it in reverse, from the bottom up.

Try to shoot holes in your plan. To eliminate familiarity and personal bias, hand the plan to someone whose opinion you trust who hasn't seen it, and ask him or her to find the flaws.

Never present an untested plan! One flaw in your logic, and your credibility is shot.

THE THREE TESTING CHECKPOINTS

1. *Make sure that each block has an adjective, noun, and past-tense verb.*
The plan must have this rhythmic continuity. Randomly described points are confusing. If each box in the pyramid doesn't have the *adjective, noun, and past-tense verb* format, work on them until they do, but make sure that each thought is perfectly described. Remember: The right words are vital! You need clarity of expression and consistent descriptive rhythm.

2. *Test the plan for its top-down validity.*
Ask yourself: (a) Is the description of your end vision 100% clear and accurate? If not, tweak it until it is. (b) If you achieve your Empowerment Objectives, *will they produce your end vision?* If not, redo both middle row boxes' three key words (adjective, noun, verb). Once the middle row tests perfectly, drop down and test all three baseline Action Steps.

Does each Action Step help deliver the two mid-row *Empowerment Objectives* above them? The final Action Step, the middle one, should tie in a relevant way to attaining both *Empowerment Objectives*. If you can't think of one Action Step that does tie to both, make the smartest decision possible and define a third success factor that will help to contribute to attaining both *Empowerment Objectives* above it.

3. *Test the plan bottom-up for executable validity.*

When the plan is solid from the top down, test the plan the same way it will be executed—from the bottom up. Ask yourself: If you successfully complete each Action Step, will they combine to deliver your Empowerment goals? If the answer is no, figure out what's missing. Edit your strategy. Redo the three keys words in the affected boxes and test them again.

Once you've validated all three Action Steps, ask yourself: Do they deliver both *Empowerment Objectives*? If so, will those dual objectives produce the desired end vision?

If you complete the middle row Empowerment goals, but they don't necessarily produce your ultimate *Destination Objective*, there is a flaw in your plan. Pull back and rework the three key words in each box until you know that every step, every piece, is accurately described and crystal clear.

Being roughly right isn't good enough in strategic planning. The step descriptions, scope of accomplishment, and execution sequence must be perfect.

WHAT IF THREE ROWS AND SIX BOXES AREN'T ENOUGH?

Strive to protect the integrity of this process. Resist the temptation to compromise. If you feel you need to deviate, make that an exception, not a habit.

The number of boxes or words is not as vital as identifying and defining *the critical success factors*. If you need more boxes, use more. Just make sure the plan tests perfectly in both directions (up, down).

Sometimes feeling you need more boxes really means you need more pyramids—subsets of the master plan. Use your best judgment. Build your plan as smartly as possible. If that means adding words, boxes, or pyramids—do it.

Since this way of organizing strategic thoughts is process-driven, any completed box of your strategic plan can easily become the subject of a pyramid of its own. Simply create a new pyramid, with that particular element identified at the top as the end vision. Then follow the process and build down from there. This allows you to expand on any element of your strategy to whatever level of detail the customer requires.

This methodology enables you support your "big picture" plan with a series of supportive strategic pyramids, if required. The supportive pyramids answer the "How you going to do that?" questions that arise to test logic during your presentation.

Prepare for those testing logic questions in advance. Keep supportive pyramids in a folder, to pass out if a question you have anticipated arises during the meeting. Hopefully you will never need your supporting pyramids. If you do, thank the customer for asking the question and pass out the specific sheet you need. This advance preparation sends a very strong, silent message to the customer: You are well prepared and thoroughly understand the critical success factors of your proposed solution.

SEE THE END: ORDER OF COMPLETION

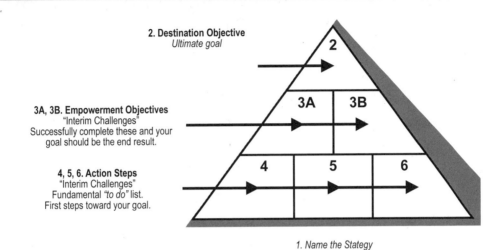

2. Destination Objective
Ultimate goal

3A, 3B. Empowerment Objectives
"Interim Challenges"
Successfully complete these and your
goal should be the end result.

4, 5, 6. Action Steps
"Interim Challenges"
Fundamental *"to do"* list.
First steps toward your goal.

1. Name the Stategy

Often it takes a ton of foundation work to build a great, complex sales strategy.

1. ***Name the strategy.*** Use the customer's phrases if you're building for external use. This skill development example is internal, so call it *Strategic Planning Improvement*.

2. ***See the End Vision.*** Define it (adjective, noun, past-tense verb). This is your *Destination Objective* (example: "Strategic Process Utilized").

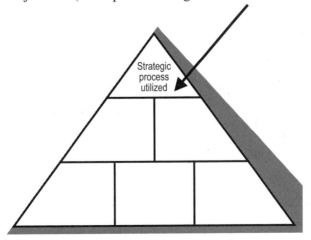

Strategic
process
utilized

STRATEGIC PLANNING IMPROVEMENT

3. *Next, decide on the two middle-row Empowerment Objectives that will produce success.* When you complete these, your Destination Objective should be the direct result. Use unique descriptions. Do not repeat words inside your pyramid.

For this particular working model, two things must occur to produce an environment in which Strategic Planning Improvement is clearly demonstrated: *Method Mastery Demonstrated* and *Ongoing Validations Inspected*. Together, these achievements certainly *should* combine to produce improvement.

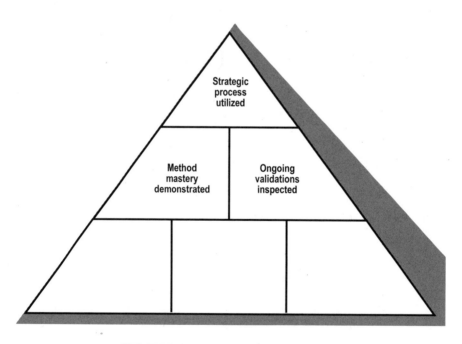

Strategic
process
utilized

Method
mastery
demonstrated

Ongoing
validations
inspected

STRATEGIC PLANNING IMPROVEMENT

4. *Completing the Action Steps will deliver mid-level success.*

Now that the example's Destination and Empowerment Objectives have been defined, move down to the pyramid's bottom row. Brainstorm and laundry list key ideas. If it helps, sketch words or phrases in the margin as you think of them. The perfect description is often elusive.

The list of Action Steps can be short or long, depending on what you're trying to accomplish. When building your overall plan, list and categorize essential achievements. Remember, it's easy to isolate any topic and build a pyramid of its own.

For the sake of our sample pyramid, look at three Action Steps that should complete the plan:

- *The first (lower left)* feeds up into *Method Mastery Demonstrated.* The obvious question: "What must occur in order for someone to be able to demonstrate that he or she has mastered the process?" Answer: *Success Elements Proved.*
- *Bottom right.* What must you do to be able to deliver on the need to have ongoing, validated inspections? Inspection assures that the people on the team use the desired technique. Answer: *Inspection Program Implemented.* If proficiency is proven and the tools used are part of the inspection program, will they help position you for success? Yes.
- *Baseline center box.* With the two bottom-row corners complete, shift focus. Ideally, this step feeds positively into attaining both middle-row goals.

What ties together both the proficiency and inspection? Answer: *Repetitious Utilization Reinforced.* Proper repetition is the key to proven proficiency; reinforcement is a key element of inspection. *Repetitious Utilization Reinforced* bridges the two.

Testing by combining the three Action Steps to see if they team to produce the Empowerment steps. If proficiency is proven, the program inspected, and repetition and utilization reinforced, will the combined results be process mastery and compliant utilization? Yes, they should.

Following is how the plan looks when the separate steps are put together:

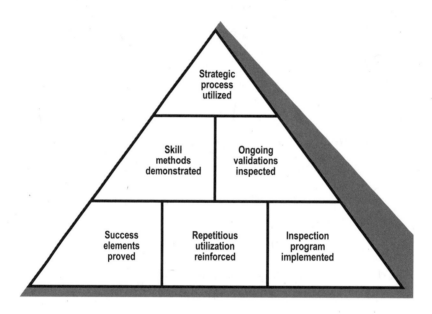

STRATEGIC PLANNING IMPROVEMENT

REMINDER TIPS

- *See the end first.* Building a thinking-person's strategy is not a speed race. The precise crafting of an airtight winning plan is cerebral, like chess; not a speedy reflexive exercise like checkers.

- *Pinpoint the two milestones that must occur to produce your desired end goal.*

- *If something is missing in your plan, don't proceed until you figure out what it is.* You cannot build these plans from the bottom up! Plans must be built from the top down. Work in sequence. If you hop around, you'll get all balled up.

- *There are 455,000 words in the unabridged English dictionary.* Your plan only requires eighteen. Don't repeat any you select.

- *Brainstorm your plan's "do-ability" with someone you trust.* Have them test your plan to make sure it's logical, doable, and sound.

- *A great plan breeds confidence.* Airtight strategies motivate execution with a strong anticipation of success. Confidence means *everything* when you're selling, and clients can sense confidence in a sales presentation as well as content. When it's obvious that you would buy what you're selling, so will they. A flawed plan will not sell, nor will a plan with a flaw in logic.

- *When presenting, first explain the end goal.* Although you always execute plans from the bottom up, you must explain the plan from the top down! After describing the ultimate goal, drop down and cover the two Empowerments. After them, the Action Steps. When you do, explain how the three Action Steps feed up to the attainment of both *Empowerment Objectives.*

- *Rehearse your presentation delivery.* The three words inside each box are thought starters (not a TelePrompTer). When presenting, do not read the words. Dialogue interactively. Encourage discussion, opinions, input. Your pyramid plan is a talk *outline*, (carefully scripted to gain a consensus agreement). Don't rush through it. Take your time.

- *When a question arises about how to achieve a particular point, peel off that point and construct a new pyramid, describing the supporting strategy with the area of concern at the top.* Build from there. React to questions as they arise. Facilitating questions effectively by using a practiced teaching style is a powerfully influential and consultative technique.

THE WATCH OUT

Remember, the American Management Association shares an ominous statistic in its strategic planning seminar: Seventy percent of all strategic plans are never executed.

Part of the reason for this colossal number of failures is that "old school" planning methods create complex, grandiose plans that are way too complicated [the SWOT approach is vulnerable to this; listing Strengths, Weaknesses, Opportunities, and Threats can get way too cumbersome to be "doable."] Insist that your sales organization build sleeker, leaner strategies. The art is in the simplicity, not complexity. From a customer point of view, simple sells. Complexity scares.

THE ART IS IN THE SIMPLICITY, NOT COMPLEXITY.

If you cannot clearly see a road map to success, do not commit resources to chase it. When you can see it, use a lean process, strategize for success, and test your plan for "do-ability." If the plan *is* doable, commit to it and execute flawlessly. Flawless execution, step-by-step, produces the desired results.

Once you commit to a plan, strive for relentless progress. If progress is derailed during execution, examine which block of the pyramid needs reexamination. Isolate that specific Action Step or Empowerment Objective and, to get back on track, build a pyramid strategy of its own.

Effective sales strategies can be executed quickly, efficiently, and cost effectively. When presenting to senior executives, knowing your plan *cold* is critical. Your message—your vision—is recommending *what* they should do. The body of the pyramid explains *how*. Clearly communicating a crystal-clear plan will have maximum impact.

Staying true to the past tense completion process is vital for one big reason. Which lands with greater authority: "I am *going* to do this," or "I *have done* this." Obviously the latter. A performance track record always lands with greater impact than the empty world of a future promise. The past tense format shows customers that you can visualize a future in which their end goal has been met. The psychology of the visualization is very important to its sales influence.

The strategic pyramids integrated throughout this workbook illustrate how vital success elements are broken down into easily achievable assignments. Master this technique and teach it to your people. Since this is a methodical process, it is easy to scale and replicate.

If you sell in a competitive world of value, coach your organization to integrate this methodology into their consultative sales approach. Focus, clarity of thought, strategic direction, winning execution, and time utilization all improve. Wasted motion and effort will decrease.

This process has broad applicability. While the example pyramid we built maps a cost-effective strategy for developing sales talent, the *process* used to build this plan can simplify far more complex business challenges to drive sales victories, career success, and financial reward.

Whether this planning process is used for business or family life, it teaches how to "see the end and work backward." Invest the time to learn, practice, and master the process and it will pay off beautifully, guiding you and your salespeople to sequential-step sales solutions. It also works perfectly as a valuable life skill.

How do you get to Carnegie Hall? Practice, practice, practice!

How do you become superbly proficient at strategic sales planning? The exact same way: *practice!*

THREE KEY WORDS

(select words from here)

To develop the proper word-order rhythm of adjective, noun, past-tense verb, select first from Column A, then Column B, then Column C. The more you practice, the better you'll get a picking exactly the right word combination to describe the point you are trying to make.

A	B	C
ADJECTIVES (descriptive words)	**NOUNS** (subjects: people, places, and things)	**PAST-TENSE VERBS** (action words)
Annual	Accounts	Achieved
Bad	Ambition	Approved
Competitive	Barriers	Attained
Conventional	Behaviors	Begun
Critical	Challenge	Challenged
Critical	Clients	Completed
Discretionary	Departments	Decided
Existing	Dream	Delivered
Fiscal	Findings	Demonstrated
Foremost	Fitness	Ended
Hurtful	Friends	Finished
Important	Funding	Halted
Improved	Goals	Hurdled
Initial	Habits	Improved
Lifelong	Hobby	Initiated
Necessary	Installation	Mastered
Negative	Money	Measured
New	Performance	Overachieved
Old	Precautions	Penetrated
Older	Products	Proposed
Performance	Recommendation	Replaced
Personal	Relationships	Researched
Physical	Responsibility	Retained
Potential	Risks	Sharpened
Prudent	Savings	Started
Quality	Skills	Stopped
Retirement	Strategies	Surveyed
Superior	Talent	Taken
Unnecessary	Thinking	Terminated
Wasted	Well-being	Validated

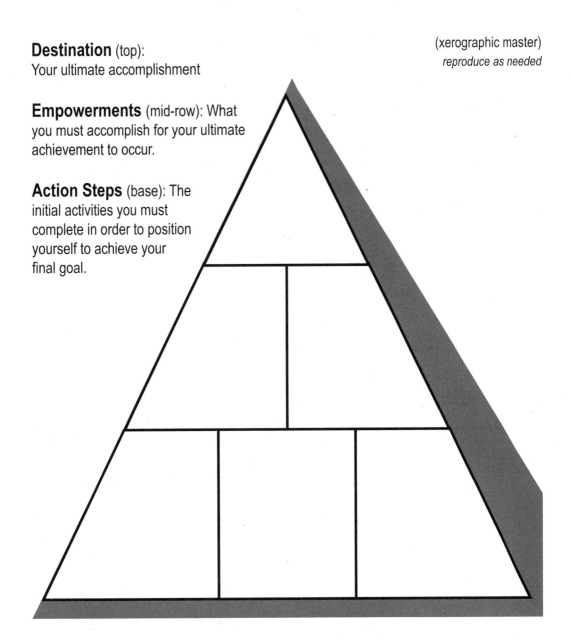

Destination (top):
Your ultimate accomplishment

Empowerments (mid-row): What
you must accomplish for your ultimate
achievement to occur.

Action Steps (base): The
initial activities you must
complete in order to position
yourself to achieve your
final goal.

(xerographic master)
reproduce as needed

NAME OF YOUR STRATEGIC PLAN
(Clearly identified, easily understood. Use customer phrase if appropriate).

7

CHAPTER

THE EIGHT STEPS TO MAXIMUM HORSEPOWER

TIPS & WATCH OUTS

The fastest, cheapest, and most effective way to build top-notch sales talent is to follow a tight eight-step process that methodically injects developmental equity. MAXIMUM HORSEPOWER sales leaders must become fluid with the process and apply it to whatever skill priorities the company identifies. Your end goal is to develop your revenue generators to be "unconsciously competent"— performing automatically, without the need to refer to the process.

THE EIGHT STEPS TO MAXIMUM HORSEPOWER

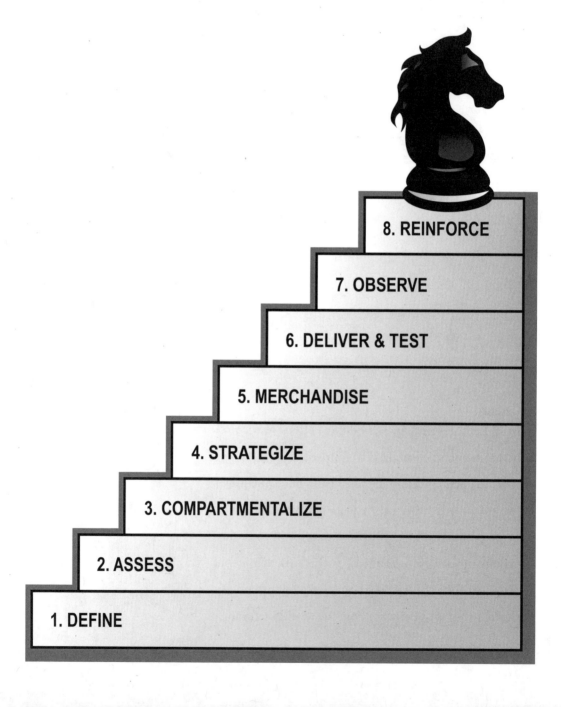

8. REINFORCE

7. OBSERVE

6. DELIVER & TEST

5. MERCHANDISE

4. STRATEGIZE

3. COMPARTMENTALIZE

2. ASSESS

1. DEFINE

1. **DEFINE.** Visualize your sales force the way it needs to be. Think collectively and define the future desired state of a MAXIMUM HORSEPOWER sales organization. Set measurably realistic objectives for the specific Knowledge, Skills, and Attributes (KSAs) you want to strengthen. MAXIMUM HORSEPOWER occurs when the KSAs of the job match the KSAs of the people. This definition stage requires pinning down the KSA objectives that, once delivered, will propel the sales team up the effectiveness curve.

2. **ASSESS.** Map your people against (future) role-model proficiency. Compare the desired future state against the current strengths and weaknesses of your people.

3. **COMPARTMENTALIZE.** Break down what is needed into properly sized KSA "buckets" that can be repetitiously executed with a high probability of success.

4. **STRATEGIZE.** Strive to be really smart about identifying the learning content that must get transferred to the team or individual. Same with skills. Same with inspiring attributes. Gap closure is the bridge between the current state and desired state.

5. **MERCHANDISE!** More companies mess up here than on any other step. *What your salespeople need to learn hugely influences the best way to teach them!* Therefore, each of the three KSAs is best taught differently. Salespeople bore quickly, so impactful learning experiences demand creative ingenuity. Building great learning experiences is crucial to keeping salespeople actively engaged. Packaging what you need to teach smartly has a huge impact on success.

6. **DELIVER & TEST.** Showmanship is everything! Great delivery drives home the message. Poor delivery shuts down listening and learning. If a salesperson checks out, it's hard to get him or her back. Because of decreasing attention spans, this step is increasing in importance and will continue to do so. You will never—*ever*—get a MAXIMUM HORSEPOWER impact from blasé delivery. The success burden shifts from the instructor to the student. They are responsible for demonstrated progress. If you're teaching Knowledge topics, test your sales talent and score their work. Objective measurement reveals whether your program is a hit or a miss. Skill development is more subjective than knowledge, thus harder to measure. When possible, use video to record

the skill work. Play it back and discuss the strengths and weaknesses of what you see on the screen.

7. **OBSERVE.** Has your message been retained? Are the key behaviors being practiced? Are the desired traits in evidence? If not, they will not resurface later. Repetitive practice helps the salespeople grow from competence to excellence. Let the reps know "Big Brother is watching."

8. **REINFORCE.** Disciplined execution drives absolute results. Make relentless improvement part of your culture. Re-emphasize the key elements—*the necessaries*—that must become integrally automatic to the work efforts of a high-performing individual. Ongoing repetition increases the "stick factor."

HOW TO METHODICALLY DEVELOP SALES TALENT

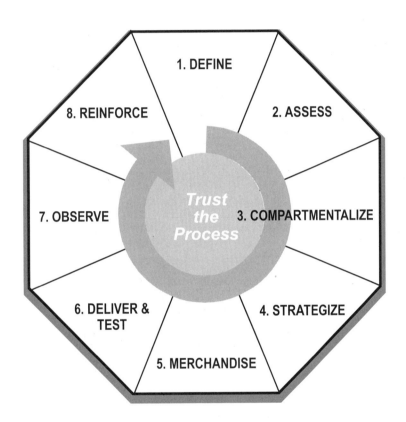

AMPLIFYING EACH OF THE EIGHT STEPS

Step 1. DEFINE

What do you want to accomplish? What is your end vision? If you succeed in transforming your sales organization, what will it look like? Two years from now, when things are cruising on autopilot and the revenue is steadily hitting the monthly numbers, what will be driving your success?

Is your sales group being micromanaged or given latitude to maximize results on its own? What traits fuel the overachievement that defines your high-performance sales brand? Will you achieve market wins by playing checkers with customers or high-stakes chess? Or does your team play both?

One year out, two years out, five years out, will your sales team be orchestrating consistent success, or praying for it? *If your team doesn't get better, then what?* Will they scrambling to make plan, run ragged juggling pipe-dream bid responses and slim-chance, no margin reverse auction price deals?

Maintaining the status quo is a loser's blueprint, because the market has no conscience about leaving laggards behind. Future success might demand proactive consultative selling, impenetrable account relationships, and the ability to control complex selling cycles.

MAINTAINING THE STATUS QUO IS A LOSER'S BLUEPRINT, BECAUSE THE MARKET HAS NO CONSCIENCE ABOUT LEAVING LAGGARDS BEHIND.

Define what must change in order to get your people where they want to be. Whatever you must accomplish, write it down. Decide on and prioritize three skills that you want your sales force to master. Aspire to be great. Do not shortchange the vision of what your organization is capable of becoming. Build a *trademark of excellence* that your competition will envy. Get so good that top performers seek to work for you.

The Watch Outs: Guard against being too general, too non-specific. Know precisely *how* you want your sales force to excel. Map your success keys in *explicit* terms. If you are too close to the action today to see precisely what you need, call in an unbiased resource to help figure it out. Seek multiple opinions that either affirm or reject your vision and help refine it.

This first-step objective defines your top three improvement milestones in a *Did it—Didn't do it* way. "Getting better" isn't measurable. The vague phraseology is not tight enough. Define positive change in measurable terms. For example, instead of "Getting better," perhaps: "Having a high-performing, low-turnover sales organization, with all key accounts happy and locked up on five-year renewals." If you want to be even more specific, tag numbers to performance and percentages to turnover.

After defining your desired state, you will begin advancing through the change process. Don't worry that change is uncomfortable. It always is, even though change is relentless. [*note:* Managing change is discussed in detail in Chapter 10].

Also, stay within realistic expectations. If change involves a massive overhaul, don't abandon your vision. Break it down into doable stages.

STEP 2. ASSESS

Once your end vision is clear, determine how your people's talents rate today. This is a macro organizational assessment, not a micro rep analysis. For example, if your team is excellent at customer service but weak at orchestrating new opportunities, and new opportunities matter, flag that deficiency immediately.

The Assessment step is an interrogatory one designed to dissect the status quo of your sales organization. The goal is to figure out what you've got and better understand—for better or worse—precisely why your sales team is where it is. To dissect your status quo, take a hard look at the competency bell-curve distribution of your sales organization. Why do your salespeople fall on the curve where they do? Why are too few at the high-performing right side of the curve and so many in the middle? Are your salespeople largely self-trained? Were they cobbled together at random, hired in common images, vacuumed into the organization through merger and acquisition, or sourced strategically with diverse and complementary skill sets? In a sentence, how would your competitors describe your salespeople?

Disassemble your current collective KSAs to understand why your group functions the way it does. Backtrack hiring histories, too. There is a lot to learn about where your sales organization is, based on the sourcing origins of the individuals. Study the point of entry of both your high and low-performers. Where have your best reps come from? How were your worst ones sourced? This is very important stuff to find out.

THERE IS A LOT TO LEARN ABOUT WHERE YOUR SALES ORGANIZATION IS, BASED ON THE SOURCING ORIGINS OF THE INDIVIDUALS. STUDY THE POINT OF ENTRY OF BOTH YOUR HIGH AND LOW-PERFORMERS.

The Big Question

Is the current crop of talent capable of doing what you envision?

IS THE CURRENT CROP OF TALENT CAPABLE OF DOING WHAT YOU ENVISION?

You've got five possible answers: Yes, probably, maybe, probably not, and no chance. The farther down the ladder you descend, the more development work you'll need to do. If your answer to the Big Question is "probably not" or "no chance," you have just told yourself that you need to face some hard calls on personnel.

Every profitable company does some things better than others; the same holds
true with sales organizations. Some are better hunters than farmers; some are great
at nurturing account relationships, but do so reactively rather than proactively. Some
companies sell price, not value, leaving themselves vulnerable to the vagaries and
shifting decisions of whimsical dollar-squeezers. Other sales teams talk value, but
they don't close well and lose too many winnable opportunities. Operationally driven
businesses often manage to a pure P&L, refusing to concede short-term margin points
for long-term opportunity. Others, especially mature businesses that feel the competitive
heat, go the other way—sometimes retaining clients by authorizing renewal deals that
offer little or no margin, tie up resources but make no profit. This is the "dollar on the
corner" syndrome. You can stand on the corner sunrise to sunset, trading dollars all day
with a thousand people passing by. By the end of the day, you've had your hands on a
thousand dollars—but all go home with is one lousy buck.

Based on the market space in which you compete, do a "plus and minus" assessment
of how your salespeople stack up. Match what you see with what your customers are
telling you. Ask your customers how they see their business changing over the next few
years. Seek their opinions in order to understand how your team can better serve your
market's expected evolution. Some customers might not have recommendations, but
some will. All will be glad that you asked.

Aside from the customers, compare your sales team with other sales forces whom
you admire. Don't benchmark to match them. Benchmark to *leapfrog* them.

The Watch Out. Don't be soft on the status quo. Self-congratulatory *attaboys* do
not add value. Measure yourself against the absolute best. You are building a plan to get
better, so raise your expectation of what *good* really is, and redefine *great* in loftier terms.
Aim too low and you'll be operating beneath your organization's production capability.
Hold your expectations to a higher standard and some of your people will rise to meet it.

What Specifically to Assess

When you've finished your pluses-and-minuses analysis, frame what you've learned against three points of view: Knowledge, Skills, and Attributes.

Knowledge

Knowledge creates the inside edge in an increasingly competitive marketplace, which is why so many successful companies build vertical industry sales organizations. In this context, knowledge is described as what you know, relative to what you need to know, in order to succeed. Knowledge encompasses a body of information that needs to be ingested, digested, retained, and applied. Knowledge, of course, can be taught. *What* needs to be taught must be determined, as well as *how* to teach and test it.

Also important to discover is what you *don't* know. What resources can you find that might shed light on what your competitors know that you don't? A common phrase is, "I don't know what I don't know." If necessary, hire someone to find out and tell you.

If you know your business well, trust your instincts on your vision of where the industry is headed. If you're new to the business, research and solicit multiple and diverse points of view from industry experts (both internal and external) whose insight you respect. Process these multiple views but manage by fact-based analysis.

Skills

In professional selling, I define Skills as the demonstrated ability to deliver the desired results over time. Consultative greatness requires integrating, utilizing, and flawlessly executing multiple deft skills. If your team is flawed and must get stronger, pinpoint the specific skills that must be strengthened in order to improve. Identify the key skills (listening, creative problem-solving, strategic planning, etc.) and prioritize them. Focus on the ones that will clearly move the performance needle.

Sustained excellence demands relevant practice, but don't worry (yet) about how to teach in order to strengthen the identified priorities. For now, just isolate the critical few. If you aren't sure of the smartest way to prioritize what you need, bring in resources who can.

Attributes

Attributes are the intangibles that each salesperson has when he or she walks through your door, the invisible traits that make him or her unique. Attributes and attitude differ. Attributes are a singularly complex interwoven fabric of a thousand traits. Attitude is how people feel. Beware of assuming that attitude drives performance. It doesn't. *Talent* drives performance. The need to *win* drives performance. The world of sales is overrun with happy losers, most of whom blame every defeat on price and not because they were outsold.

> THE WORLD OF SALES IS OVERRUN WITH HAPPY LOSERS, MOST OF WHOM BLAME EVERY DEFEAT ON PRICE AND NOT BECAUSE THEY WERE OUTSOLD.

Don't mistake attitude for aptitude, either, nor its correspondingly intrinsic behavioral DNA. Attributes can't be taught, but they can (and should) be inspired. Motivation is an attribute. Salespeople *must* be self-motivated. Motivational speeches, *the rah-rah fire 'em up feel-good warmth of temporary bliss* cool like campfires when there's no internal wood supply to keep the flames crackling.

Throughout the evolving global market, the clockspeed of change is accelerating. Human change, of course, requires a *willingness* to change, which is a personal attribute. Some folks embrace change; others struggle against it. The successful salesperson who works hard and makes the quota today, but resists change, will not win in the future. The willing adaptation to changing circumstances, both customer-driven and market-driven, is a must-have championship attribute.

What are the top five high-performance attributes that your business demands? Identify them, list them, prioritize them. If your current roster is thin on what you need (competitiveness, intensity, etc.) craft a new strategy to inspire your sales force. If that fails, go outside and hire who you need to play the game at the level you expect to play.

Motivated people accomplish great things. Inspiring good talent is a lot easier than churning and burning through a merry-go-round of replacement hires. Get good at nurturing the high-performance attributes of your sales team and they'll deliver better business results for you.

**INSPIRING GOOD TALENT IS A LOT EASIER
THAN CHURNING AND BURNING THROUGH A
MERRY-GO-ROUND OF REPLACEMENT HIRES.**

STEP 3: COMPARTMENTALIZE

Once you've sorted out your assessment findings into the three key change categories (Knowledge, Skills, and Attributes), focus on each separately. Change dynamics are significantly different for Knowledge gaps than for Skills, and strengthening Skills is a radically different challenge than inspiring an adult's latent Attributes.

Knowledge improvement involves the digestion and retention of an educational body of work. It, therefore, is a challenge of the mind.

Skills development is more mechanical, practice-driven, and coach-reliant. Stronger selling skills come from the willingness to work hard to get better. Skill habits require a discipline (and ego need) to relentlessly improve. Betterment is a challenge of the heart.

Attribute nurturing is part art, part science. It doesn't come from education and it doesn't come from practice. Attributes require inspiration—food for the soul. Not all managers are good at it but every one can try.

COMPARTMENTALIZE: KNOWLEDGE

Once you've identified the general, broad-based Knowledge topics your team must learn more about, peel back one level at a time. As you do, focus solely on what your sales team *must* know. Don't worry about what would be *nice* for them to know. Focus on what they *need* to know in order to become great performers.

Also, when do they need to know it? Immediately, short-term, mid-term, long-term? Scrutinize each Knowledge topic from these four points of view:

1. *New hires coming aboard.* What content must someone new to the organization learn in order to become functionally effective? By what timeline do they realistically need to know it? The quicker a new hire becomes proficient, the quicker he or she starts earning his or her keep.

2. *Current salespeople.* What must your existing reps learn in order to raise their value in the external marketplace to a best-in-class status? Enhance their knowledge in two ways: internal things they need to know more about, and external marketplace smarts that will provide more winning insight. Becoming proficient at providing consultative value to customers requires teaming broad macro industry understanding with insightful micro customer awareness. Great salespeople can always frame advice in a way that clearly illustrates to customers how specific changes will affect *them.*

3. *Consistent, consultative top performers.* What must they learn in order to remain the best? Ego propels top performers. The status quo is never good enough. What creates expertise?

4. *Changes over time.* As internal and external change dynamics reshape the marketplace, how will these changes impact what new Knowledge is necessary for all three levels—new hire, current reps, top performers? Money doesn't sleep, nor does competition. Knowledge gleans insight. Insight shapes strategy. Smart strategy, flawlessly executed, wins.

The Knowledge Watch Out. Avoid getting dragged down into the quagmire of things that are "nice to know." Maintain a disciplined focus on what your salespeople *need* to know. Don't waste time or money teaching trivia; non-essential learning should come from self-discovery (reading and research). Invest in the core. Know what that core consists of and how to smartly transfer it to new hires, existing reps, and your superstars. Then mark your boundaries. Never let your people waste time or money straying into the wasteland of minutiae.

COMPARTMENTALIZE: SKILLS

Skill gaps lend themselves to easier topic identification than Knowledge. Stack-rank the high-performance skill traits that matter the most. Focus on the critical few that drive actionable interest and behavioral change. Pinpoint the specific skills that generate better results. Keep the goal in front of you, and stay focused on reaching it. When the team is strengthened to where you want them, they'll win the deals they're supposed to win and some of the ones they're supposed to lose.

The Skill Watch Out. Don't set your bar too low. Skill enhancement, especially with veteran salespeople, requires tough love. Raise the expectations and you'll raise results. According to a comprehensive study by the prestigious Washington, D.C. Sales Executive Council of the Corporate Executive Board, the number one reason salespeople leave a company is because they aren't growing professionally. Tough love is a growth vehicle. Drive it. Everyone benefits from a talent's progression, including customers.

COMPARTMENTALIZE: ATTRIBUTES

The most inspiring gift you can sprinkle over your sales team is a heightened sense of urgency for chasing their greatness. Challenge them to become what they are capable of being—never satisfied with what is easy or comfortable.

Attributes play a huge role in the big picture of compartmentalizing change because of people's inborn reluctance to change at all. Big picture: What is the Attribute message you want to convey? Which Attributes are cornerstones of the future greatness for your high-performing, self-sustaining sales organization? List these traits and prioritize them. From this list will come your customized strategies that will help you methodically inspire your team.

The backbone of your new sales "brand" is how consistently your people close deals. Leaders shape a culture, so carefully study, then decide, which attributes matter the most for the brand you want to build. Once you pinpoint those elements, own them. Advertise them. Teach them. Coach them. Reinforce them. Those elements constitute your *brand*.

The Attribute Watch Out. Don't be too grandiose. Keep your list of prioritized Attributes simple. Grandiose dilutes and sabotages progress. Choose Attributes that are relevant, recognizable, easy to advertise and inspire, easy to role-model. Maintain and inspire good people and they'll propel you where you need to go.

STEP 4: STRATEGIZE

You've pinned down what to build toward. You've assessed how your people map against your higher standard. You've evaluated your areas of deficiency. Now you will strategize. Strategy starts with knowing your business.

What *kind* of business are you in? Is it fast paced and ever-changing, or static and predictable? Is it a hard or easy business to learn? Are you competing in a high or low-turnover industry?

Deciding big picture stuff is hard enough. Deciding what is realistically "do-able," in view of the realistic growth factors of your personnel, is even harder. Whatever you build has to be relevant to both the business and the people. Deciding what to work on with little wasted time requires a good strategic plan. The following five categories will help you create a smart strategy:

1. Topics

What areas of your business must your people gain more insight? Clearly pinpoint what is *necessary* for them to know and draw a line of separation between it and what would be *"nice"* to know. The "nice to know" they can learn on their own time.

2. Complexity

How deep can you go? Depending on your people, their proclivity for learning might not be as ambitious as you would like. Make sure that whatever you build will be within their capabilities to master. For example, never expect a salesperson who doesn't write well to learn to write better. He or she won't. Salespeople sell with their mouths, not with their fingers (so shifting to a email sales would be foolish, moving from strength to weakness).

Despite great intentions, job requirements often change faster than people. The market moves, customers evolve, competitors rise and fall. As market forces collide, your people move in one of two directions: either closer to or further from proficiency.

Keep in touch with realistic expectations, based on your populace. If turnover is high, you may need to lower your expectations to a level beneath what you could expect from a more tenured and stabilized force. Be conscious, too, of whether or not you are asking people to do things for which they have no demonstrated propensity.

AS MARKET FORCES COLLIDE, YOUR PEOPLE MOVE IN ONE OF TWO DIRECTIONS: EITHER CLOSER TO OR FURTHER FROM PROFICIENCY.

3. "The Why"

Why does the topic matter? Why does each key element matter? Why is this relevant to teach, learn, and reinforce? Why will learning these things help them sell more?

Great programs pound home the *Why*, because the *Why* teaches insight, and insight increases a willingness to embrace. Without embracing new ideas, new behaviors simply don't happen.

4. Chronology

Sequence is important, because successful adult learning requires a building-block approach. What builds best upon what? Does one module inspire the next? Half of the battle to inspiring people to learn is triggering their curiosity. Smart sequencing prods professional evolution.

5. *Money*

Eagles soar. Sheep don't. Who and what is worth investing in? Keeping people is cheaper than replacing them, but invest your development money wisely. Plow your relevant resources into people who have a track record of inspired good work.

> KEEPING PEOPLE IS CHEAPER THAN REPLACING THEM, BUT INVEST YOUR DEVELOPMENT MONEY WISELY.

What people think drives how they feel. *How* they feel drives what they do. Getting better at selling requires hard work and a disciplined commitment. Invest in the reps from whom you'll get the best return, since their strengthening self-image (what they think of themselves), shapes their self-esteem (how they feel about themselves). Truly motivated reps, driven to improve, visualize themselves at the top of their peer group.

When salespeople believe that a change will be positive, they will change. When they can't see it or feel it, they don't change—and throwing money at them, hoping they will, is a waste. Inspired, motivated people who want to grow will find a way, either with you or with another company. Invest in the good ones.

Creating a strategy brings some science to KSA gap closure, and probably will involve constructing several strategy pyramids. As you build the comprehensive plan, each pyramid pins down what needs to be taught individually and collectively to the team, boundaried by two things: *realistic expectations* and *relevance*.

Can your team *realistically* be developed quickly and well? Or do you need to clean house and bring in better people, perhaps at a premium, in order to raise the long-term performance bar? Will you be asking your people to do things they have never demonstrated? If they *have* done it, how often? In selling, like life, once is an accident, twice a coincidence, three or more is a trend. Promises mean zero.

Without *relevance,* you waste energy, time, and money. Build for relevance. Test for it and deliver it. Avoid "off-the-shelf" programs that do not cut to the core of a very specific learning objective. If a sales team sniffs irrelevance in what you're teaching—either in content or delivery—they'll tune out your program. You'll lose them. They'll pull out their BlackBerries, killing time doing the two-thumb *cha-cha-cha* on their tiny keyboards.

Another key—a big one—to smart, real-time field relevance, is knowing your marketplace well enough to identify precisely what drives your people's success. Does consistent success hinge mostly on Knowledge, rather than Skills or Attributes? If so, strategic sales differentiation is key. Customer insight and understanding are vital. What specifically must your people know in order to gain a competitive edge?

Or does your organization's success rely primarily on Skills? If there is little product or service differentiation between you and your competitors, the best salespeople will make the difference. If your people are better, you will win. If yours are inferior, you will lose. If you leave it to chance, you will lose.

When opposing sales forces are quasi-equal, sales force Attributes make the difference. After all, people buy from people. They buy the most from competent, happy, well-dressed, and persistent people: people who are inspired, nice, grateful, conscientious, respectful. Shape your salespeople in positive ways and they will impact the marketplace accordingly.

When deciding what gap-closing improvements are realistic, think carefully about sequence. Remember: According to the American Management Association, 70 percent of strategic business plans do not get executed. Don't let yours become a statistic. Insist that the goals your team decides to build toward are realistically attainable.

On the following pages are five strategy pyramids that help peel back the work and sequencing for *Topic Selection, Complexity, Teaching the Why, Sequential Chronology,* and *Spending Money.*

TOPIC SELECTION

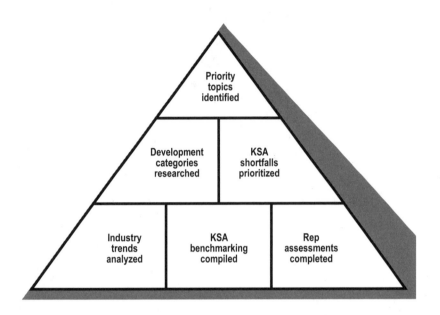

FOCUS ON WHAT TRULY MATTERS

Identify macro (general) topics first. Keep more specific micro topics second. "Communication skills" is general. "Listening" is specific.

Do your homework. What are high-focus learning areas inside your industry that clearly have value to your customer base? What are the trends? What do those trends mean? Where is the business headed?

Use a tough-love approach. Raise your sights and expectations. Communicate a clear goal to your sales force: It is up to them to *leapfrog* the talent offered by your competitors.

What do your competitors do well? What can you learn from them?

What is your vision? Can you describe future excellence to your salespeople? How do they stack up? Are they worth investing in or not?

COMPLEXITY

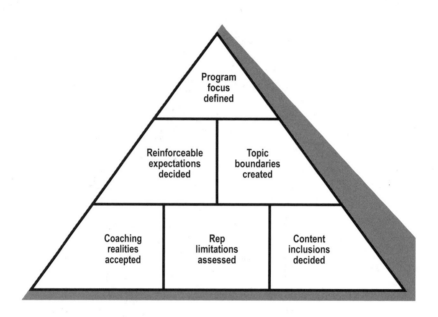

WHAT IS REALISTICALLY DO-ABLE?

Complexity matters. Whatever you do needs to be administered within the abilities of your salespeople to embrace, process, practice, and apply. Make very specific decisions on program focus and scope.

What can you reinforce simply and well? Without reinforcement, new learning is less likely to stick. Topics need clearly defined boundaries. Also, the content within those topics needs specific containment boundaries.

Know your people. Your reps have limitations. Never put them in a position to fail unless you've tried all else and they've reached the point where their future hinges on moving up or moving out. Same with your managers. Managers must own the coaching responsibility for ongoing reinforcement.

TEACHING "THE WHY"

ADULTS MUST UNDERSTAND THE WHY

1. *Build no module without clearly explaining the specific object of the module and why the attainment of that objective matters.*

2. *Adults are grown kids. As such, they are more likely to learn once they understand The Why. Shape it into every module. Script it into every program overview. At every info share (vertically and horizontally) go out of your way to explain each topic and Why it matters. You cannot over communicate the Why. This is vitally true to the stakeholders who hold the purse strings, too. If they don't understand where their money's going and why that investment is so important, the money will disappear.*

3. *In order to get the developmental programs embraced, communicate the Why on multiple levels.* Explain it big picture when discussing future expectations; share it with the management investment required to reinforce what matters most; and discuss the Whys relentless in audience of one meetings whenever the situation warrants. Teach the Why and the "what" will be embraced.

SEQUENTIAL CHRONOLOGY

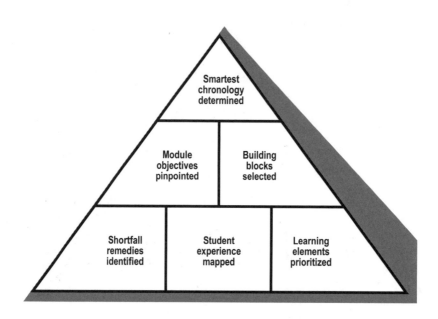

WHAT BUILDS ON WHAT? THINK IT THROUGH.

Sequencing is a huge contributor to success. Invest the time to understand your designed learning experience from the sales organization's point of view. The reps must know the objective of the overall strategy, as well as each component's objective.

Building talent equity in salespeople is the same as building a house. Start with the foundation (Knowledge, Skills, Attributes) and focus on the *need to knows*. The type of business you are in dictates where to start. Begin with what drives sales in your industry: Knowledge, Skills, or Attributes.

Remember, all programs involve and revolve around students. They have the most energy early in the day, the least shortly after lunch. Sequence accordingly. Get them involved early and often. Keep them hopping, especially after food. Field salespeople are allergic to sitting, so smart sequencing and shingled learning (one relevant lesson building upon another) pay big dividends. To keep the class fully engaged, keep things moving at a brisk pace.

SPENDING MONEY

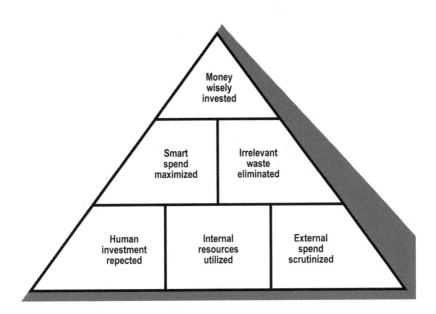

YOU DON'T HAVE TO SPEND MORE TO GET BETTER.

Spend smart! The biggest misconception about getting better is that it costs a lot. Nonsense! Crafting a relevant plan that's strategically clever hangs upon two things: investing dollars (not wasting them), and managing human capital.

Internally, use subject-matter experts and high-equity employees as consultants. Respect their time and recognize their contributions. For many, helping to strengthen the sales force serves as a much-appreciated developmental opportunity. Everyone wins when put in a position to contribute in a meaningful way.

Externally, be hard when sourcing suppliers to help realize your vision. Be firm and specify what you want. Don't bend. Drive hard for maximum value. Trust but verify on issues of competence. Insist on performance guarantees.

Remember Neil Rackham's definition of value: Value = Benefits minus Cost. Benefits are tangible and intangible. Costs are direct and indirect. Maximize the value of what you get for your money by squeezing every element.

STEP FIVE: MERCHANDISE!

Just like the Thanksgiving Day turkey that we aspire to carve, plowing forward with merchandising programs to develop our people doesn't work without a strategy. The power of programs comes from merchandising the message in order to "sell it" to sales reps with maximum impact. To do this, switch your point of view to that of the sales team. Your reps take time out of the field and show up wanting to learn. They hope to net a good return on their time invested in the workshop. You owe them valuable, relevant insight or skills that adds to their competitive edge. Give them that, and your company will maximize its return on investment dollars.

Now more than ever, merchandising your messages to teach a dynamically-changing sales audience is a vital success step. Technology, changing demographics, and shorter attention spans mean you cannot let your people teach the way it was done ten or twenty years ago. So, listed on the next page are ten smart information-merchandising tips.

TECHNOLOGY, CHANGING DEMOGRAPHICS, AND SHORTER ATTENTION SPANS MEAN YOU CANNOT LET YOUR PEOPLE TEACH THE WAY IT WAS DONE TEN OR TWENTY YEARS AGO.

TEN ELEMENTS OF GREAT MERCHANDISING

1. Understand the three primary ways that people learn: audio, visual, and kinesthetic.

2. Factor into your message-design the two different ways people process ideas: detail-to-concept, or concept-to-detail.

3. Master all four components of effective communication: sender, receiver, channel, message.

4. Pack value into every program module.

5. Smartly use your time allocations and clock management, especially as they relate to the performance peaks and valleys of the evolving workday.

6. Remove distractions and barriers to learning performance.

7. Keep everyone engaged.

8. Test and assess the progress of each participant.

9. Stay vigilant for anything that helps to maximize their retention, application, and positive change of your people—individually and collectively. Strive to learn a *better* way to teach these vital elements.

10. Open strong. Finish strong. Salespeople evaluate a session based on how it goes from its onset to the first coffee break. Same with a strong close at the end of the day. Leave them positive and upbeat with infectious energy as the day draws to a close.

EXPANDING ON THE TEN ELEMENTS

1. Understand the three ways people learn: audio, visual, and kinesthetic.

Audio learners learn best by *listening*, so they tend to take verbal instructions well. Visual learners do best by *watching*; they learn best by replicating actions that others show them. Kinesthetic learners do best by *doing*; they prefer active engagement and often figure things out on their own by hands-on trial-and-error. In meetings and during sales calls, kinesthetics tend to keep their hands busy. Pen spinners are an example. So are doodlers and note-takers. In any work group, chances are you'll have some of each.

For example, think about how people ask for directions. Some listen to spoken words without notes, repeat them verbatim, then set off en route. Others write down the directions. The third type says, "Which way is north? What's it near? I can find it."

Often attendees cue their learning styles by the words they use. Audio learner tip-offs include phrases like, "I hear you. I like the sound of that. Sounds good to me." Visual learners may say, "Looks good. I see what you're saying. Crystal clear to me." Interactive messages denote a kinesthetic learner: "You paint a nice picture. Seems worth investigating. Let's pull apart the elements and tackle them one at a time."

As you build your KSA development programs, make sure that every module is crafted to appeal to all three learning styles. PowerPoint is often ineffective because its primary appeal is to the visual learners in the audience. Audio learners and kinesthetic learners bore quickly, because the information is not presented in a learning style that suits them. Once bored, they tune out.

2. Factor into your message-design the two different ways people process ideas: detail-to-concept, or concept-to-detail.

Because people have different learning styles, they use different thought processes to arrive at conclusions. If you send a detail person to explain something to a high-concept thinker, within minutes the concept person will be cross-eyed with confusion. *Where are you going with this? Spit it out.*

Same on the flip side. If you go high-concept to a detail person, he or she won't even bother trying to follow. *Where are the facts? There are a thousand things missing here. Why are you wasting my time?*

Big problems stem from cerebral shutouts that arise when learners cannot embrace a concept due to the way an idea is packaged and presented. While like-thinkers communicate easily, unlike-thinkers do not. They struggle to communicate, exchanges are forced and stilted, and awkward discussions are speed bumps to learning. To proactively avoid communication failures, build every module so that it is presented in ways relevant to both concept and detail thinkers.

> **BIG PROBLEMS STEM FROM CEREBRAL SHUTOUTS THAT ARISE WHEN LEARNERS CANNOT EMBRACE A CONCEPT DUE TO THE WAY AN IDEA IS PACKAGED AND PRESENTED.**

3. Master all four components of effective communication: sender, receiver, channel, and message.

While recognizing different learning styles helps to assure that your salespeople will receive a message well, the most important *merchandising* element is this one. Each of these four components plays a vital role in MAXIMUM HORSEPOWER selling.

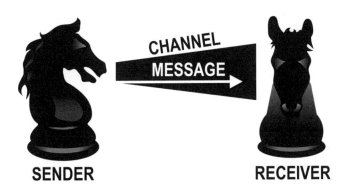

SENDER   RECEIVER

Sender

Selling ideas in a sales workshop is the same as selling ideas to prospects and customers. Whoever talks the most is losing. As a sender, strive to facilitate a *dialogue* (interactive communication). Salespeople like to talk. Build modules that let them. Design from *two* points of view: the facilitator as the sender, the learner as the sender.

Receiver

Receivers (audiences) process ideas differently. During interpersonal communication, 55% of a message is transmitted by nonverbal body language, 38% by voice and tone, 7% by the words spoken. Study your objectives, and factor in receiver management. Few program builders do.

Channel

How you transmit a message is its delivery vehicle or *channel*. Channels are verbal (spoken), written (handouts, fax, etc.), visual (PowerPoint), digital (email, web-based, PDAs), voice mail, and interactive two-way digital (telephone discussions, webinars, videoconferencing).

Every communication channel has strengths and limitations. Know those pluses and minuses. Always select the best delivery channel for the learning objective. When appropriate, multiple channels work better than a sole channel, because you are more likely to be relevant to the three different learning preferences of the audience.

Wrong channel selection or channel abuse (the over-dependence of a single channel, regardless of circumstance) can destroy a presentation's impact. Death by PowerPoint is a prime example. PowerPoint is quick, easy, and convenient for senders, but not for most receivers. They bore easily and quickly and tune out the presenter (sender).

Another example is e-learning; okay for transferring and testing knowledge, useless for skill development which, by nature, is best when interactive. Master your communication channels and you'll maximize the impact of your messages, while minimizing wasted time and potential audience boredom.

Message

Make your statements short and clearly understood, scripted in the language your salespeople use. Remember that some people process ideas detail-to-concept, and others concept-to-detail. Make every message statement relentlessly relevant to everyone present—or as many as possible. This is absolutely vital when creating lasting, high-impact learning experiences. Whether in a workshop or presentation to senior executives, your messages must hit the relevance bullseye.

4. Pack value into every program module.

Salespeople have itchy bottoms. They prefer to be in motion and don't like sitting in a room all day while sales are being made beyond the four walls. Teaching a sales class can quickly become a lion-tamer's challenge. From their chairs, the reps roar and wave their paws.

ROAR! TEACH ME SOMETHIN'!

Treat each module you deliver like its own unique value proposition: What is the benefit the reps will derive from the module? What are the direct and indirect equities? What is it costing the company in time and money for the salespeople to attend?

Respect each of these pivotal considerations. Deliver to the attainment of each specific objective and you'll end up with a series of solid, well-appreciated modules that will produce positive change. To create value, every module's objective must be important and relevant to the receiving participants at the sales workshop. Define that objective and build toward it. Make sure it is attainable.

Because in-person skill development is costly, also dole out your knowledge modules in less-expensive delivery methods. (The exception is when information is complex and best taught in an interactive environment facilitated by subject-matter experts.)

Skill work is best accomplished interactively via practice, so create a smart environment. Invest the associated class time in teaching the *what,* the *how*, and the *why*. Urge the reps to practice the techniques they value most, on their own in specific social settings (cocktail parties, at lunch, while waiting in line, etc.). As simple as this suggestion sounds, many reps appreciate the steerage and most are willing to practice when they have ideas about how and where to do it: in the office, at home, with friends and strangers—but never with customers. Never encourage your salespeople to practice on the customers. Customers are show time!

> **SKILL WORK IS BEST ACCOMPLISHED INTERACTIVELY VIA PRACTICE.**

> **URGE THE REPS TO PRACTICE THE TECHNIQUES THEY VALUE MOST, ON THEIR OWN IN SPECIFIC SOCIAL SETTINGS (COCKTAIL PARTIES, AT LUNCH, WHILE WAITING IN LINE, ETC.).**

5. Use smart time allocations and effective clock management, especially as they relate to the performance peaks and valleys of the workday.

Clock discipline is important for a multitude of reasons: It keeps you on schedule, rations time according to the percentage focus you want a module to represent, enables the right modules to be delivered at specific times of the day, and sends a very strong message to the class that the program is professionally run. All of these help you to "sell a salesman."

Map your program to a time calendar. Block time for startup, intros, expectation setting, lunch, and breaks. Also plan time for reviews upon return to class, at the end of the day, and the beginning of future days.

First impressions are vital, so start strong. Be punctual at resuming after your first break, and don't wait if some of your people are missing. Start anyway. Ignore the latecomers as they straggle back. But as they get settled, call on them quickly. Treat them as if they've been there the entire time. They won't like it, but the people who were punctual will. Your message is subtle but clear: There is punishment for non-compliance.

If the latecomer can't answer what you asked because he or she missed the material, that person will not be late a second time. No one likes looking bad to peers. If the latecomer manages a correct answer, he or she now knows that being late means getting called on. Most of the time this risk of embarrassment cures the problem. If someone's tardiness is chronic, take that person aside at the break and reset your expectations. Run a tight, professional program.

The post-lunch crash is the toughest slot, so avoid lectures. Lectures are one-way "sender" dumps, and the food-sated "receivers" won't process your words. Fill the post-lunch slot with interactive, involved work. Keep them busy and moving. Ratchet up the energy.

THE POST-LUNCH CRASH IS THE TOUGHEST SLOT, SO AVOID LECTURES.

If you don't, the group's enthusiasm will wane. When students waddle back from lunch, stuffed by too much food, they engage or disengage based on the value of the material immediately before them. If the module is interactive and valuable, they will dial in. If left to sit and listen while their food digests, many tune out.

How to carve up time blocks

Build every module systematically so that the learning objective can be comfortably attained before its scheduled completion. Pitfalls to good clock management include straying off-topic, lack of focus on the specific learning objective, and losing control of who's doing the desired talking.

Design every module to have specific, targeted speakers handling the facilitation. Alternate teacher speeches, sales rep and guest presenters, and interactive group dialogue. If you are dedicating an hour to robust discussion, how many participants will be involved? Ten contributing equally during one hour provides six minutes each, assuming zero time is wasted; time use is never linear, discussions go sideways, so budget half that amount (three minutes) per person. How many questions or topics can you adequately cover based on that allocation?

Peeling back the desired group dynamic into a methodically dissected expectation per participant enables you to build tight, focused modules that will run efficiently. Attaining every specific learning objective is the end game of every module. Know what the objective is, and build the appropriate dynamic well *inside* the time allocated. If you are using handouts for group exercises, do your salespeople (and yourself) a big favor and always put the time allocation under the header.

For example:

PAIRS LISTENING EXERCISE
Time allocation: 20 minutes

As a general rule, the more the group talks and the less you do, the better the learning experience for the participants, especially salespeople. They like to talk, so let them.

AS A GENERAL RULE, THE MORE THE GROUP TALKS AND THE LESS YOU DO, THE BETTER THE LEARNING EXPERIENCE FOR THE PARTICIPANTS, ESPECIALLY SALESPEOPLE.

Factor discussion time into *every* dialogue, and create exercises that underscore the learning dynamic. Role playing, for example, helps salespeople *feel* what works and what doesn't. Factor in time to do what you want, then talk about what they experienced. Then test to see if the practiced behaviors are making them feel what you intended. Telling them what they *should* feel isn't worth two shelled peanuts. Shepherd each participant through the experiential learning exercise.

6. *Remove distractions and barriers to learning performance.*

Some success inhibitors are visible, others are invisible. Saboteurs include venue selection, room and class size and set-up, high ceilings and acoustics, module design *faux pas,* mistakes with food, poor seating assignments, interruptions, tardiness. These inhibitors negatively impact listening comprehension and learning, and tie directly to the same three barriers to performance that are commonly found throughout every level of selling: Either a rep *can't* learn, *won't* learn, or is *prevented from* learning.

SOME SUCCESS INHIBITORS ARE VISIBLE, OTHERS ARE INVISIBLE.

Can't learn issues are troubling because they demonstrate shortcomings in Knowledge and Skills that may not be bridgeable.

Won't learn barriers stem from people perceiving that either there's no real payoff for doing the work required to learn what is new, or there's no downside penalty if they don't. They also might suspect that mastering what is being offered could lead to more work, which unmotivated people abhor.

Prevented from learning issues can be visible disruptions (e.g., bad venues, locations, interruptions) or invisible inhibitors such as poor instructional merchandising or overloaded battles for mindshare (work problems, home problems, financial or health problems).

One expectation I set with sales professionals I meet with is simple: "When you're here, I need you *here*." I am asking for their total attention, which is an increasing challenge compared to a decade ago. We are a sound-bite society and behaviors have changed. Retraining someone to focus isn't always easy. This vital issue—the ability to concentrate for an extended period—is one of sales' greatest behavioral erosions in the new millennium.

7. Keep everyone engaged.

Class size impacts your teaching options, which can limit the reps' learning experience. Strive to teach *The Ripken Way:* Keep it simple, make it fun, celebrate the individual, and explain why. Do all of these and you'll be able to keep everyone involved. When they're involved, they commit. When they commit, they improve.

The overriding element in keeping your sales talent engaged is being almost fanatical about leading them in ways that will maximize their positive emotional experience individually and collectively. Do this and they will sell each other (as much as themselves) as your learning sessions gain momentum.

THE OVERRIDING ELEMENT IN KEEPING YOUR SALES TALENT ENGAGED IS BEING ALMOST FANATICAL ABOUT LEADING THEM IN WAYS THAT WILL MAXIMIZE THEIR POSITIVE EMOTIONAL EXPERIENCE INDIVIDUALLY AND COLLECTIVELY.

Sales reps can quickly read whether or not a program is designed to maximize a great learning experience for their benefit. They also can tell whether or not you care. If both readings are affirmative, they'll dive in.

SALES REPS CAN QUICKLY READ WHETHER OR NOT A PROGRAM IS DESIGNED TO MAXIMIZE A GREAT LEARNING EXPERIENCE FOR THEIR BENEFIT. THEY ALSO CAN TELL WHETHER OR NOT YOU CARE. IF BOTH READINGS ARE AFFIRMATIVE, THEY'LL DIVE IN.

8. Test and assess the progress of each participant.

The downside of large classes is the loss of connection with each participant.

Managers and business leaders want to know, for better or worse, what they have or don't have in the way of sales talent. Big classes can stymie your assessment, so factor *pulse-reading* checkups into your program design, to find out whether or not your salespeople are absorbing the module's objectives. Some will, some won't.

You *never* want to finish a skill session without knowing who has progressed and who hasn't. Checking who gets it and who doesn't is critical to becoming a great molder of talent. Embrace that responsibility and you'll find creative ways to get results. Bake positive emotional messages and tones into everything you say and you'll maintain a positive, non-threatening learning environment in which the salespeople are excited and thriving on improving their professional skills. *Do a better job. Make more money.* That's how they're thinking. Just help them get there.

9. Stay vigilant for anything that helps to maximize the retention, application, and positive change of key learning principles for everyone.

Life skills are the Trojan horse of sales talent development and I frame all of my key sales lessons inside them. Life skills produce higher retention, and foster a greater post-learning incorporation of ideas, than any other teaching method I have used or seen. In other words, life skills help maximize the "stick rate" of what you're striving to teach.

LIFE SKILLS HELP MAXIMIZE THE "STICK RATE" OF WHAT YOU'RE STRIVING TO TEACH.

Make your learning principles important to "real life" and sales reps are far more likely to embrace them than if the concepts are perceived as "business only." Sales is, after all, about influencing behaviors. Teach salespeople what influences their own life choices and they'll gladly apply that insight to their business.

The same holds true with problem solving and listening. Frame as many *business* lessons as possible in the context of *personal* life skills and you'll grow a sales team of unstoppable winners.

10. Open strong. Finish strong.

Great sales programs linger in the mind long after a session ends, if your reps leave with at least one legitimate technique that will make them better forever. But in order to have a memorable learning event, get off to a quick start—and finish with a bang. Don't leave strong starts and strong finishes to chance. Know *precisely* what you will say and do. Hook them quickly, work hard throughout the day, and turn them loose in an upbeat and positive way.

Salespeople decide very quickly whether to dial into or out of a mandatory training program. Often this occurs in the first hour (for a daylong session) or the first morning of a multi-day seminar. Begin immediately with a great *interactive* learning dynamic and you'll set the stage for a momentum-building experience.

Whenever possible, close each half-day session with a thought provoker: a strong, positive message that inspires the listeners' personal attributes.

This is doubly important at the program's end. Leave your salespeople with something to think about, a lingering memory that will persistently reaffirm their value to their family, friends, community, and company. Closing strong *matters*. People motivated to change, will.

This concept—celebrating the individual—is step three in the late baseball coach Cal Ripken Senior's teaching methodology. Use it. As a leader, you must do your best to inspire your people to chase their potential. Potential is latent in way too many salespeople.

There is greatness in everyone. Many people who work for you don't know that or can't see it. It's your job to tell them. Inject positive emotional experiences into their

> THERE IS GREATNESS IN EVERYONE. MANY PEOPLE WHO WORK FOR YOU DON'T KNOW THAT OR CAN'T SEE IT.

hearts and minds and you will propel your people toward a new, more powerful future.

STEP 6: DELIVER & TEST

Delivery

Done well, this step helps motivate your reps' commitment to grow. A *blah* delivery inspires no one and, more often, creates disinterest.

When it comes to delivery, credibility is everything. Salespeople expect legitimacy, so give it to them. Individually and collectively, they are different than the surrounding cubicle colonists who support them. Salespeople prefer to learn from salespeople, battle-tested kindred souls who have survived the echoes of *no* often enough to create cheers of *yes*. They are noble warriors who generate revenue for a living. Salespeople respect peers who honor and excel at the craft.

> SALESPEOPLE PREFER TO LEARN FROM SALESPEOPLE, BATTLE-TESTED KINDRED SOULS WHO HAVE SURVIVED THE ECHOES OF NO OFTEN ENOUGH TO CREATE CHEERS OF YES.

Delivery requires sales credibility and skilled proficiency, so it belongs in Sales, not in Organizational Development or Human Resources. Credibility is unimpeachable and, without the scars, it's tough to fake. The same with proficiency; it is impossible to fake.

Years ago at Xerox, I worked with a guy who stood up in front of new hire classes and lied about his credentials. He had never sold as much as a single bottle of toner. He was a nepotism hire who stood up there and faked it. New trainees didn't know any better, but veterans did and quickly smoked him out. While it's easy to *tell* people how to sell, getting them to focus, listen, care, and improve is a totally different persuasion.

In the context of advancing the skills of salespeople, there are two aspects of credibility: the sales side, and the instructional side. Does the instructor have the KSAs (Knowledge, Skills, and Attributes) to role-model professional selling? Has he or she mastered, in a sales context, the profession of classroom management? Does he or she deliver with high impact?

Hand-in-hand with credibility goes proficiency, the glue that makes improvement stick. Salespeople are an itchy sort. They are ego-driven adults whose professional lives evolve on emotional rollercoasters. Some deals are won in glorious upsets; others are lost in crushing defeats.

Many salespeople enter a classroom close-minded from being told that they need to improve, so their learning process must be one of self-discovery or they will have no discovery at all. Great instructors create a motivating environment of self-discovery. Here are the critical success factors:

Proficiency in Adult Learning

Xerox taught its sales trainers that there are four stages of adult learning. Experience has taught me that there is also a fifth. Here are those five, framed against the context of a whitewater-rafting trip.

Stage 1: Unconscious incompetence. The first-timers in the raft don't know what they're doing, but they don't realize it yet. A non-salesperson trying to teach sales falls squarely into this category and will fail miserably. Fledgling salespeople are often clueless about the realities of the life they are about to enter. The rafting trip looks like a lot of fun on the website and brochure. After all, the people in the photographs are smiling. How hard can it be?

Stage 2: Conscious incompetence. The paddlers don't know what they are doing, but the moment the current grabs the raft and shoots it down-river, they instantly realize it. The raft bounces and jostles in the swift hydraulics. A giant boulder suddenly looms. The rafters panic, jolted by fear and concern; they now understand that the journey is governed by the powerful whims of a fickle river, not by what's promised on a four-color brochure.

Stage 3: Conscious competence. By listening to their guide and doing what they're told, the rafters focus, concentrate, and execute. With guidance, they can emulate appropriate behavior, with a reasonable chance to perform as expected. But it's tepid execution, not yet automatic. At this stage—Stage 3—a million mediocre or worse salespeople hide behind canned PowerPoint presentations. They depend on their slides to usher them safely through a big presentation's stressful emotional whitewater, since the focus is on the screen, not the presenter. In rafting terms, at this stage the team is executing behaviors based on the instructions the guide barks out. If they execute properly, they will safely navigate the dangerous, roily hydraulics. If they don't listen— and fail to execute—they will get dunked, maybe even drown. And they know it.

Stage 4: *Unconscious competence.* At this point, the bounding raft is guided downriver by rafters who are flawlessly executing paddling and steering decisions without guidance. This stage is the goal of all talent developers and sales leaders, because it is now that the workers have mastered the learnings and do what is needed reflexively, without thinking. This was the pinnacle of the four stages of learning that Xerox taught and expected of its instructors. Talent development excellence that produces *unconscious competence* blends a motivated sales force with a clever instructional design and a delivery that has program relevance and instructional credibility.

Stage 5: Subject-matter expert. In rafting terms, these are your master river-runners, the men and women who train great paddlers into top-notch guides. They can read a river like Tiger Woods reads a putting green. Subject-matter experts (SMEs) are relentless in their need to separate from their peer group and do so via talent and performance. Unconscious competence is nice, but to an SME, being great is better. These people are the best there is at what they do and work hard to make sure they never fall below that standard. The difference between unconscious competence and subject matter expertise boils down to ego and work quality. Watching them work, the consistency of a SME's exemplary performance is humbling and inspiring. Their proficiency comes from true and demonstrated mastery of the trade. These people define greatness. SMEs are made, not born, and truly are "the best of the best."

CREDIBILITY

Credibility's definition is simple: Whoever is in charge must have earned the right to be there. Internally, you know who these men and women are. Externally, you don't; you have to learn. So, *caveat emptor* (buyer beware): There are a whole lot of fakers out there pretending to know what they're doing. Thoroughly check backgrounds and references. Know where your money flies. Here are three key points concerning instructional credibility:

1. *Don't fake beyond your credibility boundaries.* Sales audiences own the world's most accurate electric fences and BS detectors. When expertise is bluffed, the fence buzzes, the noses sniff, and mouths bark. Great instructors never need to fake it. Honor yourself and your audience by staying inside your core of special insight. Engage SMEs in areas outside your expertise.

2. *Honor the profession. Respect the participants.* Build time into the discussion modules to *listen* to what the participants have to offer. Subject matter experts

know more, have more accumulated knowledge, than others. That doesn't mean that they know more about *every* element. They *compile* expertise. They aren't know-it-alls, nor do they pretend to be. All great delivery artists learn as much from their classes as do those they teach. They are open and willing to learn from anyone, at any time, about anything.

3. *Never be an expert in something that requires no expertise.* A friend, Jan Heckmann, coined this phrase for me twenty years ago. We were in a Xerox training lab, watching a stuffed suit know-it-all pretend he knew how to clear a paper jam from a high-volume electronic duplicator. The *suit* shredded the stuck paper to confetti, trying to remove it, and never bothered to ask for help.

Rather than volunteer, Jan and I stood by and watched. When ten minutes elapsed and the suit's classmates started mercilessly toasting him, Jan moved in to intercede. As he did, he turned to me and whispered, "There's a lesson to be learned here. Never be an expert in something that requires no expertise." I broke up laughing. Pure poetry and words to live by.

Without a word, Jan lifted a small lever. A wide cavityopened and freed the paper to drop loose. The suit's face turned as red as Jan's tie.

Smart people don't do dumb things.

When it comes to integrating external delivery suppliers into your strategic development plan, seek, and pay for, Stage 5 people (subject matter experts). If you have to, settle for Stage 4 people (unconscious competence). Never accept Stage 3 people (conscious competence). Your salespeople deserve better—and they need it. Positive results come about only when you give your reps a better-than-mediocre performance.

When it comes to how quickly your reps escalate up the five stages of learning, remember that development is a process. Making them better isn't an instant on/off, especially in the world of skill development, which takes practice and does not come with a diploma. Changing behaviors isn't easy—especially when the new standard is significantly higher than the status quo.

INSOURCE OR OUTSOURCE YOUR PROGRAM DELIVERY?

DIFFERENT FACTORS SHAPE WHAT'S BEST

INSOURCE	OUTSOURCE
Familiarity breeds ho-hum.	A natural incentive to perform.
Cheaper.	More costly. Are you investing this money or spending it? How solid is your ROI?
May not be SME on what's required.	Generalists abound. Specialists are worth a premium. It only costs a nickel more to go first class, but you have to spend the nickel.
Often good, not great. Which do you aspire to be?	Inquire and verify their delivery style and classroom-management effectiveness.
How skilled are your internal teaching resources? (Amateurs aren't good.)	Outsource providers can *sell*. But can they *teach* as well as they sell?
Terrific developmental opportunity for the right individuals.	Candid third-party feedback opinions are often worth a premium to managers and leadership teams.
Excellent retention tool.	Good ones inspire your people differently and more profoundly than co-workers.
Participants are often overtly politically correct, which compromises a straight-shooting approach.	Must be professional, but their lack of internal political baggage is often a big plus. Candor is refreshing and helpful.
Who can teach it better? Someone with internal knowledge of the business idiosyncrasies?	Who can teach it better? Someone with a different, unbiased point of view?
How painful will the learning be? If it's easy and painless, consider keeping things internal.	If "tough love" is required, hire an unbiased black hat to deliver the news.
Is what's required internal in nature, company stuff that needs to be shared?	Is what's required foreign and new to the organization or not in great abundance?
What's the upside of good execution? Where's the downside of poor execution?	How much is at stake? A lot or a little? How do you minimize risk?

TESTING

If you've ever cupped a dancing grasshopper, then slowly opened your hands to see if you caught it, you know what it's like to test your salespeople during and after a workshop. Sometimes the hopper is in there. Sometimes it ain't.

"NOW YOU SEE ME...
BOING!
NOW YOU DON'T!"

Tests are part of every vocation, so sales is no exception.

Every ballplayer in the major leagues earned his way there thanks to thousands of hours of work for over a decade under the watchful eyes of busloads of coaches. But which coach taught the star each facet of the game? Which helped him get good enough to reach the big leagues? Who gets credit for his home runs? Who is to blame for his strikeouts?

A similar debate exists in selling. Bean counters want to measure the ROI on "training." The m-word (measurement) causes some talent professionals to shudder, because talent development is not an instant gratification business: It's an investment business.

TALENT DEVELOPMENT IS NOT AN INSTANT GRATIFICATION BUSINESS: IT'S AN INVESTMENT BUSINESS.

Multiple answers exist to the bean counter's question: the revenue line, customer satisfaction, sales-employee turnover rate, new-hire referral figures, and industry reputation. Developing talent is subjective, so it isn't easy to measure. None of the data bubbles up from a spreadsheet—so testing *is* essential. Without proof that the lessons are sticking, you don't know whether you are blowing money or investing it.

Testing Knowledge

Breaking down the testing-and-evaluation process into the three performance elements (Knowledge, Skills, and Attributes), Knowledge is by far the easiest to measure. It's what you know, relative to what you need to know in order to be successful. If something is important enough to teach, it's important enough to test.

Don't horse around with this step. If the reps need to know something, teach it. Then test it. Hold everyone accountable, salespeople *and* managers. Yes or no, true or false, fill in the blanks. See who is making strides and who isn't. Don't tolerate slackers. Install and administer penalties for substandard performance.

Testing Skills

Skills are the demonstrated ability to deliver desired results over time. Knowledge is easy to measure in a quantifiable form; skills aren't. Improvement is subjective. So judging sales talent from a skill development perspective calls for multiple points of view: the reps, the managers, the customers, the instructor. Judging good or bad, better or worse, more effective or less, are all open to varying degrees of debate. A fair assessment should be an unimpeachable tenet of any corporate development strategy. The key is figuring out how to do it.

Kirkpatrick's Theorem is a common formula used in the training business to identify four levels of measurement, each offering a different perspective. In theory, when all four perspectives yield positive results, positive change in skill level has occurred.

Level one consists of student evaluations, often called *"smile sheets."* If you use them, make sure your opinion surveys are judging relevance and competence.

I am lukewarm on smile sheets for two reasons: One, being hard on someone in class usually leads to angry, vitriolic penned retribution on the smile sheet. Second, an instructor whose performance or chance at repeat business is judged by student opinions tends to pander to those students. Rather than make the hard call and insist on top performance, the instructor settles for less, rather than risk getting dinged on an opinion survey. If you use smile sheets, take them for what they are: convenient data points with built-in limitations.

Level two in Kirkpatrick's process incorporates teacher observations. A smart instructor can quickly read who is advancing concepts in the class and who isn't. Pros have no axe to grind with anyone. They only care about tangible progress.

Level three measures progress as gauged by manager observations after a salesperson has returned to the field. Is he or she using the new techniques? Application is important to notice and to reinforce in repetitively positive ways.

Level four, Kirkpatrick's final measurement, is one that senior execs care about most, but it takes the longest to produce: absolute results, the tangible fruits of successful good work. In the end, after all of the money is spent and the hard work invested, is the net result more business? If so, measure it. The ROI sometimes can be astronomical, because the difference between winning and losing is sometimes *one technique*, smartly executed.

IN THE END, AFTER ALL OF THE MONEY IS SPENT AND THE HARD WORK INVESTED, IS THE NET RESULT MORE BUSINESS?

Russell Jones, a highly respected London-based financial services sales executive, has closed individual deals worth upwards to a billion dollars, deals that have redefined the company for which he works. "Big deals are hard," he says. "They are a lot of work. Nights, weekends, whatever it takes. You must know what you're doing, because one mistake can lose it. One *sentence* can lose it."

Jones is a student of the profession of selling, forever searching for one more trick, one tiny edge that will tip a deal in his favor. "This is what I do," he says. "I must do my best."

Over time, the key credibility factor to your talent development organization revolves around your company's ability to fairly assess its people. Sometimes this can be done well by using internal resources. Other times, you're better off going outside for unbiased views.

Testing Attributes

Attributes are the invisibly intrinsic "DNA" factors that make every salesperson different. Talent development programs should strive to inspire attributes in its people. You can't teach attributes, but you certainly can inspire them.

YOU CAN'T TEACH ATTRIBUTES, BUT YOU CERTAINLY CAN INSPIRE THEM. SYSTEMATICALLY EXECUTE TACTICS AND TECHNIQUES THAT INVEST EMOTIONAL EQUITY IN YOUR PEOPLE.

Systematically execute tactics and techniques that invest emotional equity in your people. During one-on-one sessions and group observations, your reps' behaviors accurately signal who is motivated and who isn't. The goal is to inspire what matters most to each individual, so he or she will maximize his or her personal contribution to the organization. Do that and you'll change lives. You also will be building a better business and everyone, in turn, will benefit.

STEP 7: OBSERVE

The cardinal rule of observation is simple: *Know what you're looking for, or there's no chance you'll ever see it.*

The second rule of observation deals with stern accountability. At this stage, the burden of professional development shifts from the company to the rep. He or she must demonstrate commitment to the newly learned techniques. It's the rep's burden to demonstrate. The organization should not have to remind, encourage, cajole, or hope any salesperson decides to role model what is expected. Reps owe the company a return-on-investment (R.O.I.). Observation is a great way to inspect that return.

Without inspection, and reinforcement, long-term growth via behavioral changes will be minimal because many people quickly tend to slip back to their old, comfortable habits.

WITHOUT INSPECTION, AND REINFORCEMENT, LONG-TERM GROWTH VIA BEHAVIORAL CHANGES WILL BE MINIMAL BECAUSE MANY PEOPLE QUICKLY TEND TO SLIP BACK TO THEIR OLD, COMFORTABLE HABITS.

Observations should be both macro and micro: the organization's improvement, and each individual. The following is an overview matrix that nets out the absolute minimum to look for at the three stages of a salesperson's career. Each box offers an opinion for how long your tolerance fuse (patience) should be.

OBSERVATION: WHAT TO LOOK FOR

	Low-tenured	*Mid-career*	*Veteran*
Low performer	Look for a clearly visible and ongoing effort to consciously demonstrate multiple learning priorities. *Burn a little longer fuse due to their newness to the business.*	Expect an improvement urgency that demonstrates a hunger to get better. Inspect quality practice. These reps must demonstrate an unquestionable effort to improve. *A short fuse.*	Tenure means zilch without leadership and performance. Vets must urgently work toward positive change. They also must own better absolute results. *A short fuse.*
Mid-level performer	Watch for the proactive repetitive practicing of their next key learning priority. Hold them to a higher standard. *Medium-to-short fuse.*	Seek proof of conscientious work. Some will never advance beyond the middle of the bell curve. *Medium fuse.*	Have zero tolerance for horsing around. Vets know the game. Look for the demonstrated willingness and work commitment to get better one skill at a time. *Short fuse.*
Star performer	Expect relentless practice tied to one specific thing at a time. *Stars deserve longer fuses than others.*	Inspire stars to a higher level. Challenge them to get better. *Medium fuse for getting going, a short fuse when they are trying.*	Pride drives the star's need to relentlessly improve. Appeal to the ego. They'll get it done. *Long fuse.*

With so much at stake, working hard to get better must never be optional. Everyone owes it to their organization to improve. Calibrating your expectations of your salespeople goes hand-in-hand with the KSA changes you're looking for. With regard to what they are capable of doing, your talent portfolio will be all across the board. Manage their change within their capabilities.

Low Performers

Low tenure. Low-tenured low performers deserve the benefit of the doubt—unless they aren't trying. Adults are aging kids, which means each learns at a different pace. If you aren't seeing effort, however, cut your losses and counsel them out of the business. If they *are* trying, keep encouraging them. Oprah Winfrey was a noble failure in her first job as an on-camera newsreader and she got fired. She's proven to be pretty good ever since.

Mid-career. Reps at mid-career who perform at a low level better be working with a heightened sense of urgency (and effort), because investing development time and money in them is a gamble. It's up to them to validate that worthiness and they must feel the heat of that ownership.

Low-performing mid-career reps will smother you with their good intentions. So what? *Show me the effort. Do better work. This is a results business. Deliver better results.* Customers vote with their money. Every job in every company is nothing more than a temporary custodial spot. Low performers at mid-career either must move forward or move out. Make it clear to them that the status quo just isn't good enough and that no team stays intact forever.

LOW-PERFORMING MID-CAREER REPS WILL SMOTHER YOU WITH THEIR GOOD INTENTIONS.

Veterans. When it comes to accountability for performance, veteran reps should receive zero advantage over less-tenured people. Vets are *expected* to deliver results. Vets understand the business and the accountability that comes with a quota. If a vet is tanking performance-wise, he or she better be working harder, smarter, and more effectively than ever before. If not, start looking for someone who will.

> IF A VET IS TANKING PERFORMANCE-WISE, HE OR SHE BETTER BE WORKING HARDER, SMARTER, AND MORE EFFECTIVELY THAN EVER BEFORE.

In every case with a low performer, effort is an attribute. If the person's attributes aren't fueling the need to practice, you're coddling a bad investment. Make the hard call and move on. Business is not a country club. Ours is a ROI universe in which every sales organization is a planet, and whose revolving results keep feeding the warmth of the sun.

Regardless of experience, your observation expectations with a low performer must be clear and consistent: Step up. Get better. Show me the effort. Get the job done. Don't care enough to try? Then don't waste my time.

Reinforce loudly (and often) that the burden of proof of positive change sits squarely on the shoulders of that individual. At this step of the improvement process, the pendulum has swung. No longer is the organization investing *in* the person. The investment has been made. Now he or she is expected to pay back the organization.

In summary, when it comes to low performers, be firm, be fair, and be consistent. Burden them to demonstrate positive improvement and better absolute results.

Mid-Level Performers

Low tenure. When dealing with mid-level reps, shift your expectations. For people who are new to the sales business and are performing okay, ratchet up their sense of urgency to hone their craft. Rarely will a newbie enter and peak; often they face a performance ramp. Feed their knowledge, emphasize their skill practice, and inspire their attributes. Never let a new rep sit comfortably in the middle of the bell curve.

Mid-career. Many of your mid-career, mid-level performers are destined to stay in the middle of the bell curve forever. Even so, improvement practice remains vital, because status-quo skills lose ground in a tightening market.

Because many salespeople are working within KSA limitations that create a low ceiling for growth, know *your* people's limitations. Most organizations benefit from workforce stability in its "role player" environment; so inspire improvement, and inspect each person's effort—but do not expect your backup singers to someday star on Broadway.

Veterans. Veteran mid-packers are habit-driven, and breaking old habits and creating new ones often seems tougher than teaching a buffalo to skip rope.

Some vets try to skate, figuring, *"Ah, another program of the month. I don't need it. I'm me. Soon enough, this too shall pass."*

AH, ANOTHER PROGRAM OF THE MONTH. I DON'T NEED IT. I'M ME. SOON ENOUGH, THIS TOO SHALL PASS.

Have zero tolerance for lack of effort. No mid-packer gets a scholarship, nobody skates, everybody plays. This might involve staying on top of people, some more than others. Vets don't like this. So what? Ignore the grumbling. What's comfortable doesn't always get the job done. With mid-pack vets you operate under jungle rules—which means there are no rules. Do whatever it takes until there's proof the work is done.

Star Performers

Stars get different treatment, and there's a simple reason why: They've earned it.

Thoroughbreds thrive on competition and love to win. Some are more reluctant to enter the starting gate than others; some walk right in, others need a slap on the flank, a few need a generous shove. In the end, they'll get where they need to go, because that's what thoroughbreds do. They compete, the very best they can.

Every star has a method to his or her madness, so your tolerance fuse should burn longer for them than the others. My guess is that four-fifths of your stars will practice new concepts without so much as a gentle reminder, because it's in their best interest to get better and professional growth feeds them. A few of your more recalcitrant prodigal sons and daughters might fuss about practice, because their success formula already works—but they'll do what it takes to advance.

> **EVERY STAR HAS A METHOD TO HIS OR HER MADNESS, SO YOUR TOLERANCE FUSE SHOULD BURN LONGER FOR THEM THAN THE OTHERS.**

Stars showcase stylistic differences en route to common ambitions. Tolerate it. The key is: Make sure they know you're watching.

Sometimes the most efficient way to make sure your stars are rehearsing is to partner them with an up-and-comer, as mentor and mentee. This lets the star grow and teach at the same time and gives the other rep access to a role-model performer.

Managing stars is a nice challenge to have. Sales superstars are like rare coins—so dig deep, polish their talent, and collect as many of those rare coins as you can.

THE SIX KEY POINTS

1. The burden shifts 100 percent over to the rep to demonstrate mastery of new and better methods. The rep owes the company a solid R.O.I. for what the company has invested in that rep.

2. Low performers must proactively try with an obvious sense of urgency.

3. Mid-performers need to be nurtured or inspired, depending on the individual.

4. Stars get special treatment. Stay in touch—but don't badger them.

5. Everyone is accountable for his or her results.

6. If you do not police them, slackers will slack.

STEP 8: REINFORCE

Most adults are repetitive learners, so the primary way to help most reach the *unconsciously competent* stage is by creating an environment that inspires and encourages practice. When Cal Ripken Sr. was teaching his sons to play baseball, he hammered home a message he echoed a thousand times: "Practice doesn't make perfect," he'd say. "*Perfect* practice makes perfect."

Senior's almost fanatical insistence that his sons Cal Junior and Bill play the game fundamentally right meant spending thousands of hours on millions of drills that involved billions of baseballs. The brothers' tireless commitment to meeting the strict demands of their father steeled both of them to the big leagues. Thousands of far more physically gifted players than the younger Bill never made it to the majors. Cal Junior became an American sports hero; countless are the number of tremendously gifted natural athletes whose careers ended at the foot of the stairway to greatness, which Cal Junior methodically ascended.

Junior is a big, powerful man who coupled his physical skills with mental toughness to prove his father's mantra right: Perfect practice *did* make for perfect play.

As the memory of Cal Junior's career now fades to legend, his legacy will forever link his iron will with his professional approach, discipline, and methodical, almost robotic, flawless execution. His stardom at the highest level is a direct result of honoring what his father preached to so many for so long: By being perfectly prepared to play the game *right,* you'll be perfectly prepared to play your very best.

Putting the onus on the company to reinforce learning is a recipe for failure. Far better results, both short and long-term, occur when reps are *self-motivated* to practice. The key is making practice fun and easy, by encouraging practice techniques that fit the daily activities of people's lives outside the office. As you encourage these practice habits, emulate "The Ripken Way." Cal Senior's rules were simple but comprehensive, as relevant to teaching salespeople as they are ballplayers.

- Keep it simple
- Make it fun
- Celebrate the individual
- Explain why.

PUTTING THE ONUS ON THE COMPANY TO REINFORCE LEARNING IS A RECIPE FOR FAILURE. FAR BETTER RESULTS, BOTH SHORT AND LONG-TERM, OCCUR WHEN REPS ARE SELF-MOTIVATED TO PRACTICE.

The art of this marvelous profession comes from the disciplined execution of a thousand little things that matter. Together, these talent differentiators separate a top performer from a salesperson in the middle of the bell curve—or worse.

Better baseball players win more games. Better salespeople win more deals. Regardless of the profession, a true pro *practices*. When game time arrives, like Cal, a true pro can flawlessly execute under pressure. It's that flawless execution, under pressure, that wins deals and changes careers.

THE ART OF THIS MARVELOUS PROFESSION COMES FROM THE DISCIPLINED EXECUTION OF A THOUSAND LITTLE THINGS THAT MATTER.

HOW QUICKLY CAN YOUR PEOPLE GET BETTER?

How quickly can positive change take place? The MAXIMUM HORSEPOWER process is scalable to any size sales organization, so it doesn't take long to do smart, great work. Time is impacted by the scope of what you need, the numbers, and the clockspeed of the organization's execution. Pilot programs can quickly be built in parallel. Below are realistic major account expectations. Assume accelerated timelines for smaller sales organizations.

TIME PERIOD	MILESTONE EXPECTATION
30 days	*Strategic plan developed.* Great work can be accomplished quickly by following the described process.
60 days	*KSA profiles constructed. Current value propositions redefined.* The faster you get the smartest and best available stakeholders together, the quicker you can reach this milestone.
90 days	*Priority pilots delivered.* Modularity feeds execution. Follow the building process to create relevant programs quickly. Properly built pilot classes should be excellent right out of the chute. Pilot classes should expect tightening. Good is nice; great is the objective.
Six months	*Program continuum in place.* The attendee pipeline should be in place with sales reps coming through. Vested internal stakeholders should be well-apprised already of the progress. Trumpet your successes. By now, the programs should be strong enough that good word-of-mouth is driving demand. The way to judge your support is by whose phone is ringing. If the field is calling to enroll, you're on the right track. If the field is calling to cancel, you're getting bad publicity. If that's the case, stop and fix whatever is broken.
One year	*Modular updates integrated.* Good is never good enough. Stay relevant all the time. Expect to update programs regularly. Ownership of every module is important. Someone must be accountable for its excellence. You should be seeing good talent referred into your pipeline.
Two years	*Process-driven high performance sustained.* The company's reputation for talent excellence and development should be well respected in the field and by your customers. Good talent should be migrating steadily into your pipeline.

8

CHAPTER

THE THREE SKILLS OF INFLUENTIAL PERSUASION

USE "REAL LIFE" SCENARIOS

Skills of persuasion are to a salesperson what sports skills are to athletes. Neither is turned on and off like a light switch. Polished skills must be automatic reflexively and every skill you want your reps to master is learned best when you are able to tie its practice to a social setting the rep frequents. Rehearsing behavioral drills in real life eliminates barriers to practice, since salespeople hate to experiment while meeting with customers. Because of the safe, non-threatening social setting, practicing in a life skill context eliminates this "fear of failure." Since harmless interactions become a bit of a game, every dedicated salesperson is happy to practice new techniques on anyone who's not pay-related. The practice goal, of course, is getting them smooth enough with the new methods to use them confidently with customers.

Following are real-life practice scenarios I have used with great success when teaching the three skills of sales persuasion: (1) learning to listen more effectively, (2) learning how to develop a problem, and (3) learning to disagree properly.

In each case, the important behavior is tagged for practice inside a common social setting that could otherwise be perceived by salespeople as "dead time." By creating utility for these scenarios, each situation takes on a specific learning purpose. By framing a skill to hone inside a "real-life context," you provide the *where* to practice, *what* to practice, and *how* to practice. Armed with a purpose, a rep will practice new techniques.

> **BY FRAMING A SKILL TO HONE INSIDE A "REAL-LIFE CONTEXT," YOU PROVIDE THE WHERE TO PRACTICE, WHAT TO PRACTICE, AND HOW TO PRACTICE.**

SKILL #1: LEARNING TO LISTEN MORE EFFECTIVELY

Practice Setting: The lunchroom, restaurant, or dining room.

Practice Objective: Virtually nobody in the sales business actively teaches listening, which is shocking to me, because it's the *number one most important skill* a great salesperson possesses.

Listening *can* be taught and it *can* be improved. Smart organizations insist that their people get better at it.

I learned a five-step process, which I strongly endorse, from Denver behavioral communication specialist Dr. Sherod Miller. Perfect practice for better listening relies on following Dr. Miller's fives steps, while *listening* for two specific things: content and emotion. Dr. Miller's work teaches participants to *feel* precisely why this five-step process works. What a rep learns by going through the exercise is that a great listener can positively influence someone by not saying a single word.

Dr. Sherod Miller's Five-Step Listening Drill:

1. **Attend.** As the speaker talks about something that matters to them, dial into them nonverbally. Eye contact, rapt attention, the whole deal. You are locked into a universe of two. Nothing else on the planet exists. You are at a social distance, three feet or less.

2. **Affirm.** Head nods, wide eyes, smiles, etc. Send an ongoing series of nonverbal signals that you get the message.

3. **Encourage.** Don't interrupt. This step is designed to keep the person talking. If you *must* speak, get in, utter a word to keep them talking, and immediately jump back out. Do not judge. Do not summarize. Never interrupt their train of thought. *"Wow!" "Then what?" "What else?"* are common encouragers. This encouragement keeps the speaker rambling while you process the content they share and gauge the emotional peaks of their message.

4. **Summarize.** When the speaker has finally finished, summarize back what you heard—*without judgment.* Use his or her words, not your own. *Paraphrase nothing.* "Parrot back" exactly what you heard, the way you heard it, emphasizing the areas of highest emotional resonance.

5. **Ask a relevant question.** Salespeople are told from Day One to ask questions, but rarely do mediocre reps master the three specific reasons to ask them:

   - To seek information
   - To clarify what was heard
   - To test understanding.

Based on what is heard during the social role-play, have the rep pick one of these three types of questions. Good listening provides bountiful opportunities for relevant, insightful, and pointed questions. When you listen well, it's easy to select the right *type* of question and direct it to the speaker's emotional peak.

SALESPEOPLE ARE TOLD FROM DAY ONE TO ASK QUESTIONS, BUT RARELY DO MEDIOCRE REPS MASTER THE THREE SPECIFIC REASONS TO ASK THEM.

Practice Method: Have the rep seek out someone who is willing to talk about a topic that matters to him or her. I prefer practicing during mealtime, because people are bottled up from working and are often quite chatty. Political opinions are easy topics, as are moral views and life experiences. Have the rep choose a topic someone will gladly and passionately ramble on about. The goal is for the rep to listen without interrupting and archive what he or she hears, plus gauge the emotional high/lows of the message. When salespeople *listen* for emotional amplitude, they will hear it. If they don't, they won't.

A huge selling takeaway that comes from experiencing this exercise is how difficult it's become for most people to listen without interrupting the speaker or judging what they hear as right or wrong, good or bad, agree or disagree, etc. *Just listen.*

As listening is a great salesperson's number one most valuable skill, Dr. Miller's exercise is a great process to master.

SKILL #2: DEVELOPING A PROBLEM INTO A NEED

Practice Setting: The backed-up checkout line at a store.

Practice Objective: I am a big advocate of Huthwaite's SPIN® methodology for developing needs in the professional sales marketplace. Have the rep study the process (via the book or Huthwaite's excellent training program) and then practice all four steps of the model while waiting in line. Huthwaite's SPIN® methodology relies on four types of questions: Situation, Problem, Implication, and Needs Payoffs. For example:

- *Situation* question: *"Looks like the lines are clogged again. Do you have other stops to make?"* This often draws an affirmative response.

- *Problem* question: *"Frustrating, isn't it? How long do you think we'll have to wait?"* Again, a quick response. Problem questions are designed to identify an area of dissatisfaction and zero in on the pain.

- *Implication* question: *"Delays are always an inconvenience. What is this keeping you from?"* This question seeks to unearth the ramifications of the delay.

- *Needs Payoff* question: *"It sure would help if they opened more registers to get us out of here so you could get on to that next appointment, wouldn't it?"* Here the rep summarizes what they've heard that has true relevance when problem-solving for a customer.

The goal, of course, is for the rep to become "unconsciously competent" with the ability to develop a customer problem into an actionable need.

Practice Method: Waiting-in-line time is dead time, so urge your reps to take full advantage; they've got a captive audience in front of them and behind them. A line in a store is a perfect practice setting, because no one likes to wait. The person *behind* the rep is the ideal unknowing practice partner because he or she is captive and can't leave first. These practice exchanges should be quick, polite, and non-stalkerish. They are also very structured, which is what "perfect practice" is all about. Armed with a disciplined commitment to perfect practice, a professional salesperson can soon make the four-step SPIN® process automatically conversational.

SKILL #3: LEARNING HOW TO DISAGREE PROPERLY

Another element of the SPIN® model I really like is how to properly disagree. Skilled reps in a finesse type of selling environment *must* learn how to disagree properly, which includes avoiding the use of negative prepositions such as "but" and "however." The word "but" is, in many cases, a contradictory term. It is amateurish, yet uttered a billion times a day in selling scenarios across the globe. Few things grate a smart customer more than hearing a salesperson say, "I agree with you *but* . . ."

FEW THINGS GRATE A SMART CUSTOMER MORE THAN HEARING A SALESPERSON SAY "I AGREE WITH YOU BUT..."

Practice Setting: A cocktail party or social mixer. The lunchroom works just as well.

Practice Objective: When selling into the multiple level complexities of a major sale environment, learning to disagree properly requires excellent listening, coupled with smart segues that are specifically designed to make someone listen to your point of view.

Replying with a quick, reflexive, "No, because" or "Can't, because" spurs the client to push back emotionally (and defensively). Once customers hear a reflexive negative stance from us, pertaining to an issue that matters to them, they have no burning reason to know (or care about) why we don't agree. As soon as they know we disagree, they shut down and stop listening. When the customer knows we disagree, our *reasons* don't really matter. Our goal is to make sure our *reasons* are heard, before we convey a statement of disagreement.

"I disagree for several reasons" lands negatively on a customer. So, the goal of practicing *influential persuasion* is to master a smooth flow of dialogue that eliminates a negative emotional response. *Influential persuasion* requires making someone listen to your reasons first. Then, follow those reasons with a smooth, non-confrontational statement of disagreement. This technique sounds easier in concept than it is in reality. This disagreement methodology is totally counter to a rep's normal, knee-jerk, reflexive behavior. It's a tough skill to master.

Reasons first. Disparate opinion second. Never use the words "but" or "however." In their place, substitute the word "and."

Practice Method: Have the rep pick a popular movie, TV show, or news item to broach with someone. Solicit an opinion, then listen with rapt attention and nod appreciatively as the person explains why he or she feels the way they do. Regardless of what position the person takes, the rep's challenge is to respond with the *opposite* point of view. Respond by acknowledging the solid points of what was heard, then smoothly segue from the other person's key points to the rep's own, spoken non-judgmentally. The rep should offer one or two differentiating reasons to explain their contrarian view, and close by saying something like, "So, I guess our views are slightly different."

The art form is learning to avoid a confrontational disagreement. The cocktail party venue (or similar social setting) is great for this because the sales pro can work the room and practice dozens of times during a single event.

Because most salespeople are repetitious learners, identifying social practice venues creates a learning lab in real life, which means this traditional "downtime" is invested rather than wasted.

THE GOAL OF PERFECT PRACTICE

Purple squirrel sales performers never *practice* in front of a customer. They *perform* in front of customers. In each of the above sample scenarios, the goal is identical: to have fun learning new things in a relaxed, no-pressure setting—so when the stakes rise in a sales situation, the rep is ready to perform his or her very best, most influential work.

The payoff is the confidence to perform perfectly when it matters the most—in front of the customer. When the time comes for the value-added sales cycle to wind to a close, the customer will choose with whom to do business. Perfect practice yields better delivery, and better delivery increases the sales reps' odds of being selected.

To perform their best, your sales team must invest in practice—perfect practice—well ahead of time. Few companies invest a lot of time or money in reinforcement workshops. Smart sales leaders always reinforce the key learning methods; especially during call debriefs, one-on-one coaching sessions, and ride-along days. When offered in a positive vein, such interactions are important contributors to your salespeople's permanent improvement.

PERFECT PRACTICE YIELDS BETTER DELIVERY, AND BETTER DELIVERY INCREASES THE SALES REPS' ODDS OF BEING SELECTED.

In the end, change must come from within. Coach your reps to practice in social settings and inspire them in positive ways. Those who are motivated to practice on their own will get better—assuming they know *where* to practice, *what* to practice, and *how* best to pursue perfect practice with professional discipline.

The success of reinforcement directly relates to your rep's emotional experiences. What they think shapes how they feel. And it is how they feel that drives their desire to practice or not. Great coaches inspire better habits that deliver superior results.

EIGHT TRAITS OF GREAT SALES COACHES

1. Great coaches *Teach*. They don't just do.
2. Great coaches *Motivate*. They do not threaten.
3. Great coaches *Encourage*. They do not disengage.
4. Great coaches *Reward*. They do not blame.
5. Great coaches *Stand Tall*. They do not wilt.
6. Great coaches *Create Value*. They do not meddle.
7. Great coaches *Help*. They do not hover.
8. Great coaches *Inspire*. They do not badger.

WHO TO COACH

The best coaching results come from investing your time with the right people at the right time.

In a recent comprehensive study of good sales organizations, the Washington D.C. Sales Executive Council's findings on sales coaching concluded that the best results come from coaching the right people early in the selling cycle (the strategy stage) and again during the latter stages of a sale. They recommend investing three hours a month on medium and top performers, less time with low performers.

Make your low performers earn their time. Invest in the middle of the bell curve—but don't neglect your top performers. Stay in touch with your big guns, especially concerning new learning opportunities. Strong performers have a naturally inquisitive nature that makes them aspire to learn new techniques, because sometimes it only takes one new idea to help make a sale.

At the *reinforcement* stage, the ongoing sales coaching message must be about rep ownership and accountability. The reps own their improvement, and we owe them caring leadership. Caring means scheduling skill reinforcement into a structured day, in a positive environment conducive to coaching.

Stay consistent with the reinforcement message and be professional about it. Let no one be flippant about the work or the expectation of disciplined practice en route to subject matter mastery.

If you craft a bell curve of your sales performers, here's what to do:

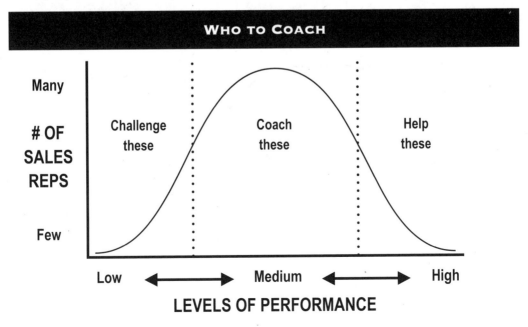

STEP 1. THE DEFINITION STAGE

(Read the plan from the top down. Execute the plan from the bottom up.

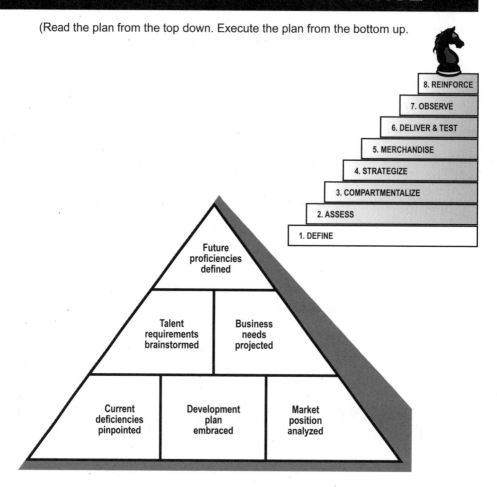

| 8. REINFORCE |
| 7. OBSERVE |
| 6. DELIVER & TEST |
| 5. MERCHANDISE |
| 4. STRATEGIZE |
| 3. COMPARTMENTALIZE |
| 2. ASSESS |
| 1. DEFINE |

Future proficiencies defined

Talent requirements brainstormed

Business needs projected

Current deficiencies pinpointed

Development plan embraced

Market position analyzed

VISUALIZE YOUR TEAM'S "BRAND" OF SELLING

Focus solely on visualizing where you want your sales force to be at a future point in time. How do you want your brand of selling to be described in the marketplace? Measure the future needs of your business, then dissect those needs into the key talent elements it will take to deliver those results at a sustained level of excellence.

Study your current deficiencies mapped against the current competition. Study your market position and build a solid development plan that clearly defines the traits you need your salespeople to role model in order to deliver great performance.

This is a vision step. Until you can see where your team needs to be, you can't begin building a straight-line strategy to get them there.

STEP 2. THE ASSESSMENT

(Read the plan from the top down. Execute the plan from the bottom up.

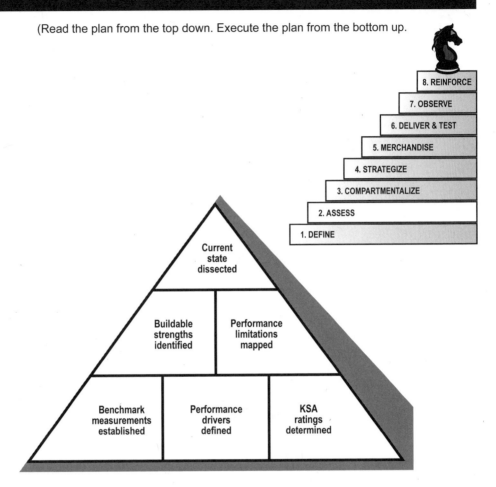

WHEN ASSESSING, BE HARD BUT FAIR

Once your future vision is clear, step back to where you are today. What do your people do well? What don't they? List buildable strengths. Prioritize performance inhibitors. Benchmark externally against the best in your field. Learn *how* they do what they do and why they're good at something you admire.

During the glory days of the IBM and Xerox sales machines, the global reputation of these powerhouse sales forces came from the respect expressed by the two giants' customer bases. That perception was shaped by design, not by accident. Nobody earns premium pricing by generic performance. Both titans invested in their salespeople and trusted those representatives to produce premium value for their customers, a value for which the customers were happy to pay.

Seek to learn and stack-rank the key Knowledge, Skill, and Attribute traits that drive absolute results.

Dissection of your current state is a "tough love" exercise. Be hard, but fair. If you're too close to the action, engage resources who aren't. You need a good, accurate read.

STEP 3. COMPARTMENTALIZATION

(Read the plan from the top down. Execute the plan from the bottom up.

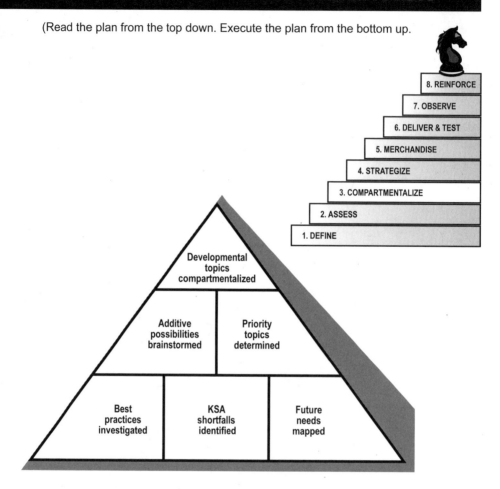

8. REINFORCE
7. OBSERVE
6. DELIVER & TEST
5. MERCHANDISE
4. STRATEGIZE
3. COMPARTMENTALIZE
2. ASSESS
1. DEFINE

Developmental
topics
compartmentalized

Additive
possibilities
brainstormed

Priority
topics
determined

Best
practices
investigated

KSA
shortfalls
identified

Future
needs
mapped

PINPOINT SPECIFIC PRIORITIES

This step pinpoints topics to hone that are intrinsically relevant to moving your sales talent forward. It involves dissecting what matters most.

After you compartmentalize your Knowledge, Skill, and Attribute priorities, brainstorm each topic horizontally and vertically. Repeatedly ask why questions. "Why does this matter?" "Why do we need to be great at this?" "Why is *this* more important than that?"

Map your answers against what you learn from external best-practice research.

When your specific topics sit on top of existing KSA shortfalls, in conjunction with the future needs of your business, you've positioned yourself to move forward with precision. Smart execution clears the quickest, cheapest path to better performance.

STEP 4. DEVELOPING A SMART STRATEGY

(Read the plan from the top down. Execute the plan from the bottom up.)

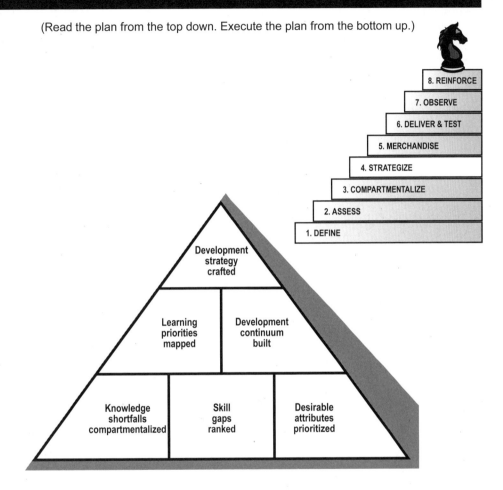

8. REINFORCE
7. OBSERVE
6. DELIVER & TEST
5. MERCHANDISE
4. STRATEGIZE
3. COMPARTMENTALIZE
2. ASSESS
1. DEFINE

Development strategy crafted

Learning priorities mapped

Development continuum built

Knowledge shortfalls compartmentalized

Skill gaps ranked

Desirable attributes prioritized

SUSTAINED GREATNESS REQUIRES A CONTINUUM

Building a winning strategy with long-term legs requires a continuum of interrelated programs built to serve relevant priorities. By compartmentalizing and dissecting the big three (Knowledge, Skills, Attributes), your portfolio can systematically usher your sales team through the development process in a prioritized order that your experts decide matters most.

Each KSA must have its top five category priorities stack-ranked. Once they are, systematically build your prioritized continuum.

Every strategy element should be modular in design and easy to change over time. Think them through with an easy-to-edit "D.A.S.H." formula (Delete, Add, Subtract, Hold). Real-time program modifications will keep your work timely and relevant, while helping to minimize costly waste and obsolescence.

STEP 5. MERCHANDISING THE DEVELOPMENT MODULES

(Read the plan from the top down. Execute the plan from the bottom up.)

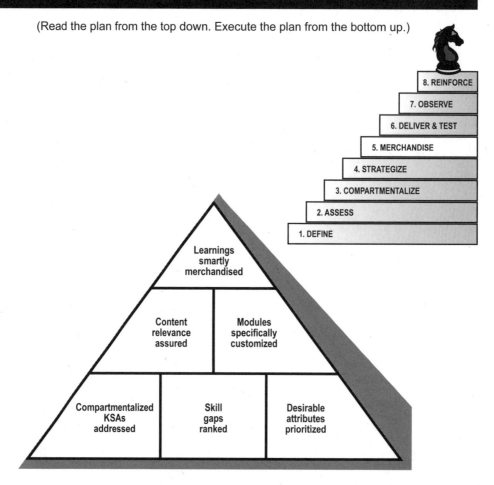

BE SMART ABOUT HOW YOU TEACH WHAT MATTERS MOST

The art starts here. To this point, your analysis work has been scientific and systematic. Now the heavy lifting of positive change shifts, because nothing you attempt to do will matter one iota if the learning doesn't stick (hence, the vital importance of smart merchandising). Shaping a maximum-impact learning experience must combine relevance with shrewd customization.

Relevance must come from ideas, topics, and skills that your sales force values. Greatness hinges on blending increased knowledge with stronger skills. So, nurturing the individual and collective Attributes of your people is vital. Don't make the mistake of not treating Attribute development as seriously as Knowledge or Skills. Attribute nurturing injects emotional equity in your employees and helps to fuel their positive motivation.

Merchandise every module for maximum emotional impact. Each participant will embrace or reject behavioral change based on how he or she receives that learning. Maximize the positive emotional experience of every participant into everything you build.

STEP 6. DELIVERING & TESTING THE WORK

(Read the plan from the top down. Execute the plan from the bottom up.)

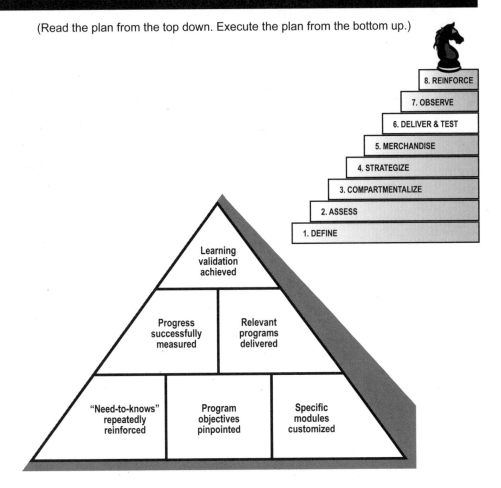

8. REINFORCE
7. OBSERVE
6. DELIVER & TEST
5. MERCHANDISE
4. STRATEGIZE
3. COMPARTMENTALIZE
2. ASSESS
1. DEFINE

Learning validation achieved

Progress successfully measured

Relevant programs delivered

"Need-to-knows" repeatedly reinforced

Program objectives pinpointed

Specific modules customized

IF YOU TEACH IT . . . MAKE DARN SURE THEY LEARN IT

Measurement is a must. The relentless *ying-and-yang* debate of this nearly invisible business—developing sales talent—usually comes from how best to *measure* it. The Kirkpatrick Theory recommends a four-step process:

1. *"Smile sheets."* How did the attendees feel about the session? It's nice if they like it, but it's better to be effective than liked. When instructors start teaching to happy scores and not the needs of the business, they will fail.
2. *Facilitator observation*. What did the coach or teacher notice about the attending constituency? Did they get it or not? Was their grasp a short-term memorization or an internationalization that's likely to last long-term?
3. *Post-training*. What do the managers see? Are new behaviors evident in the reps? Are they using their new techniques out in the field?
4. Absolute results. Are their sales result improved or not? Bottom line: Do they sell better?

STEP 7. POST-LEARNING OBSERVATION

(Read the plan from the top down. Execute the plan from the bottom up.)

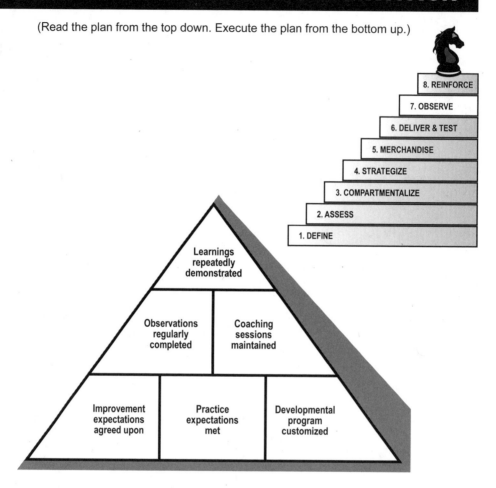

MONITOR THE ONGOING USE OF NEW TECHNIQUES

Maintain a very high profile of ongoing inspection. Let the reps know you're observing their specific actions, reactions, behaviors, and techniques.

The Washington, D.C. Sales Executive Council study recommends that skilled coaches invest a minimum of three hours per month per rep on skill-development issues. Teams that continually outperform others are coached smartly at the strategy stage, then again near the late-cycle closing stage.

Coaching does not mean jumping in and taking over! Coaching involves teaching, inspecting, and reinforcing the sales techniques that matter most in your industry.

Reps who know their managers care about their performance extend the effort it takes to do more conscientious work. Share expectations, help where needed, monitor progress, and coach in a positive way. Reps handled this way will grow stronger.

STEP 8. ONGOING REINFORCEMENT

(Read the plan from the top down. Execute the plan from the bottom up.)

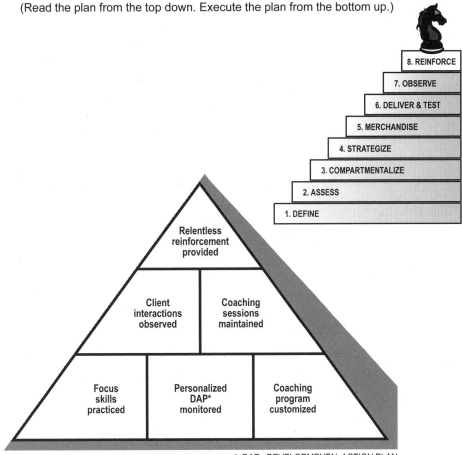

* DAP: DEVELOPMENTAL ACTION PLAN

SUSTAINED GREATNESS REQUIRES A CONTINUUM

To relentlessly reinforce the key success elements, you must create a cultural coaching climate.

Never miss a chance to debrief and critique, especially after a client interaction. What worked and why? What didn't and why? Which statements landed with high impact? Which bounced? What did the rep do or say that generated the greatest customer interest? How did the customer's body language or animation change? Was that animation positive or negative? Why did it change?

Incorporate scheduled coaching sessions into the plan-and-review calendar. Make sure the sessions are customized to the wants and needs of each rep. Every sales rep should have an action plan customized to his or her focused priorities.

When you teach and reinforce, follow the Cal Ripken Sr. coaching model: Keep it simple. Make it fun. Celebrate the individual. Explain why. If the reinforcement process isn't fun, you aren't doing it right. Remember: They are *coaching* sessions, not *chiding* sessions.

9

CHAPTER

FIVE DEFICIENCY AREAS TO STRENGTHEN

UNDERESTIMATED AND OVERESTIMATED SKILLS & TECHNIQUES

I n order to sustain a MAXIMUM HORSEPOWER selling environment, it is imperative to strengthen five common deficiency areas. Hammer these home and you'll strengthen your individual reps as well as the collective skills of the team. Do that, and you'll benefit from better results. Following the discussion on these five essentials are two reference tables that list *Underestimated* and *Overestimated* traits and techniques.

The vital five area you must drill your sales reps to master are:

1. *Message management*

2. *Actionable interest*

3. *Value formula*

4. *Controlling the sales cycle*

5. *The need to win.*

NECESSARY #1. MESSAGE MANAGEMENT

Objective: Maximize your team's effectiveness with all four elements of communication: sender, receiver, channel, and message.

Sender. These four priorities are vital to teach:

- *"Pedestal statements."* These words and phrases have a positive emotional resonance with customers and prospects.

- *Avoid creating negative emotional experiences.* Many of these are unintentional. Whenever interfacing with a customer, a salesperson must maintain a strong sense of awareness that how his or her communication is framed ["what they say and how they say it"] has a huge impact on how a listener receives it. For example, my good friend Emmett Reagan loved to make this point in Xerox sales class by singling out a female class member and saying, "You look twice as pretty today as yesterday." The recipient beamed with pleasure at his kind compliment. Emmett would then point out he could say basically the same thing differently: "You ain't half as ugly as you used to be." The first example, the class member heard as a pedestal statement—a compliment—while the second was taken as an insult. Emmett's simple example underscores that the words you choose in selling have a dramatic impact on the whether the customer's receptivity is positive or negative. "That's a great idea!" is a compliment. "I'm surprised you thought of that" is not.

- *Learn how to disagree properly.* Not "I disagree because" or "You're wrong because." Teach your reps to express reasons first and a differing perspective last. This is counter to typical sales behavior, which is why this technique is so hard to master, yet so wonderful effective when used. True selling starts, as we all have experienced, when the customer balks. The mark of a great rep, therefore, is how smoothly he or she turns that "no" into a non-threatening arena of professional discussion. Very few reps are great at this technique.

- *Learn to give flawless presentations to attain the envisioned outcome.* Teach your reps the science and art of superlative delivery. A great presentation, skillfully delivered by a smooth and polished presenter, can steal a deal that a boring one would lose.

TEACH YOUR REPS THE SCIENCE AND ART OF SUPERLATIVE DELIVERY.

Receiver. Reinforce the following three things to improve the impact your salespeople's messages have upon their sales audiences:

- *Listen without judgment.* Jumping to conclusions or making quick assumptions during a conversation with a customer runs a strong risk of creating a negative emotional experience. The best way to positively impact a customer is to listen carefully, seeking to understand rather than judge. Learning to listen constructively involves breaking bad reflexive habits. Doing that requires practice. It's incumbent upon sales leaders to provide ongoing reinforcement.

THE BEST WAY TO POSITIVELY IMPACT A CUSTOMER IS TO LISTEN CAREFULLY, SEEKING TO UNDERSTAND RATHER THAN JUDGE.

- *Adults learn best in one of three ways*: audio (listening), visual (watching), or kinesthetic (learn by doing). When in doubt about which style best matches a potential customer, teach your salespeople to *ask*. Presentations have maximum impact when pitched using the preferred method of the customer.

- *People tend to process information in one of two directions:* the big picture to the granular details, or via a string of details that lead to a conclusion. In pressure situations, when detail people try to communicate with concept people, they often struggle because *how the two people process information* is radically different. This is common in high-stakes selling because many value-adding salespeople are concept-people by nature; yet many senior financial decision-makers with whom they deal are risk-averse and analyze business deals by scrutinizing the details.

Like-minded people tend to communicate very easily. Unlike-minded people often struggle. Teach your salespeople to be adept at "flexing" their messages and delivery into both concept-oriented and detail-oriented presentations. Doing so will maximize the sales effectiveness of their pitches.

TEACH YOUR SALESPEOPLE TO BE ADEPT AT "FLEXING" THEIR MESSAGES AND DELIVERY INTO BOTH CONCEPT-ORIENTED AND DETAIL-ORIENTED PRESENTATIONS.

Channel. Every communication channel has strengths and limitations. Insist that your sales reps become masters of multiple delivery methods, since alternative types of media sell best in certain situations. Recommendations for the commonly used sales channels are explained later in this chapter.

From a strategic standpoint, teach your sales force that everyone is expected to develop the expertise to sell via a combination of channels and creative presentations.

Too many sales reps "show up and throw up," using the same message and channel (ex. PowerPoint). While this might be easy for the rep, it's boring to a savvy customer. Your sales talents must be taught which channel to pick—plus when and why—and practice their delivery skills to a strong level of proficiency. All great salespeople have multiple-channel mastery.

> **INSIST THAT YOUR SALES REPS BECOME MASTERS OF MULTIPLE DELIVERY METHODS, SINCE ALTERNATIVE TYPES OF MEDIA SELL BEST IN CERTAIN SITUATIONS.**

Message. High-impact messages may be scripted—but must *sound* smooth and natural, not "canned" or *"sales-y."* Here are the three vital success elements of strong sales messaging:

- *Elevator speech.* Everyone in sales should know how to craft a polished *twenty-second* descriptor of what they do, how they are different, and why it matters to the person with whom they are speaking. The reason for the twenty-second target is simple: It's about as long as someone can speak without having to pause to take a breath.
- *Value script.* Value is a perception, shaped by what people think, how they feel, and how those conclusions map to their different priorities. In professional selling, it is *vital* to know what value means to each customer and how to describe that value for maximum persuasive impact. This is a hallmark skill of every MAXIMUM HORSEPOWER performer.
- *Liberal benefit statements.* Benefit statements are high-impact phrases that are shaped for and delivered to vested stakeholders in order to have a maximum, personalized impact. Great salespeople sprinkle them liberally throughout a call or presentation. Mediocre reps utter them by accident.

As a sales leader, you must *insist* that your reps become students of all four elements of effective communication. Winning depends on it, now more than ever. Customers have options in the marketplace. The company whose people best communicate a high-impact, relevant message in a compelling fashion will have sales advantages over companies that rely on boilerplate talk tracks and tepid efforts. Hold your reps to a higher standard. Tell them you expect them to *separate* from the competition by being the best communicators their customers will ever meet.

> **THE COMPANY WHOSE PEOPLE BEST COMMUNICATE A HIGH-IMPACT, RELEVANT MESSAGE IN A COMPELLING FASHION WILL HAVE SALES ADVANTAGES OVER COMPANIES THAT RELY ON BOILERPLATE TALK TRACKS AND TEPID EFFORTS.**

NECESSARY #2. ACTIONABLE INTEREST

The better your reps are at persuasive communication, the more likely they will be to be able to create actionable interest with customers. Actionable interest is vital, because without it, no deal gains a champion or advances to the close. Customers only buy when they *decide* to. Farming that action—getting the customer to "Yes"—requires converting *possible* interest to a want level high enough that the customer is willing to take action. The key elements to creating actionable interest are:

Know what triggers human behaviors:

- What people *think* drives how they feel.
- How they *feel* drives what they do.
- To influence their behavior, a customer's collective thoughts must shape— and then trigger—an emotion strong enough to act upon. Action-taking emotions typically come from the positive reward gained by the action or the avoidance of a negative penalty. The insurance business, for example, is built upon the negative "what if" world of hypothetical loss.

Listen, without interrupting, for content and emotion. As we have marched swiftly toward being a sound-bite society, interrupting has become increasingly common. Being interrupted is irritating . . . and loses sales. *Teach your reps never to interrupt their prospects.* Instead of interrupting, have them focus on listening intently for two things as the customer speaks: content and emotion. The content provides a salesperson *context*. The emotional peaks a good rep hears tell him or her where to aim the message. Interrupting is a habit—a bad one—so make sure you coach your people on trading this hurtful technique for a positive one.

AS WE HAVE MARCHED SWIFTLY TOWARD BEING A SOUND-BITE SOCIETY, INTERRUPTING HAS BECOME INCREASINGLY COMMON.

Know the three reasons to ask a question, and remain disciplined in their proper use:

KNOW THE THREE REASONS TO ASK A QUESTION, AND REMAIN DISCIPLINED IN THEIR PROPER USE: TO SEEK INFORMATION, CLARIFY, OR TEST UNDERSTANDING.

- *Seek information.* A series of systematic information questions requires discipline to produce relevant insights. Asking too few questions does not generate enough data. Asking too many haphazard questions, seemingly at random, quickly becomes irritating to a prospect, especially when lacking a smooth segue from one topic to the next. Advance preparation maximizes a sales rep's chances of high-quality information gathering.
- *Clarify what was heard.* Not enough salespeople have the discipline to do

this well. They usually assume a prospect's intent rather than re-check for clarity. To demonstrate, ask six people in your office to define the term "good service." You'll get six different responses. Clarity comes from crystallization and quantification. Reps should be specific when asking customers to share insight and should always put the onus back on themselves when asking.

For example: *"Hearing you say good service is a very important part of your decision-making process is extra important to me, too. Could you please take a moment to help me better understand what "good service" means to you and how you prefer to measure it?"*

The customer's answer to the clarification question will provide far more insight than we'd otherwise leave the meeting with. Drill your reps on clarification questions aimed at all the key elements of your typical customer decision-making criteria. Strive to gain clarity in an *objective* form. The phrase above, *" . . . and how you prefer to measure it?"* enables us to hone in on good service from the same point of view as the customer.

New reps, especially, don't clarify as well as they should. Mediocre ones don't, either, and misinterpretations are a consistently big reason why they lose winnable deals. Insight gleans a competitive edge, so make sure the clarification technique is taught, coached, and reinforced regularly.

Aggressively discuss the value of clarification questions during post-call debriefs. How often did the rep ask questions? How effectively did he or she crystallize a vague idea or gain a new insight? The strategic use of clarification questions in a selling context is a professional yet under utilized technique, vital when following up on parts of a presentation that clearly land on a customer with emotional resonance.

When selling, it's rarely what you know that beats you; it's what you *don't* know. Insist that your reps clarify what they hear in order to expand the amount of shared insight they have with their customer.

WHEN SELLING, IT'S RARELY WHAT YOU KNOW THAT BEATS YOU; IT'S WHAT YOU DON'T KNOW.

- *Test understanding.* Testing is also underutilized—and should be taught, coached, and inspected on an ongoing basis. Testing a customer's understanding of how he or she hears the rep's message goes a long way toward helping accurately gauging the emotional weight of a customer's statements.

    People buy based on emotion, yet salespeople too infrequently verify a customer's emotional buy-in by testing their spoken words.

PEOPLE BUY BASED ON EMOTION, YET SALESPEOPLE TOO INFREQUENTLY VERIFY A CUSTOMER'S EMOTIONAL BUY-IN BY TESTING THEIR SPOKEN WORDS.

For example, the English language does not convey emotional expression and degree nearly as well as other languages such as Spanish. Experiencing this is easy: Provide a group of men and women a list of English adjectives commonly used when describing varying types and degrees of emotion. Ask them to sort the words into five *types* of emotion—anger, fear, joy, sorrow, and love—and then three *levels* of emotion (high, medium, low).

What you'll find is that the people will sort these words differently. The same word will often be categorized as describing different emotions, and various audience members will slot the same word into different *levels* of emotional intensity. This is not a sex-specific phenomenon, either. *Everybody* sorts them differently.

This word sorting exercise underscores a vital lesson in selling: People *communicate* and *interpret* emotion differently. So, when selling, it's vital to clarify what you hear and test your understanding. When it comes to gaining emotional insight with customers, rather than have your reps guess, train them to have the customer rank their feelings about key issues on a 1-10 scale, with 10 being highest in intensity. That way, nothing is left to misinterpretation.

> **PEOPLE COMMUNICATE AND INTERPRET EMOTION DIFFERENTLY.**

NECESSARY #3. VALUE FORMULA

Pound Neil Rackham's value formula into an automatic reflex in your salespeople: Value = Benefits minus Cost

- Benefits can be *tangible* and/or *intangible*.
- Cost impact can be *direct* and/or *indirect*.
- Sell the definition first. Then craft a strategy to deliver to it.
- Make value creation and sustenance a hallmark of your sales *brand*.

Value is a perception and perceptions vary, so what matters to one person may not matter to another. The key is to teaching your salespeople that value in the eyes of the customer, is very much a math problem with four possible buckets to maximize:

- If the rep's solution offers tangible and/or intangible benefits that the customer perceives to be better than current levels, there is at least some value to the solution.
- If direct cost is reduced and/or indirect cost is lessened, the value of the solution again has increased.
- Positively impacting all four elements maximizes value and offer the greatest chance of success.

Nevertheless, since customer perceptions are shaped by their accumulated thoughts, they can be influenced and strengthened by better selling. It's the salesperson's job to focus on the four value elements [tangible and intangible benefits, direct and indirect cost] in order to do so. The most powerful, yet commonly neglected, sales tool at a rep's disposal is at the heart of Rackham's work. Every sales rep should be able to identify a customer problem, learn its ramifications, and develop that problem well enough to motivate the customer to solve it.

> **EVERY SALES REP SHOULD BE ABLE TO IDENTIFY A CUSTOMER PROBLEM, LEARN ITS RAMIFICATIONS, AND DEVELOP THAT PROBLEM WELL ENOUGH TO MOTIVATE THE CUSTOMER TO SOLVE IT.**

As a process-advocate myself, I prefer the logic and clarity of Rackham's SPIN® model (now owned by Huthwaite, Inc. out of Herndon, VA). The SPIN® process has a flexible structure that enables great salespeople to control important sales calls, while systematically building value under pressure.

Expect your reps to master the value formula process and hold your salespeople to a higher standard than the competition. When they operate that way, you will gain a consistent advantage when selling deals that really matter.

NECESSARY #4. CONTROLLING THE SALES CYCLE

Time is irreplaceable, so controlling the sales cycle is a mandatory part of MAXIMUM HORSEPOWER performance. The highlights:

- Pre-call planning must be efficient.
- Command of the needs-development process is essential.
- Quick recognition of barriers to performance is vital. The four impediments most

likely to derail a sales cycle are:

1. *Can't do it.* Willing but not able, often due to a knowledge or skill gap.

2. *Won't do it.* Able but not willing.

3. *Prevented from doing it.* Willing and able, but stymied by extenuating circumstances.

4. *Performance punishment.* If the solution will cause penalty work, the rep won't push the initiative unless it preserves his or her job or increases political capital.

- Must resolve tough issues without caving and ASK for the order, more than once if necessary.

- Negotiate to close in a positive, professional way.

NECESSARY #5. INSPIRING THE NEED TO WIN

"How could I lose to such an idiot!"

—shouted chess grandmaster Aaron Nimzovich (1886-1935)

Moral victories don't ring the cash register. A great salesperson lives to win, so a moral victory is nothing but a loss sprinkled with deodorant. No matter how long you have been selling for a living, the customer's decision is the ultimate judgment. It validates and rewards all of the time, work, and effort invested in pursuing what is often a long and difficult sales opportunity.

In the sales profession, winning matters! Never let anyone who sells for you get used to or comfortable with losing. Losing stinks. Losing is a colossal waste of everything— time, money, energy, *everything.* MAXIMUM HORSEPOWER sales professionals win the ones they're supposed to win . . . and some of the ones they were supposed to *lose.*

MAXIMUM HORSEPOWER SALES PROFESSIONALS WIN THE ONES THEY'RE SUPPOSED TO WIN . . . AND SOME OF THE ONES THEY WERE SUPPOSED TO LOSE.

When a winnable deal progresses to the point of decision, inspire a culture that hustles harder than ever to win. High-performance sales organizations that consistently outperform their competitors typically invest time and resources in coaching at two distinct stages of the sales cycle: front-end plan strategy and late-cycle closing. *Collaborative mind-share is a beautiful thing, because great closers know when they have earned the right to ask for the order.*

When approaching the point of end-of-cycle negotiations, the key tenet from Roger Fisher's book *GETTING TO YES* and the Harvard Program on Negotiation is: *Know the customer's best alternative other than yours.* Fisher and Harvard terms this the customer's *BATNA* (Best Alternative to Negotiated Agreement).

Your reps must know the customer's BATNA. Quiz them on it. Make sure they know their own, too. Part of one's BATNA means knowing the walk-away point. Deals sometimes erode to the point of diminishing returns, yet something inbred in a salesperson struggles to cut the cord on a deal they've invested emotional energy in.

With a good reading on both BATNAs, a skilled rep will negotiate a bridge between the two. The deals that your brand should strive to create are good for the customer, good for your organization, and fair to all parties involved. Hard work in good faith crafts a deal that both sides can live with—forged with energy, zeal, and a positive attitude.

When all the selling is done and it's time for the customer to decide between close alternatives, often they choose the company who wants their business the most, and demonstrates that desire strongly and consistently late in the selling cycle. There is a certain amount of late-cycle stick-to-itiveness that winners have but others don't. Make sure that positive, resilient negotiation is part of your brand.

THE HIGH COST OF LOSING

An effective way to instill a sense of urgency-to-win in your sales reps is to make them calculate the cost of a loss. Make them see it in dollars and cents. Divide their typical W-2 earnings by their number of hours worked. The result will be their effective value-per-hour. Multiply that by the number of hours they have spent on defeat. Then make them stare at the number.

> AN EFFECTIVE WAY TO INSTILL A SENSE OF URGENCY-TO-WIN IN YOUR SALES REPS IS TO MAKE THEM CALCULATE THE COST OF A LOSS.

Losing is expensive. A *loss review* helps your reps to avoid losing the same way time and time again. To a rep, a loss review is like going to face the dentist's drill. But in the end, it's a good pain. You learn more by dissecting a loss than you do toasting a win.

YOU LEARN MORE BY DISSECTING A LOSS THAN YOU DO TOASTING A WIN.

Coach your people to ratchet up their effectiveness late in the sales cycle. Close hard, close often, and close in good faith. When people sell professionally, their work leads them to a point where they have earned the right to ask for the order in a frank and fear-free manner. Teach that, encourage that, and celebrate that. It's what the profession is all about: winning the business.

Winning matters and you cannot win if you don't close. Echo that expectation throughout the halls of your organization. Make the phrase "Winning matters" more than a bumper sticker. Make it the backbone of your sales culture. We find in life what we look for. Look for wins, search diligently, and you'll find them.

MAKE THE PHRASE "WINNING MATTERS" MORE THAN A BUMPER STICKER. MAKE IT THE BACKBONE OF YOUR SALES CULTURE.

TWELVE UNDERESTIMATED TRAITS & TECHNIQUES

UNDERESTIMATED	WHY
Listening	So few do, it's an art. When you find it, hire it. A salesperson's greatest skill.
"In the Moment" Effectiveness & The Ability to Totally Concentrate	As we become a sound-bite society, attention spans are short on both sides of the desk. Focus and concentration are harder to find than ever. The rewards and payoffs for being effective "in the moment" have never been higher.
Objectives	Selling a complex deal is like hiking a mountain. Great salespeople break the most difficult challenges into manageable, achievable pieces. The key is to work strictly by objective.
Urgency	Tomorrow is the busiest day of the year—that's when everyone plans to get things done. Find, recruit, hire, and inspire people who live with a sense of urgency. When they live that way, they work that way, too.

Personal Selling Style	Great reps have a personal style. They know what it is, what comprises it, how to define it. Those who don't know are at a competitive disadvantage. To know how *customers* see you, know yourself.
Professional Selling Style	All great salespeople have pride and ego. They also respect selling as a profession. Merge these two attitudes and you have a polished, thriving performer.
Distilling Information	These days there is almost *too much* information. Sifting through it to synthesize what matters is a key to sales effectiveness. Distilling information smartly is a differentiator between people who are busy and people who are productive.
Looking & Observing	People tend to see a lot but learn little. They don't gain what they should by observing what's around them. Students of the sales profession learn by watching. They study what works and incorporate key techniques and mannerisms to help them be better. Book smarts and street smarts are different assets. A smart rep is aware of the power of each.
"Q Factor"	"Q Factor" is likeability, which is *everything* in selling. Some people send out positive "vibes." Others the opposite. Hire Q Factors. People either have it or they don't but after twenty years of trying, I don't know how to create it.
Multi-generational Effectiveness	Ours is a multi-generational, cultural stir-fry workforce. People who appreciate life through the lenses of multiple generations and ethnicities have a competitive advantage because decision-makers are changing, too, demographically. Evolving social values, behaviors, technological tools, and generational differences are accelerating. Being socially interchangeable puts a rep in the position to add credibility and value in an increasing number of sales cycles.
Significant Emotional Events	Major life events have a huge impact on behavior. They shape, reshape, motivate, and crush people. On the other hand, when inspired, ordinary people can do extraordinary things. A great leader inspires positive emotional events in the lives of their people. These boosts are life-changing for everyone.
Telephonics	As more people hide behind computer screens, fewer are sharp on the phone, and that includes voice mail. Excellent telephonic skills are a *big advantage,* since most practitioners in the sales world are mediocre (or worse). Most salespeople who listen to a playback of a long-winded voice mail they've left someone else find it a very valuable learning experience.

EIGHT OVERESTIMATED TRAITS & TECHNIQUES

OVERESTIMATED	WHY
Questions	Few reps know the three specific reasons to ask questions when selling, which means that even fewer ask them shrewdly. Customers process questions to judge the salesperson. Dumb questions = low opinion of the salesperson.
"Talking Brochures"	Prospects expect salespeople to know their products and services and where they fit into the prospect's business. Talking Brochures, a term coined by Neil Rackham, are people who show up to yak about their products—not to learn about the customer's business. Customers no longer respond to these "information dumps." They want solutions.
Call Activity	Activity is nice. Call *quality* matters more. Quality activity trumps thirty unskilled calls every time. Many managers equate activity with results. To a certain extent, activity matters, yes. But call volume alone won't generate results. It's *quality activities* that drive results. This point vitally underscores the difference between telling someone what to do and teaching them. Few reps ever learn to be great on their own. Smart coaches develop MAXIMUM HORSEPOWER sales talent by teaching their people how to improve the *quality* of their efforts.
Tenure	Many managers and reps equate tenure with proficiency. *Phooey.* Tenure is good for two things: leadership and performance. You want *both*—and must get at least one. If not, a tenured rep has absolutely zero advantage over a motivated new hire, often at a higher cost.
Attitude	Attributes matter more than attitude. There are a lot of happy losers who sell for a living. Winning must matter. I'll trade two *Happys* for one competent competitor. Too often, nice but lackadaisical "Have a nice day people" who lack a competitive hunger lose to more aggressive sales opponents who have a stronger, burning need to win. A positive attitude is always good, but success will still boil down to a high-performance blend of all three KSAs: knowledge, skills, and attributes.
Email	An overused channel that can't transfer feeling, emotion, voice or tone. Email is vulnerable to spawning busywork and fostering a CYA mentality. Salespeople sell. They don't type. They make their money with their mouths and ears, not their fingertips. It's a lot easier to sell in person than it is electronically. People hide behind email.
Tactics	Directing people to "Do this . . . and do this next" is not coaching and not strategic thinking. Such task activity directives are fine in simple sales or non-differentiated commodities, but telling people what to do does not build talent or sustainable results.
Accumulating Information	Collecting information is easy. But having it all is useless unless you can synthesize what truly matters into a solution with strategic relevance. The art of the sale is distilling what you know into a compelling value proposition that someone will champion on your behalf. One must be coached in order to do this well.

CHANNELS OF SALES COMMUNICATION

Channels are the methods sales reps use to convey messages. When selling to customers, we have many channels from which to choose. Each has strengths and limitations. Here are a baker's dozen:

- In person (interactive)
- Telephone (two-way)
- Conference calls
- Voice Mail
- Fax
- PowerPoint presentations
- Handouts
- Preprinted collaterals
- Whiteboards
- Flip charts
- Business letters
- Email
- Text messaging

In person (interactive)

Strengths. A salesperson's best shot, an in-person presentation provides all three key communication elements: body language reading, voice and tone judgments, and the opportunity for substantive, interactive dialogue. People talk, on average, 180 words per minute, so face-to-face provides a salesperson's best chance to cover a large body of information and to create actionable interest with a customer. Also, *listening* to the customer is vital in large opportunity selling—it cannot be overstated—and nothing beats the listening opportunity of an interactive exchange.

Limitations. In-person presentations increase in difficulty during the latter stages of the sales cycle, thanks to pressure and increasingly larger audiences. The rep must be confident when addressing groups, especially in the face of tense discussions. Call objectives must be clearly known prior to the meeting, and pre-call prep is essential. Because discussion points can change during a meeting, reps who are not quick on their feet are susceptible to losing control if the discussion changes scope or direction. Face-to-face meetings are also expensive in direct and indirect costs, so tight budgets mean that every opportunity must be maximized.

Telephone (two-way)

Strengths. A phone discussion is the next best thing to face-to-face. Telephone presentations provide spontaneous, real-time interactive discussions that allow salespeople to judge voice and tone. Enable the salesperson to seek information, clarify what he or she heard, and test understanding. Allow the use of supportive collaterals, which can be referenced and examined by each party during the discussion. The phone is cheap to utilize, and calls are personal in nature.

Limitations. Reps lose the ability to read the customer's body language, which is important when building trust and a relationship. Telephone discussions are word reliant, and not the best for explaining complicated concepts. It's also hard to sell on the phone, almost impossible when you have no relationship with the person on the other end of the line. At Xerox, we were told to use the phone to close for face-to-face appointments and to do our selling *then*. Also, some salespeople are not good on the phone, and their voice and grammar skills are not polished or professional. It's important to remember that in selling, the greatest impact in a face-to-face meeting is non-verbal—the reading of body language. It is *not* the words the rep and customer chooses to use. On the telephone, however, the non-verbal cues are stripped away. Salespeople are totally word and voice-and-tone reliant.

The other big problem with phone calls is they leave the participants susceptible to distractions. These can include emails, passersby, background noise or music, in-transit traffic noise—you name it. Each of these impedes a quality conversation. As great as the spontaneity of a good phone call can be, it's not a salesperson's panacea. It's got limitations.

Conference Calls

Strengths. Conference calls enable the engaging of multiple stakeholders simultaneously. With a skilled facilitator, this channel can be very effective to gain group understanding and consensus; and they are relatively inexpensive, especially compared to travel.

Limitations. These calls depend on corralling the focus of all attendees, because people frequently multi-task, which diffuses their attention. Also, attendees can dominate the call, excluding others who remain silent. Conference calls need two things: a tight, relevant agenda, plus good call-leadership. Too often people drone on way too long, dwelling on a topic or contributing because they feel obligated to do so. When this happens, other attendees bore quickly, quit caring, stop paying attention, and freefall into the abyss of Conference Call Purgatory.

Voice Mail

Strengths. Voice mail gives salespeople the opportunity to leave a recorded message of their own creation that can be advanced to others. When scripted and smoothly delivered, a voice mail message can be very effective. A recorded message is never as good as an interactive discussion, but a vibrant voice—*a happy, positive voice*—is better than no voice at all (i.e. an email). The more important the message, the more important it is to have your salespeople script their words *pre-dialing* in short, concise sentences. Doing so enables a specific message to be practiced, then delivered, precisely the way the salesperson desires. Since most voice mail systems allow for message "playback," the salesperson can hear a replay of his or her voice before committing the message to the customer's inbox. If the rep isn't satisfied with the playback, he or she can re-record their message and listen again. Good, tight, quick voice mails add a professional touch.

Limitations. Voice mail is one-sided messaging. There is no body language "readability" on how the message is received. Messages are taken literally. There is no chance to clarify or test understanding. Also, unscripted, people tend to ramble and, when they ramble, they deliver a low-impact message that is sometimes deleted even before completion. When you leave a voice mail, cut to the chase quickly.

Fax

Strengths. A hard-copy document has permanence that an electronic one does not. More and more interactions are shifting to electronic content, so a printed fax affords a quick, spontaneous, and inexpensive way to create and transmit a hard-copy message that usually finds its way to the intended recipient. Faxes with a tangible legitimacy are delivered, not filtered or "block deleted" like many emails. Fax is a nice communication option when you want an important message to land on a desk.

Limitations. Because a fax will be delivered where it is intended, the specific message must be perfect, written precisely as desired prior to sending. There is no back-up, "reverse," or do-over button to rescue a sent fax.

PowerPoint Presentations

Strengths. PowerPoint presentations are fast and simple to create, easy to use, simple to replicate and modify. This portable, computer-generated slide-show tool is excellent for audience information sharing that requires images, explanations of networks, systems and/or solution complexities that don't lend themselves easily to verbal description. Used properly under the control of a skilled presenter, PowerPoint can be a great tool. Because the presentations are computer-driven, the tool is ultra-portable and allows the quick access of previous or future content. Because the presentations are constructed in advance, there is also ample opportunity to customize, rehearse, and time its delivery.

PowerPoint is often an excellent choice when presenting to large audiences. For example, Al Gore's Oscar winning film, *An Inconvenient Truth*, is basically a filmed

PowerPoint show. Gore uses charts, graphs, and images to wallpaper his words. Without the images, his words alone would ring hollow, not propelling his climate change message with anywhere close to maximum impact. Gore's film is a perfect example of maximizing the utility of this tool with a finely tuned message. He maintains complete control throughout his global-warming presentation by using the PowerPoint slides to pace, augment, and highlight specific elements of his tightly scripted message.

Limitations. By its very nature, PowerPoint is a visual tool that steers the attention of the audience from the speaker to the images on the screen before them. It is terribly overused in business, its effectiveness diluted by crudely amateurish creations shown *ad nauseum* by less-than-compelling presenters. Only a very small number of creators know how to maximize PowerPoint's capabilities, and the audiences suffer as a result.

At its best, work like Gore's underscores that PowerPoint can be a great tool to convey compelling images that supplement the speaker. Hats off to Al Gore: He has honed the integration of his slide show and message so tightly, *An Inconvenient Truth* has become an archived example of how an otherwise ordinary presenter can deliver an extraordinary presentation if he or she works hard enough on preparation and practice. The film, of course, is the lynchpin reason Gore was honored as co-recipient of the 2007 Nobel Peace Prize. His documentary film—a videotaped PowerPoint show—was built and delivered so convincingly that it caused the industrial world to face up to a course correction.

But for every man or woman who perfectly uses the tool, thousands don't. At its worst, PowerPoint foists on its audience a mind-numbing "deck," a page after page bulletized text parade that a bored audience scans at a glance but doesn't care about. Boring, irrelevant slides lose an audience. Eyes glass over, PDAs come out and people start text messaging, and little is retained when the show mercifully ends.

Too often, this approach—a boilerplate PowerPoint presentation—is the *one-size-fits-all* tool of the lazy salesperson. The rep uses the same boilerplate call after call, never customizing it carefully for a specific audience and objective, switching one customer's name and logo for another. These reps hide behind their slides and repeat what is clearly readable on the screen. Consequently, they "shut out" their audience. These one-sided monologues are so self-focused that many reps finish the presentation without a clue how well they did or did not do. Improperly used, PowerPoint is a "shut out" tool. Unless the presenter knows how to engage the audience, they will simply sit there stone-faced and unresponsive.

AT ITS WORST, POWERPOINT FOISTS ON ITS AUDIENCE A MIND-NUMBING "DECK," A PAGE AFTER PAGE BULLETIZED TEXT PARADE THAT A BORED AUDIENCE SCANS AT A GLANCE BUT DOESN'T CARE ABOUT.

In addition, mistakes on a big screen are professional torpedoes since errors are magnified for all to see. Perfect construction is vital. A typo on a giant screen is humiliating, especially in a room full of important people you are trying to sell or impress. Presenters need to know how to operate their computer and remote control, too. Incompetence is sad, an absolute deal-crusher.

Handouts

Strengths. Custom-created handouts are tangible, inexpensive, portable, and perfect for kinesthetic learners who like to take notes. They also easily augment other channels (e.g., formal comments, a PowerPoint show, a site tour). They have a feeling of permanence, a take-away factor, and are easily customizable for a very specific sales objective and audience. When possible, handouts should be customized, with the attendees' names clearly printed in **bold**.

Another advantage of handouts is that the salesperson controls the distribution. Well-prepared salespeople often go into important customer meetings armed with several customized handouts—ready to distribute what is needed, when it's needed, but only *if* it's needed. Because handouts help to focus (or refocus) a discussion back onto a specific topic, they are excellent for spurring discussions. Coach your people to take full advantage.

BECAUSE HANDOUTS HELP TO FOCUS (OR REFOCUS) A DISCUSSION BACK ONTO A SPECIFIC TOPIC, THEY ARE EXCELLENT FOR SPURRING DISCUSSIONS.

Limitations. Handouts must be accurate, relevant, and typo-free. Most salespeople earn their livings with their mouths and ears, and they don't write as well as they speak. Verbal errors are invisible (and somewhat forgiven), but printed ones are permanent. Make sure the handouts are proofread ahead of time, and printed in sufficient quantities before the meeting. Always print extras, and encourage the customers to keep one and channel another wherever it might be needed. Make sure attendees' names are spelled perfectly and titles identified accurately.

Preprinted Collaterals

Strengths. These professional-looking, carefully crafted corporate messages — brochures, pamphlets, slick folders of preprinted information — can be excellent supportive tools, especially when selling to someone unfamiliar with your company or solution.

Limitations. If done on a shoestring, competitors have slicker ones. They can be outdated quickly, especially at the clockspeed of marketplace change. Also, they are usually crafted by the Marketing Department, independent of Sales, and can cause mixed messaging. Brochures may have nice photos and slick graphs, feature-laden and advantage-rich, but light or devoid of benefit statements that relate to the customer's business. Subject-matter expertise and content mastery is expected of every rep who shares a collateral with a customer. When a rep hands a brochure out, he or she is expected to know every element in it, cover to cover.

Preprinted slicks are time-consuming and costly to create, print, archive, inventory, manage, ship, and distribute. All too often, sales organizations end up tossing half of what they've bought. Waste is high, as is cost per effective utilization.

Whiteboards

Strengths. Whiteboards are excellent for spontaneous drawing of support visuals, group ideas, and outputs generated from collaborative meetings. They are usually large enough to display far more content than a flip-chart page, plus they are correctable and erasable.

Limitations. Whiteboards house temporary messages, so its content is not permanent and not portable. Ideas worth saving must be replicated by transcription. Their use can also be somewhat distracting, as some meeting attendees will stare at something still on the board. To minimize this, erase as you go. Whiteboards also have a finite distance from which they are easily viewable. Readability is harmed by poor penmanship, marker color (black reads best) and letter size. Teach your salespeople to print legibly with a minimum letter height of three inches. Letter size increases as viewer distance from the whiteboard lengthens, a minimum of one inch per ten feet. Markers bleed out quickly, so always bring new ones when you're selling. Then be a sport and leave them behind. Customers notice.

 MARKERS BLEED OUT QUICKLY, SO ALWAYS BRING NEW ONES WHEN YOU'RE SELLING. THEN BE A SPORT AND LEAVE THEM BEHIND.

Flip charts

Strengths. Flip charts are a terrific channel for handy, spontaneous use with small and medium-sized (20) groups. The pads are inexpensive and offer plenty of pages for explanation and documentation, sheets easily removed for transcription or posting nearby. They are very helpful during meetings to explain, capture, and build upon contributions and ideas; and they can be prepared in advance to save meeting time and add professionalism. Office supply companies sell zip-up carriers with handles to accommodate and transport flip charts, so invest in one and keep it around the office.

Limitations. Limited sight range and slow to scribe, it's important to remember that black ink reads easiest, wide-tip markers are far superior to thinner points, and letters should be readable and three inches tall, minimum. Readability is also impacted by vision angles and distance. If you are in a selling meeting with a customer, bring two new markers of each color you plan to use. For me, it's black (primary), blue (supplemental), and red (emphasis). I prefer Sharpie wide-tips. They read the best from a distance. Never rely on a customer to supply the markers. You'll get fine points no one can read, bludgeon-tipped whiteboard markers, dried-out markers with barely any ink—you name it. When you head out to sell, take your tools. It's what pros do.

Business Letters

Strengths. A letter is a personal, high-impact written record of an important message. This form is underutilized—despite always being read. People don't receive a lot of authored letters any more; everything seems boilerplated, computer-generated, or poorly written. A great letter, beautifully written, is a marvelous selling tool.

A GREAT LETTER, BEAUTIFULLY WRITTEN, IS A MARVELOUS SELLING TOOL.

Limitations. The more vital the message, the more important that the letter be written perfectly. Errors crush credibility. A well-written letter is not verbose. Use the newspaper technique of "who, what, when, where, why, and how" to craft a tight message that cuts to the core. Write to be clearly understood. Rambling, "salesy" doublespeak goes straight in the trash, which is where it belongs. Write tight and use a proofreader.

Email

Strengths. Email is quick, easy, and cheap. It enables real-time communication around the planet. A brilliant tool in so many ways, personalized digital messaging has shrunk the world, yet expanded the global marketplace. Email is excellent for instantly sending a specific message to stratified audiences of any size.

Limitations: Email has largely obsoleted the handwritten word in business thanks to rising global popularity. Along with its sometimes-addictive use has come the CYA (Cover Your Arse) mentality that exists on every continent. It also is a severe talent-inhibitor. No sales professional and writing amateur becomes better by sending digital smoke signals.

Email is a one-way communication medium that cannot convey voice or tone. It is *terrible* for expressing emotion, which often leads to being misinterpreted. Plus, slow creation output makes email a poor substitute for the telephone (e.g., 180 words-per-minute spoken, versus 20-30 wpm typed); slowness is a detriment in selling, where interactive dialogue is greatly beneficial. Because few salespeople write well or quickly, this easy tool often hampers sales productivity. Growing problems with email addiction increases dependence while shortening the attention span, especially in middle-aged workers. People read less now, and because of it, command and proper use of the language is on the downslide. Writing is a craft but email is a tool of convenience. Abuse in selling—or thinking that selling via email is a cheap panacea—is a highway to failure.

BECAUSE FEW SALESPEOPLE WRITE WELL OR QUICKLY, THIS EASY TOOL OFTEN HAMPERS SALES PRODUCTIVITY.

Text Messaging

Strengths. This immediate means of virtual access to intended recipients is easy and cheap.

Limitations. Texting has the same inherent sales problems as email—but amplified, since addiction problems are growing dramatically. This form of "digital shorthand" is chronically overused and contributing to declining language skills, especially grammar, spelling, vocabulary, and punctuation. This is a most unsuitable vehicle for long messages. Excessive texting messages can be chronically intrusive.

From a sales point of view, what's most disturbing about the texting reliance young people have developed is that managers will soon inherit a workforce of people who are used to hiding behind a tiny keyboard. Recent study findings published in a national newspaper indicated that nearly half of college males have asked girls out via texting and nearly one-fourth of females have broken up with their boyfriends via texting—a statistic that does not include Britney Spears, who dumped husband Kevin Federline this way.

As a sales leader, you can't stop the text-messaging trend but you can certainly study its ramifications in the world in which your people sell. You'll have an uphill road to success if you rely on chronic abusers to win a strategic sale.

> **FROM A SALES POINT OF VIEW, WHAT'S MOST DISTURBING ABOUT THE TEXTING RELIANCE YOUNG PEOPLE HAVE DEVELOPED IS THAT MANAGERS WILL SOON INHERIT A WORKFORCE OF PEOPLE WHO ARE USED TO HIDING BEHIND A TINY KEYBOARD.**

When delivered properly, a great sales message achieves its intended objective—or more. Just as people tend to process ideas in one of two ways—concept-to-detail or detail-to-concept—some channels are better suited to one person than another.

Also remember the three types of learning styles: listening (audio); watching (visual);

and doing (kinesthetic). Some channels are better suited than others to effectively reach these different ways of processing information. Phone is great for audio learners. Charts, graphs, and documentation works for visual learners. PowerPoint won't work for kinesthetic learners.

Experience and attention to detail will help your people grow stronger. Urge them to expand their range of channel delivery excellence and wean them away from a boring and predictable "one size fits all" presentation approach.

When making a sales presentation to multiple members of a customer company, chances are there are both types of thinkers in the audience—concept and detail—plus all three learning styles. The smart salesperson builds the sales message using multiple channels—to reach *every* member of the audience.

Great sales presentations must be *relevant* to attending stakeholders. When you put your message in a format and presentation package that matches how those stakeholders process ideas and prefer to learn, you will have maximum impact. Mix and match channels to create maximum impact and your sales team will win more, sell more, and— of course—make more money.

This is a vital area of differentiation between run-of-the-mill sales organizations and great ones. Hold your people to a higher standard—expect them to be the best in their competitive space—and you will quickly achieve greater success. Channel mastery, creatively used, helps everyone on the team sell better.

Any customer will tell you that a terrific presentation can tip the scale to victory. Teach your people the merits of multiple channels, have them practice, demonstrate, and be critiqued, and challenge them to become superb practitioners.

This, too, will make them stronger. Few things in selling are more fun than nailing a big presentation with a lot on the line. Multiple channel effectiveness helps make that a reality.

CHAPTER 10

MANAGING THE NOISE

HOW TO DEAL WITH THE FOUR STAGES OF CHANGE

Sales is a profession that consistently rewards a competitive edge in financial ways. Change occurs often in high-performance sales organizations: coverage models, territory reorganizations, budget adjustments, compensation plan reconfigurations, resource allocations, mergers, divestitures, and competitive repositioning—just to name a handful.

MAXIMUM HORSEPOWER sales organizations deal with change better than mediocre competitors by accelerating through it quickly and effectively en route to the post-change effectiveness stage. Dealing with change professionally is part of the MAXIMUM HORSEPOWER culture.

Leadership tips:

1. People don't resist change as much as they resist *being* changed.

2. No leader can change anyone. Change is inevitable, growth is optional, resistance is stress inducing. A salesperson may resist, snort with bluster, square off and fight—or embrace the need to change. No one can make a person change except that particular person. A person changes only when he or she decides to.

3. Skilled leaders don't control change. They shape, guide, influence, and help their people through it.

4. Change is thorny because it pushes people out of their comfort zones.

5. People respond differently because of their upbringing, personal history, life experience, value system, personality, and perception of the environment.

6. The size, scope, complexity, and timeline of a change *all* matter. Smart leaders never forget or underestimate this. Mediocre managers often do.

7. Some people do not change. Others are change-averse.

8. Resistance to change occurs for dozens of reasons, including:

   - Lousy communication, which causes a distrust surrounding the motives of the people leading the change.

   - Loss of something valued (e.g., money, prestige, turf, span of control, political influence). Negative value may be work-related or home-related. Emotional reaction is a sure sign that one or the other is threatened.

   - Anxiety due to a suddenly uncertain future. People don't understand the impact of change on their role, their work, their life, and their future. Respect that sometimes this is the result of a negative experience with a previous change.

   - Disagreement over a change's need, scope, motive, design, selected solutions, or implementation. Office hallways are full of gossips. Squash them.

- Change recipients have different temperaments and receptivity. When change arrives, the recipients will fall anywhere along a full spectrum that stretches from change-averse to change-embracing. The bigger the change, the wider the swing of emotional receptivity. Don't expect people to react the way you want them to. Expect them to react differently.

9. Seek to understand the reasons for people's stress. Know the root causes in order to minimize, then eliminate, exaggerated emotions. Some of these emotional triggers you might easily guess. Others you must seek.

10. *Over-communicate!* Under-communicating feeds the worry monster; so, make clear, consistent communication part of your leadership strategy. The bigger a necessary sales change, the more important an open pipeline of factual information. Incomplete information or selective disclosure cause stress and trigger rumors. To prevent a fear of change and team member uncertainty, stick to the facts. Do not sanitize, embellish, or hide them under layers of corporate doublespeak.

11. Proactively urge your people, individually and collectively, to be resilient. Read your people and gauge their resilience factors. Resilience enables people to thrive during a change, especially salespeople. Coach your people's self-confidence, flexibility, and problem-solving approaches.

12. Keep people connected. The more connected someone is, and the better his or her interpersonal skills, the easier change will be to embrace. Isolationists and poor communicators often struggle. Major business change is an earthquake to workaholics who have one-dimensional lives.

13. Know the composite emotional mix of your work force. Salespeople fear managerial shakeups, territory realignments, comp changes, budgeting adjustments, anything that rearranges the furniture on the stage on which they sell.

14. Spend as much energy investigating the upside success opportunities a change presents, as others do whining about it. Broadcast what you learn.

15. Change is disruptive and inconvenient. It is also inevitable. So, dwelling and lamenting serve no positive purpose. Teach your salespeople to accept a change for what it is: a temporary disruption to their status quo. The sooner a change is embraced, the quicker it becomes the new status quo. Urge your people to take root in their reconfigured environment, or to embrace changed expectations or strategic direction. The sooner they do, the sooner they will flourish.

16. Coach your people to worry only about things in life they can control (their own behaviors) and to jettison the rest of the stress that comes with organizational change. If they aren't the ones who initiate the change, urge them to focus on what elements of the transition they *can* control: How quickly they *choose* to embrace it. Half of life is learning what not to worry about. The other half is not worrying about it.

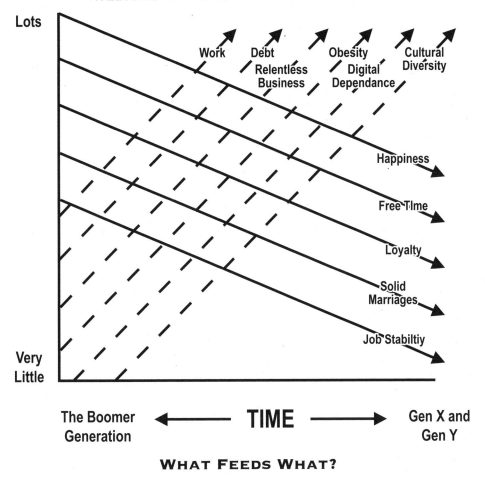

CONFLICTING BEHAVIORAL INFLUENCES

WELCOME TO THE MINDS OF YOUR SALES FORCE

Lots

Work   Debt   Obesity   Cultural
        Relentless   Digital   Diversity
        Business   Dependance

Happiness

Free Time

Loyalty

Solid
Marriages

Job Stabiltiy

Very
Little

The Boomer   ←—— **TIME** ——→   Gen X and
Generation   Gen Y

WHAT FEEDS WHAT?

The current working generation is evolving through a very dramatic series of intertwining social changes, many of which aren't good. Sourcing, developing, leading, retaining, and inspiring MAXIMUM HORSEPOWER sales performance from a diverse workforce that comes to the office each day immersed in this social upheaval requires skilled, strategic leadership.

Sales leaders must remain in touch with the behaviors that influence their workforce, since these same societal trends enmesh the customers who wade through similar distractions en route to making decisions that shape our success or lay bare our failures.

Leading a MAXIMUM HORSEPOWER sales organization requires reading, reacting, and adapting to changing social influences. It's a far bigger challenge than just tracking sales calls.

THE FOUR STAGES OF CHANGE

MANAGE YOUR SALES REPS SMARTLY

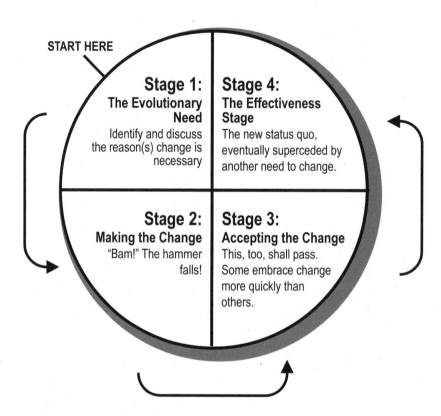

START HERE

Stage 1:
The Evolutionary Need
Identify and discuss the reason(s) change is necessary

Stage 4:
The Effectiveness Stage
The new status quo, eventually superceded by another need to change.

Stage 2:
Making the Change
"Bam!" The hammer falls!

Stage 3:
Accepting the Change
This, too, shall pass. Some embrace change more quickly than others.

Stage One: The need to change evolves over time. Depending on the reasons, impending change will create anxious expectations and/or rumor-mongering fear. Emotions rise.

Stage Two: When change is announced, people struggle with it. They push back and fight it, their first impulse negative, some vocally so. This is to be expected. The key is to let people vent, and then work to help them get to Stage Three Acceptance as quickly as possible.

Stage Three: Once people accept the change they switch their focus from the way things used to be to the way they are and can be. They see the positives and dwell less on the negatives. Resistance recedes. People settle in, adjust, and refocus.

Stage Four: Humming along. Over time, of course, things will evolve and eventually create the need to change again.

MANAGING SWIFTLY THROUGH CHANGE

(Read the plan from the top down. Execute the plan from the bottom up.)

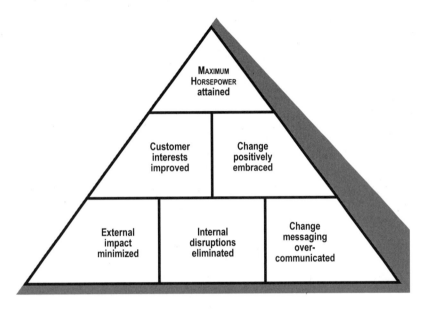

MAXIMUM HORSEPOWER attained

Customer interests improved

Change positively embraced

External impact minimized

Internal disruptions eliminated

Change messaging over-communicated

BE A BULL, NOT AN OSTRICH

In every company there are times to be bullish and times to hide. Leading change is a time to be bullish. Depending on the scope of the change, the emotional impact will be small or large. The larger the change, the more emotion. Smart internal mind management—understanding that being unsettled is typical but temporary—helps minimize the disruption. Above all, insulate your customers from any short-term chaos the change may cause.

It's easy to under-communicate during change but hard to over-communicate. Change has come about for reasons. Share those reasons and when you do, don't forget to explain the "why." The sooner people understand the why, the quicker they'll get over the disruption to the status quo.

There are four steps to change: making it, fighting it, accepting it, and flourishing after it. Usher your people to the acceptance stage as quickly as possible.

CHAPTER

HERDING CATS AND GOATS

STRENGTHENING INEXPERIENCED, MID-CAREER, AND VETERAN SALES PROS

"Anybody can change as long as they have enough extra clothes."
– Jacob Q., fourth grader

Developmentally, all salespeople are in different places at the same time, which presents a challenge when trying to figure out how best to collectively accelerate the sales team's growth.

Less-experienced reps must work on different things than mid-career performers and veterans. The lens through which tenured salespeople look at life, business, the company, and their profession is different from those with half the experience. Age, business maturity, and the scars of life have a lot to do with what people see.

THE LENS THROUGH WHICH TENURED SALESPEOPLE LOOK AT LIFE, BUSINESS, THE COMPANY, AND THEIR PROFESSION IS DIFFERENT FROM THOSE WITH HALF THE EXPERIENCE. AGE, BUSINESS MATURITY, AND THE SCARS OF LIFE HAVE A LOT TO DO WITH WHAT PEOPLE SEE.

Your goal is to have your sales team collectively engaged and advancing toward the high-performing *right* side of the performance bell curve (chart 1 below). Smart planning, coupled with differing segment priorities, helps to steer each person toward what will most benefit him or her. Career development is an incremental process; building one new, effective sales tool upon the next helps create sales stars. High performers don't sell more than others by accident. They do it because their talent is a *byproduct* of their time and invested effort.

Before building your strategic development plan for each of the following three career segments, assess where your people are now on the performance bell curve. How do they rate when mapped against the behavioral "three-headed man" (chart 2 below)?

Once you know your people's levels of performance, build a plan that creates a "tool of the month" campaign aimed at creating a common focus. Two common threads to build upon are the emotional investment of each salesperson in both his or her career and the company. Feed that emotional allegiance by focusing each month on one specific sales skill that will help to strengthen that rep's effectiveness. During that month, reinforce the topic over and over and over again. Make it so visible and so widely reinforced that your reps can't help but learn it.

CAREER DEVELOPMENT IS AN INCREMENTAL PROCESS; BUILDING ONE NEW, EFFECTIVE SALES TOOL UPON THE NEXT HELPS CREATE SALES STARS. HIGH PERFORMERS DON'T SELL MORE THAN OTHERS BY ACCIDENT. THEY DO IT BECAUSE THEIR TALENT IS A BYPRODUCT OF THEIR TIME AND INVESTED EFFORT.

CHART 1: SALES PERFORMANCE BELL CURVE

"Thrivers, Survivors & Chevrolet Drivers" ©

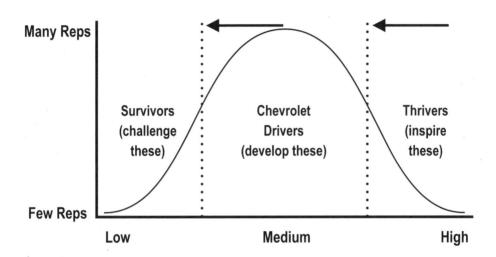

SALES PERFORMANCE

EXPECTED PERFORMANCE DISTRIBUTION FOR AN AVERAGE SALES ORGANIZATION

Left side **"Survivors"** are low, sub-par performers with substandard KSAs. They often have insufficient motivation to do good work and are easily replaceable. Survivors are "minimalists" and tend to be a negative influence on the rest of the work group. "Slugs," a friend of mine calls them.

Center **"Chevrolet Drivers"** comprise the bulk of the sales force. They are good people who work hard to carry out the company's goals. Drivers can be influenced negatively by Survivors, or inspired to greater things by Thrivers. Smart sales leaders strategically influence this group.

Right side **"Thrivers"** are high-performing sales leaders who consistently outperform all the others. They expect more of themselves, and they deliver. They are the irreplaceable revenue engine of the organization. Year after year, they are the people the field looks up to.

Goal: Move the vertical dotted lines to the left to reduce the number of low-performance Survivors and increase the number of high-performing Thrivers.

Key to success: The lines move to the left after you solidly execute a strategic KSA development plan that will gap-close the talent shortfalls. Stronger talent delivers better results.

THE SCOURGE OF THE THREE-HEADED MAN

Reps are not only in different places experientially; they are also in different places emotionally. The ability to inspire both individual and collective attributes of your sales organization hinges on successfully relating to your people's motivational triggers, which depends on their positions relative to "the three-headed man" (see figure below).

This concept recognizes that a professional salesperson's behaviors change only when he or she chooses to change them, and that decision is only acted upon where change is congruent with what matters most to that person. What matters *most* depends on how that person sees him or herself when faced with the three-headed hydra of the self-image.

The three-headed man is always awake, and chooses behaviors based on how demanding each of these three heads is:

CHART 2: THE THREE HEADED MAN

How I *want* to be perceived by others.

How I *am* perceived by others.

Who I *really* am.

Everyone in your organization, including you, juggles and reconciles the emotional hunger of these three heads differently.

Family upbringing through the early teen years hugely influences people's behavioral tendencies. Significant emotional events—unpredictable positive and negative traumas—force self-assessment (and reassessment) and reshape one's behavior as life unfolds. Think back to *9/11* and how people reacted. Volunteerism went up, charity giving skyrocketed, divorces rose, and people quit jobs they didn't like in pursuit of something more fulfilling.

Inspiring a diverse sales force hinges on getting a good, accurate reading on how these three *heads* are reconciled. Early-career reps usually focus on how they want to be perceived. Mid-career reps vary the most; they can be anywhere, and they tend to vacillate between the three heads with a somewhat unpredictable pace. Smart managers get an accurate reading on each mid-career rep as quickly as possible and accordingly manage their behaviors and development. Veterans tend to accept where they are in life and work.

This behavioral principle applies to our customers, as well as our people. Use it when shaping your sales strategy and messages.

THE REALITIES OF THREE-HEADED JUGGLING

Each time a member of your sales organization meets with you, he or she arrives with a unique between-the-ears mix of these three cognitive tug-of-wars.

For simplicity's sake, suppose a person has 100 points to divide among the three. *How* those points are divvied up directly influences behavior. As people age and/or mature, the mix can change. Teenagers, for example, are heavy in head one—how they want to be perceived by others. Older people tend to be concerned less about head one and more about head three.

All of your salespeople will allocate a different mix of their 100 points between these three heads. The following table offers suggestions for dealing with the various combinations you'll run into.

When interviewing new sales talent, strive to have your interviewers get an excellent read on a candidate's three heads. Some high-performance personality types—narcissists come to mind—can be great performers but absolute nightmares to manage. Narcissists love themselves above all else and take neither direction nor coaching very well. If you opt to hire one, *caveat emptor!* (buyer beware).

SOME HIGH-PERFORMANCE PERSONALITY TYPES— NARCISSISTS COME TO MIND—CAN BE GREAT PERFORMERS BUT ABSOLUTE NIGHTMARES TO MANAGE.

How I want to be perceived	How I am perceived	Who I really am	Comments & Recommendations
85	5	10	Out of balance. *Appeal to the ego.* Don't trust crucial deals to these people.
65	15	20	Out of balance. *Appeal to pride and ego.* Find them the right mentor to coach them toward a better balance.
55	25	30	Yellow zone. Still preoccupied with self. *Coach to maximize substance to meet or exceed style.*
25	35	40	Too much concern with uncontrollable perceptions. *Work to lower the middle number.*
25	25	50	Green zone. Nice balance. *Appeal to the long-term importance of building personal equity.*
20	20	60	Even better balance. *Coach them to expect and embrace a higher standard.*
15	15	70	Light yellow. Beware of overt self-confidence. *Coaching caution: Don't let them get complacent.*
10	10	80	Yellow zone due to personal preoccupation. *Vulnerable to misreading customer perceptions.*
5	5	90	Red zone. Out of competitive balance. *Vulnerable to defeat. Work hard on customer perception awareness.*

LESS-EXPERIENCED SALES PROS: THE "ME" STAGE

"You don't have to know anything to make something happen."
—Ted Turner, during a Notre Dame commencement address

New hires tend to divide their 100 points of the "three-headed-man" differently than veterans, skewing more toward perception issues, with heavier weighting on the image they would like to project. Veterans put more weight on personal surety. Coach and teach accordingly.

Twelve focus areas for developing the talent in less-experienced salespeople:

1. *Backbone Elements of the Profession*

- *Strategizing good pre-call objectives.* Help your people learn to sift *need-to-know* from *nice-to-know*. The need-to-know drives deals. Nice-to-know wastes time.

- *Staying client-focused and goal-oriented.* Separate the *act* of business rejection from the *emotion* of being rejected.

- *Developing an expressed, explicit need.* Your reps should know one when they hear it. Few do.

- *Controlling a sales call.* This is generally not a trait of fledging sales aspirants. Make it one.

- *Repetitious utilization of benefit statements.* Your reps need to learn and be unconsciously competent with these magic three: features, advantages, benefits.

- *Dealing with objections.* Better yet, coach your reps on how to eliminate them.

- *Closing.* Make your reps develop and own a personal closing style. Hound them about it. Every great sales professional is a skilled closer.

2. Listening Skills

Expect a weakness here. Better listening is an upside opportunity for virtually all inexperienced talent. Prior to their coming on-board, expect that they have no previous training on smart listening techniques. Hearing is a born ability. *Listening* is different. *Listening* is an improvable skill. When people haven't been taught, expecting them to be good at it is unrealistic. Stress, demonstrate, and reinforce how *structured listening* is a powerfully positive sales influence when trying to gain actionable interest with a prospect. Listening is one of the hardest skills to find in a sales employee. I recommend hiring great listeners when you do find them and to make room for them on your team. For a refresher on how to teach this, revisit Chapter 8.

 **LISTENING IS ONE OF THE HARDEST SKILLS TO FIND IN A SALES EMPLOYEE.**

3. Owning and Improving "Hit Rates"

A hit rate is the mathematical formula that represents the number of successes divided by the number of attempts, expressed as a percentage. Example:

100 sales presentations yields 12 orders = 12% hit (success) rate

Every rep must know what a hit rate is, that it exists, and what his or hers is—however good or bad that may be. Make them own the work required in order to raise their success percentage. If a hit rate never increases, success is linear, so the only way to sell more is to increase activities. Improvement should come from winning a greater percentage of a full workload.

4. Principles of Communication

Mandatory for any hope of sustained success. There are four components to master: sender, receiver, channel, message. Strive to make your people role models at the effective integration of multiple-channel communication.

5. Principles of Influencing Behavior

How can we expect our people to influence behavior if they don't know what causes it in the first place? What people think drives how they feel. How they feel drives what they do. How do your people expect to control a sales cycle if they can't astutely recognize thoughts, feelings, and the strength of emotions? How will they influence customers in order to inspire the customer to take actionable interest? A blind "gift of gab" can get lucky . . . but will never perform as consistently as someone who understands the "game within the game" of influencing behavior.

HOW CAN WE EXPECT OUR PEOPLE TO INFLUENCE BEHAVIOR IF THEY DON'T KNOW WHAT CAUSES IT IN THE FIRST PLACE?

6. Managing Time

When should reps invest extra time to pursue an opportunity? When should they make the hard call to walk away? Salespeople, especially new ones, are eternal optimists for whom every potential sales opportunity flickers like an eternal flame. Many need to be taught the difference between real opportunities and illusions. Countless billions in talent-time are wasted on pipe-dream opportunities with no real chance of closing. The sooner you teach your new people when to cut the cord on a lost opportunity, the more effective their time-utilization skills will become. Deal judgment is like racecar driving: There is a start, there is a finish, and there are countless speed-up, slow-down decisions to make in the heat of competition. Wrecks, blown engines, and flat tires are all part of the game. Don't let your people drive in circles if they have no chance of winning.

THE SOONER YOU TEACH YOUR NEW PEOPLE WHEN TO CUT THE CORD ON A LOST OPPORTUNITY, THE MORE EFFECTIVE THEIR TIME-UTILIZATION SKILLS WILL BECOME.

7. Utilizing Resources

Beware the three-headed man! Ego and perception concerns often inhibit the eager or pro-active search and acceptance for help. Too often, new reps want to "do it themselves" and don't want to run the risk of looking bad to others by asking for help during a fledgling sales cycle. In a winning culture, engaging others must not be perceived as punitive, an annoyance, or a sign of weakness. Foster a climate of unconditional team support.

Early in their onboarding process, make sure your new hires learn the who, what, when, where, why, and how of available help. If they don't know, too many times a new hire will be too timid to proactively seek help and will not ask. Broadly advertise your rep support. Keep your resources easily accessible. Create and champion a "how can we" team culture.

IN A WINNING CULTURE, ENGAGING OTHERS MUST NOT BE PERCEIVED AS PUNITIVE, AN ANNOYANCE, OR A SIGN OF WEAKNESS.

8. Accumulating Knowledge

What do they need to know? How do they plan to learn it? How are they going to prove their subject-matter mastery?

9. Pursuing Written, Prioritized Goals

Inspection helps. Teach an A, B, C priority system, with A goals as the most important. Urge time investment in A priorities, and teach strategies to complete them. This fundamentally smart time management should focus on actions that will make someone productive—not just keep them busy. *Productive* has a high ROI. *Busy* has a lower one. Make your reps map out, in writing if necessary, their best route to being "productive."

10. Owning Results

Sales ain't Halloween. Just because your reps dress up and spend the day going door-to-door, no one is going to hand them a business treat just because they ask. Selling takes work. The stark reality of the sales profession is that every single one of us is accountable for our results. The sooner a less-experienced rep learns that, the better. Winners win. Losers drink coffee, and whine.

SALES AIN'T HALLOWEEN. JUST BECAUSE YOUR REPS DRESS UP AND SPEND THE DAY GOING DOOR-TO-DOOR, NO ONE IS GOING TO HAND THEM A BUSINESS TREAT JUST BECAUSE THEY ASK.

11. Owning Improvement

If your reps stay still, they fall behind. What's the written KSA development plan to leapfrog the peer group? Where are the progress mileposts? Motivated professionals have incandescent futures. Coach your less experiences people to feel its warmth.

MOTIVATED PROFESSIONALS HAVE INCANDESCENT FUTURES.

12. Inspiring Ambition

These days people show up seeking a job, wanting good pay—while deciding what they like and don't like and whether or not to grow roots and stay. Teach them: Leave footprints, not buttprints, in the sands of time. For new hires, everything seems possible. Inspiring their ambition can fuel remarkable results. When you develop your people, what you are really selling is a marvelous profession. For many, this will be a novel consideration. Some won't make it. Others take off like rockets.

TEACH THEM: LEAVE FOOTPRINTS, NOT BUTTPRINTS, IN THE SANDS OF TIME.

MID-CAREER SALES PROFESSIONALS: THE "WE" STAGE

Mid-career people accept their role in a team structure. Focus on polish, and raise the bar of expectation as it relates to leadership through performance.

Twelve emphasis areas:

1. Savvy Pre-call Planning

Expect nearly 100 percent success with your mid-career reps attaining their pre-call objectives.

2. *Increasing Hit Rates*

Teach them how to work smarter, not harder, in order to increase their ratio of successes to failures. Coach them on how to recognize and invest effort in winnable deals, not implausible pipe dreams.

3. *Controlling a Sales Call*

Your reps should know how, as well as be able to, dissect calls after-the-fact, with an accurate analysis of behaviors demonstrated by their prospects. When call control is lost, they should know precisely why the control was lost. A professional mid-career salesperson can role-model the correct behaviors to a new hire.

4. *Demonstrating the Ability to Create Actionable Interest*

In a high-performance sales organization, every mid-career salesperson should be able to teach less-tenured team members how to influence customers into taking action.

5. *A Solid Aptitude for Creating, Communicating, Establishing, and Selling Value*

Value must be constructed. It can never be assumed. Without a clear understanding of what they are receiving for their money, customers opt to make price decisions. Selling price only works when you are the cheapest alternative in the market.

6. *Smart Strategic Planning*

Reps should be able to formulate and present to their customers a persuasive and compelling strategic plan. It's tough to sell a value-priced big deal if you can't explain, "Here's where we're going and here's how we're going to get there."

7. *Customizing Relevant Information for Multi-level Stakeholders*

Gaining matrix influence (supporters at multiple levels throughout a customer organization) should be part of their regular work habits.

8. *Enhancing Professional Presentation Skills*

"On stage" delivery effectiveness should be clearly above the norm.

9. *Maintaining a Proactive Efficiency with Evolving Tools and Methods*

Technology offers a bazillion choices. Stay current with tools that can enable enhanced efficiency.

10. *Becoming Politically Astute*

Since change is disruptive, customers must clearly see a political benefit or they will not champion the cause. Mid-career reps must be able to read the political winners and losers of all their proposed deals. Business sense isn't always enough to get a deal done. Appeasing political stakeholders is vital. The bigger the deal, the truer this is.

11. *Leveraging Life Balance as an Enabler to Perform*

Greatness over time relies on self-propulsion. Sustained performance has a lot of interlocking pieces. Having a good, balanced, and happy life provides that energy and sustaining motivation. It's tough to stay consistent in the office when the rest of your life is crumbling.

12. *Knowing When to Lead, When to Follow...or Get Out of the Way*

Great mid-career reps avoid stale habits and performance ruts by staying situationally nimble. Depending on the opportunity, they willingly adapt their role to whatever is required—leading an initiative, partnering with someone else, or engaging the right team of resources to spearhead a win while becoming a role player on the periphery. Winning takes precedence over "doing it themselves."

VETERAN SALES PROFESSIONALS: THE "US" STAGE

"A man who looks at life at fifty the same as he did at twenty has wasted thirty years."

—Muhammad Ali, three-time world heavyweight boxing champion

Priority work should focus on increasing efficiency while eliminating wasted time and effort. Have your veteran reps maximize their wins by controlling and accelerating the high-probability sales cycle through every necessary step of the customer's decision-making process.

Thirteen focus areas for experienced salespeople include:

1. Listening Without Judgment

Vets must have the discipline to listen for content and emotion without jumping to reflexive assumptions or conclusions. This talent is far more rare than common. Vets develop habits and listening without judgment is one that usually can be improved.

2. Avoiding the "Reflexive Loop"

Vets tend to overlay scenarios with a *very predictable* set of judgmental filters, biases, and assumptions. Learning to independently assess opportunities is a new and difficult challenge for many.

3. Effectively Using "Contrarian Thinking"

Assume that everything they think to be true is actually false; then what do they see? What new insight and perspective do they gain? Teach this self-analysis process. Make them use it. It's a terrific approach for strategic selling, because what we're told by the customer is rarely the entire story.

4. Strategic Planning Proficiency

You will never get everyone great at this. Some salespeople never become a macro thinker; they struggle with "big picture" strategies. Smart strategic planning saves tons of time and lots of money en route to increased results. Scale this expectation to the capabilities of the rep. Maximum Horsepower performance mandates that the salesperson controls the account, not vice-versa. Veteran reps must be able to develop, orchestrate, and execute big picture strategies that add value, strengthen relationships, and deliver profitable revenue growth. These objectives rarely happen by accident; shrewd leadership and flawless execution accomplish them. Veteran sales performers must be able to lead by example when it comes to strategic account management.

5. Leadership Through Attitude and Performance

When dealing with veterans, good work is measured by business results and multi-faceted leadership. Even though experienced sales reps may be sole contributors, their leadership qualities are demonstrated by attitude, work ethic, discipline, reliability, and teamwork. These two leadership traits—via attitude and performance—are *expected* of veteran sales professionals. Without these two things, the veteran has zero additional value over a less-experienced contributor. Too many sales managers mistake experience for excellence. The two are not interrelated. Veterans *must* provide positive leadership and consistent performance.

6. Merchandising Information for Maximum Impact

Whether your people sell to an audience of one or an audience of many, the blended art and science of great presentations drives better business. Pulling this off is the culmination of three key veteran rep KSA elements—Knowledge, Skills, and Attributes. Each ties directly to this vital work effort. Mediocrity is uninspiring, boring, ineffective, and costly. When two close-to-equal solutions are presented by rival companies to a customer, the one presented with the most sizzle earns a big advantage.

Some vets struggle to accept the need to improve. If their presentations aren't good—and you know it but they don't—videotape them. Let the replays do the talking. When you do this, make sure to follow the *positive-negative-positive* critique process. Reinforce what's working, mention what needs tightening, and close with a reaffirmation of confidence. Deliver an encouraging message: With practice and commitment, their presentations will improve—and so will their business results.

Many vets have big and surprisingly brittle egos, especially in a peer group setting of "tough love critiques." Your goals are to *teach* and encourage them, not scold or badger them.

Five years into my Xerox career, I got stuck working for a guy like that: a needling drinker whose motivation style was mockery and derision. Ours was a veteran team of proven performers. None of us cared for him or his approach. Instead of working hard to overachieve, we bided our time. He lasted barely a year before being shoved into the bubbling abyss where contemptible slave masters go to dissolve. If I seem embittered by the recollection, perhaps it underscores the point: *Nobody* is inspired by ridicule.

7. Effectiveness with All Communication Channels

Tenured salespeople should be benchmarks of proficiency when it comes to packaging messages that gain actionable interest and win deals. Appeal to a vet's ego. Challenge him or her to parlay experience and skills into better messaging in order to increase the odds of sustained overachievement.

He who *liveth* by PowerPoint *die-eth* by PowerPoint. Other delivery channels engage customers more readily. Take full advantage. Smart vets pick the right delivery tools for each situation. They approach every sales setting as a unique opportunity, and customize their message accordingly, selecting the maximum impact delivery channel, which varies by the sales call objective, message, and audience. They are neither lazy, nor predictable. They are cleverly creative.

8. *Gaining Multi-generational Consensus and Support*

Keep your tenured people current with today's multigenerational, multiethnic market culture. Here is a typical opportunity: A sixty-something relies on a fifty-something, who gets a forty-something to engage a thirty-something, who coaxes a twenty-something to help make the deal happen. Stress that your vets must stay young at heart, no matter what.

9. *Politically Astute*

Experienced sales reps understand that political savvy enables and denies more deals than any other catalyst. Successful veteran reps accurately assess political winners and losers tied to their customer proposals. They remain neutral (politically) as they progress through the sales cycle. They adjust their message as the cycle evolves and the agendas of the political stakeholders are identified. No big deal gets sold without a political sponsor. Successful veterans identify and nurture those champions, and work effectively in high stakes political climates. Politics has a hierarchy. Things that are strategically valued trump operational improvement. Vets must be able to accurately assess political truth.

10. *Impeccable Post-sale Follow-up*

Realistic expectations, delivery on a promise, and affirming the wisdom of the prospect's buying decision all lead to incremental new business, expansion opportunities, and strong referrals. A smart seasoned pro understands the word-of-mouth game very well and capitalizes on it. This falls in to the domain of "working smarter, not harder."

11. *Heightened Sense of Urgency for Work and Life*

Sustained performance demands sustained propulsion, which is produced by the rep's motivation. Work life and personal life must be in balance to avoid a resounding emotional splat. The price for failure to recalibrate is burnout. Burnout masquerades as midlife crisis, family trouble, or lousy business results. A motivated performer prioritizes *both* business and family. Lead by example to inspire your veteran reps to maintain a similar balance.

12. Managing the Midlife Crisis

Teach what it is, why it occurs, and *how* to negotiate it. One midlife-crisis hypothesis is that it's the predictable re-rearing of all three heads of the three-headed-monster, reshuffling behavioral predictability at the point where an aging, post-peak body intersects with relentlessly increasing, experiential wisdom.

Never let a sales rep off the hook for performance just because he or she is preoccupied with dueling the three-headed-monster. Empathy for the struggle is okay; sympathy isn't. Coach the rep through the process of coming to terms with all three heads—until that rep feels good about again him or herself as a person and as a contributor to the company. When you see this, don't ignore it. Step up and deal with it. If you do not, personal demons can weave a costly cobweb that can mummify a veteran talent.

13. Significant in the Lives of Others

Self-image is what we think about ourselves. Self-esteem is how we feel about ourselves. One of my favorite quotes is by romance novelist Doris Mortman: "Until you're happy with who you are, you'll never be happy with what you have." Inspire your tenured sales reps to leave a legacy of excellence. Urge them to be a positive influence on the lives of others. Challenge them through compassion, life balance, performance, and leadership. A veteran's career, in the end, is a body of work. Inspire your people to be proud of that body of work. Urge them to make it as impressive as possible.

CHAPTER 12

DEVELOPING YOUR SALES PROFESSIONALS

INSPIRING AND MOTIVATING TALENT

Newbies

When you're young, life sprawls before you. Everything is possible. One day, life passes you and you suddenly view it differently. Sales careers are that way, too. They typically unfold with a decreasing range of emotional modularity. The younger we are, the newer things are, the more things mean. Time and experience temper the highs and cushion the lows. Keep this in mind when inspiring and developing early-career talents. This will be a vexing challenge for managers saddled with younger reps new to the game. Jobhoppers will not have the same emotional ties to success and failure that reps committed to the craft will. Be warned: They will keep failure at arm's length.

JOBHOPPERS WILL NOT HAVE THE SAME EMOTIONAL TIES TO SUCCESS AND FAILURE THAT REPS COMMITTED TO THE CRAFT WILL. BE WARNED: THEY WILL KEEP FAILURE AT ARM'S LENGTH.

The two biggest favors you can do for reps early in their careers: (1) help them learn to control an account relationship, and (2) coach improvement with their success rates, commonly called "hit" rates. Controlling accounts starts with controlling sales calls. The sooner reps learn how to influence the behavior of prospects, the better they'll perform. The key pillars of influencing prospect behavior are a new rep's KSAs. Buyers of value expect a knowledgeable supplier, with skills commensurate with the responsibility. To develop a successful career, new reps must care about their profession and aspire to thrive in it.

Investing early in new sales reps helps arm them with what they need to succeed. Positioning alone does not pay the bills or buy the toys. *Winning* does. For your new people to win more, coach them toward improving their hit rates. In baseball, the standard mathematical formula for offensive success is the batting average. In selling, it's the number of successes divided by the number of attempts. The higher the percentage, the less the amount of time and motion squandered; the lower the number, the less efficient the production.

Managers, of course, want results—large ones, produced from strong win ratios that are cultivated from high activity levels. When you fish for business, you want gross tonnage on the dock.

Bluefin tuna are the world's most sought-after fish, the unchallenged king of ocean gamefish. The reason isn't sport, it's money. A single bluefin can weigh upwards of 1,800 pounds, its meat valued in excess of $10,000. The all-time record for a single bluefin is $180,000, purchased in Japan. First time fishermen are not hired to go catch bluefin. Too much at stake.

Sardines, on the other hand, are caught five to ten tons at a time, and sold by the scoop, which holds several bushels. Their price fluctuates, but generally a scoop sells for thirty bucks or less. Billions upon billions of sardines are netted each year, retrieved from oceans all around the world. Sardine fishing is a massive industry, built of a species that grows no longer than a finger's length. Anybody can catch them and losing a few means nothing. There are billions more waiting to be caught.

In the world of professional selling, some people fish for tuna, some people fish for sardines. When we go to the bank, the bank doesn't care what we caught; bankers only care about how much money we've got. It's the same with managers. When fishing for tuna, managers want a fish in the hold and another on the line. When fishing for sardines, managers want fish on the dock, fish in the hold, and fish in the net, waiting to get hoisted aboard. Whether fishing or selling, hit rates determine the success. Hit rates generate cash to the bank.

Everyone has a hit rate, though few realize it or consciously try to improve it. Multiply a rep's hit rate times the number of his or her attempts and you can tally that person's success potential. The only way to raise results is to increase the hit rate or to maintain the hit rate but increase activity. If a rep is already working hard, he or she has reached a near ceiling on activity. Improvement, therefore, requires a better win ratio.

EVERYONE HAS A HIT RATE, THOUGH FEW REALIZE IT OR CONSCIOUSLY TRY TO IMPROVE IT.

The sooner you make your new talents aware of their hit rates, and coach them to strength, the sooner they will be winning. Winning matters. In selling, it's how you keep score.

Remember, the amplitude of emotion is heightened for people early in their sales careers. The wins soar higher, the losses hurt deeper. Coach to these emotions. Trumpet and cheer successes. Coach positively through the defeats. Schedule formal loss reviews and "autopsies" in order to understand why another company got the sale. What could the rep have done better or differently? What was the critical success factor missed? How else might the rep have repositioned the value proposition in order to gain the upper hand? [Hint to newbies: It's not always *price* that beats you. Sometimes you get outsold.]

Competitors who win will replicate their talk track and behaviors. If your people replicate *their* behaviors, they're likely to lose again. Coach every new rep not to get beat the same way twice. Next time against that competitor, change the approach, the strategy, the talk track, the pricing structure or the offering. Proactively change the pitch.

COMPETITORS WHO WIN WILL REPLICATE THEIR TALK TRACK AND BEHAVIORS. IF YOUR PEOPLE REPLICATE THEIR BEHAVIORS, THEY'RE LIKELY TO LOSE AGAIN.

When a new rep blows a winnable deal due to a controllable mistake, use it to teach, not punish. Use the *"positive-negative-positive"* critiquing process.

Begin counseling with a positive message, and make suggestions on what might have been done differently and better. Don't berate people. They want to succeed and most try very hard. Consistently remind them: Selling is a *profession*. Pros beat amateurs, just like they do in every other

SELLING IS A PROFESSION. PROS BEAT AMATEURS, JUST LIKE THEY DO IN EVERY OTHER LINE OF WORK.

line of work. Embrace the profession and grow.

Reset expectations: that losing to a better sales professional is only a temporary excuse and that your sales "brand" is consistently top-notch work. Regain a shared commitment to sell to that level of execution. Lastly, make sure to close your rep meetings with a positive reaffirmation that expresses faith in your rep's ability to deliver. Scared salespeople can't sell. Confident ones can.

EMOTIONAL MODULARITY: EARLY CAREER SALESPEOPLE

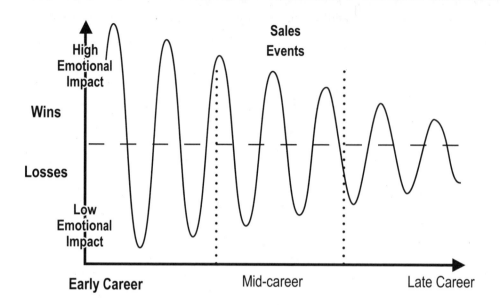

INSPIRING NEW SALES TALENT IS A *"RAH-RAH"* BUSINESS!

The highs are high, the lows are low. The emotional amplitude is the greatest it will be in the new rep's sales career. Celebrate the wins formally and informally. Dissect the defeats, then coach based on what you observe. Don't berate anyone over a loss. Nobody wins them all. Never pretend you have. Encourage the rep through inspiration, pointing out that becoming a better-than-average salesperson means doing their best to understand how they lost so they won't be beaten the same way again.

Energy and effort spent in developing a rep early in his or her career should be dedicated to knowledge accumulation, stronger skills through coaching, and inspiriting the attributes of a champion. Ego food never hurts, especially when fed to a motivated rep with big-upside potential.

The Watch Out: Don't underestimate a rep's emotional state. Maintain a close pulse reading on all of those who are trying their best. *Rah-rah* the highs. And don't crush somebody who has suffered a loss. Self-imposed pressure, the lonely feeling of personal failure, is a heavy burden by itself. Do a loss review, learn together, focus on improving, and reaffirm confidence in the rep's potential.

NEW CAREER TALENT PRIORITIES

(Read the plan from the top down. Execute the plan from the bottom up.)

"It's always been 10% talent and 90% hard work."
—Paul Newman

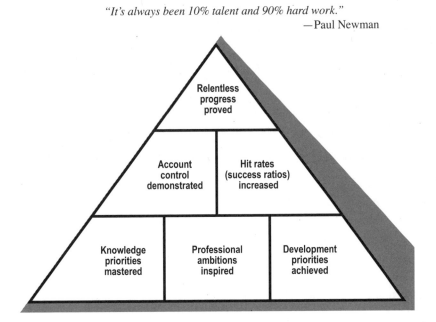

NEW TALENT MUST BE COACHED

Stay close to new reps. Be easily accessibility. Spur improvement by inspiring their attributes. Urge them to own their improvement. Celebrate their positive changes.

The two critical success factors: (1) learning how to control an account; (2) increasing the hit (win) rate. Account control requires several moving parts. Teach your people early that success comes more quickly to those who can drive a sales cycle.

Hit rates are successes divided by attempts. If a rep succeeds half the time, his or her hit rate is 50%. When a rep succeeds eight of ten times, it jumps to 80%. The only way to get better results with a flat hit rate is to drive more attempts (work harder). Growing the hit rate improves absolute results. Maximizing results is a byproduct of smarter, better work.

Ignore your people's wins and losses, they will muddle along in brooding isolation, learning mostly by trial and error. Cheerlead the development of your people early and often. When you do, they will respond.

MID-CAREER

For developing mid-career sales reps, focus mainly on accelerating advanced skills. We are selling in an ultra-dynamic global market that is liberally sprinkled with new opportunities and expanding possibilities. Maintaining the status quo is a loser's approach. Do not be shy about reminding them.

> WE ARE SELLING IN AN ULTRA-DYNAMIC GLOBAL MARKET THAT IS LIBERALLY SPRINKLED WITH NEW OPPORTUNITIES AND EXPANDING POSSIBILITIES.

Some mid-career reps grow deep roots into the comfortable soil of the fat, mediocre "Chevrolet Driver" center segment of the performance bell curve. Too few graduate to the high performance right end of the bell curve—the "Thriver" category—thanks to the investments they've made in themselves and their profession.

Attribute nurturing will inspire mid-career reps to accept the challenge to sharpen their skills, rise above the rest, and "be somebody." Two key developmental triggers propel success: a demonstrated mastery of communication skills and exemplary value selling.

At this point in his or her career, a high-performing sales rep must become "unconsciously competent" with demonstrated expertise involving all four components of communication: *sender*, *receiver*, *channel*, and *message*. Proficiency must be automatic.

Sender Management

A terrific *sender* smoothly merges effective interpersonal skills with the intentional creation of positive emotional experiences for mixed audiences of unlike thinkers. Great senders know how to influence behaviors in order to gain actionable interest and communicate accordingly.

Receiver Management

Receiver management entails smartly catering to prospects' work styles, learning preferences, and priority influence factors. It involves knowing how to gain quick, accurate reads on people at multiple levels, internally and externally, as well as being adept at assessing power brokers' personal and political motivations.

Channels

Communication channels are the vehicles a rep chooses to use in order to communicate his or her sales messages. The common ones are face-to-face, telephone, voice mail, email, fax, and PowerPoint. Each channel has its pluses and minuses. At mid-career, channel selection, use, and management must become a science.

Impactful Messaging

The fourth component of effective communication, impactful message management, involves the purposeful crafting of messages compelling enough to stimulate action. Every great salesperson knows that *what you say* and *how you say it* are both equally important, and that every message consists of both pieces.

For example, "Are you losing weight?" sounds a lot sweeter than pointing at the person's tummy and grunting, "You don't look quite as fat." Words matter, as does the delivery.

Once mid-career reps show good command of all four communication components, ratchet up your expectations of his or her presentation skills. Anne Warfield in Minneapolis specializes in what she terms "Outcome Thinking." Anne's methods involve having presenters focus on gaining a specific, desired outcome through better presentations. All mid-career sales pros should be developing their presentation skills to a higher standard. Some reps will improve quickly. Others will need classroom instruction with lots of practice. Raise the bar for what's expected, *way up*. Far too many mid-career reps are soft here, mediocre at best and boring at worst. They cannot control or inspire an audience but do not understand why.

ALL MID-CAREER SALES PROS SHOULD BE DEVELOPING THEIR PRESENTATION SKILLS TO A HIGHER STANDARD.

Stronger presentation skills positively impact all three KSAs. Knowledge comes from learning more about the construction elements of a great presentation. Repetitious practice drives the mastery of new and better skills. The strengthened attributes of grown confidence come from becoming a more polished professional.

Mid-career Summary

These days everybody is busy. But busy isn't the goal. *Productive* is the goal. So if people are diligently trying but not overly successful, what is it that's keeping them that way? Activity-wise, how do their days pass by? What are they spending time on, wasting time on, and investing time on? How can the non-productive behaviors be "Six Sigma'd" (eliminated via better processes) from their day? What must change in order to convert wasted motion into business opportunities and accelerating sales cycles that translate to more and faster wins?

Every top talent has a behavioral formula that enables him or her to consistently operate at MAXIMUM HORSEPOWER efficiency. Every mid-career rep in the organization must own the realization that this formula exists. Then they must find, practice, and protect the behaviors that create MAXIMUM HORSEPOWER. Once they own their personal high-performance formula, they need to inspire others on the team to find *theirs*, too, since inspiring others is a hallmark trait of MAXIMUM HORSEPOWER sales organizations.

EVERY TOP TALENT HAS A BEHAVIORAL FORMULA THAT ENABLES HIM OR HER TO CONSISTENTLY OPERATE AT MAXIMUM HORSEPOWER EFFICIENCY.

Don't let your mid-career revenue generators relax comfortably with the status quo. Challenge them to parlay experience and personal growth into a graduation from the middle of the bell curve to the lofty heights of high performance. Trust me: It can happen.

For several years during my Xerox career, I moonlighted as a standup comic. It is hard work, exhilarating when you "kill" the audience, but the Death Valley of disappointment when you bomb. I think that's what I love about it: like selling at its highest levels, standup is hard. You are up there, on stage, selling jokes as hard as you can.

I worked with some terrific professionals on the rise, Sinbad, Rita Rudner, and Dave Chappelle among them. Chappelle was a kid when he beat me in a contest. Fourteen, I think. Jeff Foxworthy was in Atlanta, working for IBM and honing an act full of jokes about rednecks that I thought would bomb as soon as he drove across the Mississippi River. All four of these professional performers reached stardom by paying their dues.

In every green room in every comedyclub in America is scrawled the same message on the wall: It takes ten years to be an overnight sensation. Jerry Seinfeld paid his dues. Steve Martin paid his. Robin Williams paid his, as well. Theirs is a learned craft, not an ordained one.

Mid-career reps pay dues, too. The ones worth keeping either plateau or advance. If they don't care about the profession—if selling is just a job—and you see their work habits regress, don't invest a dime. Groom their replacements instead.

If a rep has peaked, yet has organizational value, let him or her protect a low-risk customer base. But for salespeople who aspire to greater things, send a very loud message: *Great talents are made, not born.* The reps who shoulder the responsibility of improving their skill sets will be rewarded.

GREAT TALENTS ARE MADE, NOT BORN.

Your next batch of great performers will emerge one by one from the middle of the bell curve. Give those in mid-career every chance possible to become special, especially if their early years of selling did not include formal training. For the ones who are motivated to become great, invest in their KSAs.

Selling a product to a customer is not a whole lot different than selling twenty minutes of jokes to an audience. People who respect their chosen craft, work hard to improve, are open to coaching, and consistently persevere will succeed.

There are a lot of improvable talents hidden in every bell curve. Find them and invest in them. They will more than pay you back.

EMOTIONAL MODULARITY: MID-CAREER SALESPEOPLE

COMMON REACTIONS TO WINS AND LOSSES

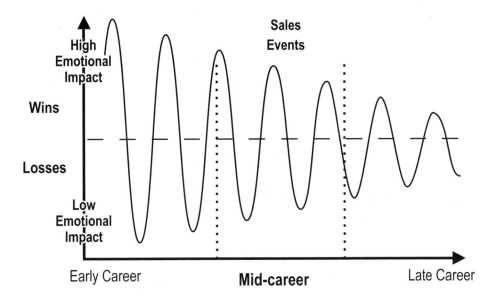

INSPIRING MID-CAREER TALENT TAKES FINESSE

Years of experience tend to temper the emotional highs and lows that are so typical of gung-ho people new to profession of selling. Since these highs and lows are less dramatic, ratchet up your leadership expectations by redefining what "good" really is at mid-career.

Communication skills must be mastered and the ability to create, communicate, sell, and maintain value over time must be performance hallmarks of every mid-career rep. Doing that takes work, hard work that requires a commitment to continuous improvement.

The Watch Out: Don't over-hype a win nor tolerate a *laissez-faire* acceptance of defeat. Never let your people get comfortable with losing. Defeat is rejection and rejection stinks. Show me a sales organization complacent with losing and I'll show you a room full of losers.

Being mediocre stinks, too, because being mediocre means you're average and when you're average you are just as close to the bottom as you are to the top. Where's the glory in that?

Challenge mid-career pros to become masters of the profession. Urge them to separate from the middle of the pack. Comfort causes plateaus. Complacency is your mid-career enemy. Squelch it. Inspire a culture of professional pride.

MID-CAREER TALENT PRIORITIES

(Read the plan from the top down. Execute the plan from the bottom up.)

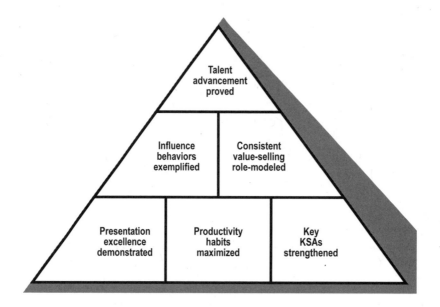

INSPIRATION CREATES PERSPIRATION

Inspire continuous improvement. With some, this is easy. For others, it will be harder than pushing a mule uphill.

Experienced reps get bored with the mundane, but tend to grab hold of behavioral principles. Focus on how to influence behaviors. Teach these principles in the context of life skills. Also, pound home the importance of selling value. Drill them on it. When the reps get tired of hearing it, drill them some more. All mid-career talent worth keeping must be able to build and persuasively present compelling value packages. If they can't, force them to learn. If they still can't, replace them with someone who can.

The vast majority of mid-career reps are mediocre or worse when it comes to presentation skills. Some don't know how; others don't like public speaking. To make them care enough to get better, appeal to their ego and raise the level of what is acceptable. Mediocre presenters rarely produce more than mediocre results.

Make your mid-career reps *prove* they are better than average. After all, mediocrity never steals a deal. Greatness does.

SALES VETERANS

Sales vets are creatures of habit. Developing them requires two things: breaking bad habits and generating new ones. Overnight change doesn't happen. Methodical progress does.

Avoid generating tidal waves of behavioral change. Vets challenge wholesale change and will resist. When dealing with experienced salespeople, change is triggered by awareness and self-discovery. Steer people to decide what current habits might impede their effectiveness. Coach, don't badger, one habit at a time in a steady pace that will facilitate permanent change.

Select the critical few new habits that will make someone better, rank them, then execute against that prioritized list with determined patience. Work on only one skill at a time. Try to do too much, too fast, and nothing will change.

Appealing to a veteran's ego makes formulating new habits easier than erasing old ones. Vets tend to be predictably ingrained in habitual thinking, trapped on a "reflexive loop" of behavioral predictability. They tend to hold the same set of lenses and filters up to every scenario, losing some of the independent vision that comes from freedom of bias. To eliminate bad habits, a rep must decide to let them erode, because behavior modification is never flip-switch simple.

VETS TEND TO BE PREDICTABLY INGRAINED IN HABITUAL THINKING, TRAPPED ON A "REFLEXIVE LOOP" OF BEHAVIORAL PREDICTABILITY.

Remind your experienced reps that tenure is good for two things in selling: leadership and performance. Leadership takes two forms: formal and informal. Formal leadership is demonstrated via behaviors. Informal leadership comes in a myriad of forms including demonstrated organizational support, voluntary mentoring, attitude, and work ethic.

Performance is all about results. Sales vets are expected to deliver. If a tenured sales pro brings neither absolute results nor positive leadership to an organization, then what's the point of keeping that person on the payroll instead of someone hungrier to improve? Absence of both means the seasoned rep is Norman Mailer's defeated Willie Loman from *Death of a Salesman*, a more costly overhead than the required resources warrant.

Just as the emotional amplitude of an early career talent rises to high peaks and falls to deep valleys, late career reps tend to experience wins and losses differently. The highs aren't as high and the lows aren't as low. Their emotional modularity is more constricted, which makes *rah-rah* coaching ineffective. Same with berating failure. Both managerial tactics bounce and roll off a vet's soul like raindrops on a freshly waxed car hood.

Motivating veteran reps works best by appealing to their leadership ego rather than offering a promise of future grandeur, since life for a veteran sales rep is lived with frequent glances in life's rearview mirror, looking back at the road traveled.

Sales veterans' attitudes vacillate. Some look ahead, some simply hang on, clinging to memories of the good old days and hoping to stick around long enough for a fat severance package or safe retirement. With them, trying to inspire visions of greatness is a dead-end street. Being frank about the need to lead and perform, and helping them do so by great coaching, is not a dead-end street—it's a two-way street. No one ever outgrows a chance to have his or her attributes inspired, especially by someone who cares. Be that person, and your vets will respond.

EMOTIONAL MODULARITY: DEALING WITH VETERANS

COMMON REACTIONS TO WINS AND LOSSES

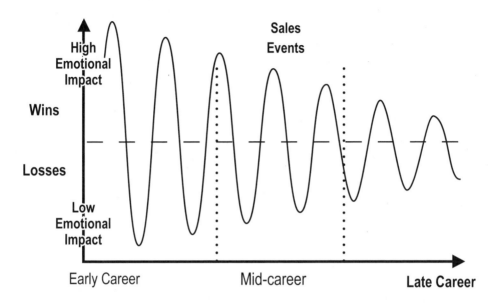

INSPIRING VETERAN TALENT TAKES COACHING

Be clear to communicate that tenure is good for two things: leadership and performance. Tenured leadership is ego-driven and can be both formal and informal. Insist that your veteran reps be positive role models, with a winning attitude and upbeat outlook. They should live and work with a sense of urgency.

Performance from vets is expected. Tenure should have created a bank of knowledge that is sufficient to win. Time should have shaped the skills that make winning more common than losing. Younger talent admires older talent who deliver results. They pity older talent that can't.

The Watch Out: If you aren't getting leadership and performance from your veterans, tenure means nothing. Clearly communicate your expectations. Work to strengthen one new skill at a time. Coach to eliminate one bad habit. Progress won't be instantaneous. Habits take time to form and time to break. Be persistent, not impatient.

VETERAN SALES DEVELOPMENT PRIORITIES

(Read the plan from the top down. Execute the plan from the bottom up.)

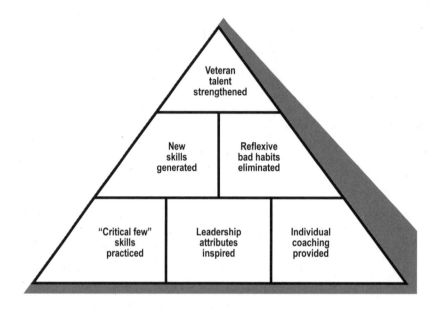

Veteran
talent
strengthened

New
skills
generated

Reflexive
bad habits
eliminated

"Critical few"
skills
practiced

Leadership
attributes
inspired

Individual
coaching
provided

VETERANS MUST LEAD BY EXAMPLE

Old dogs and new tricks aren't mutually exclusive unless the old dog hasn't shown a previous interest in learning any. Top performers evolve over time, largely because they have added effective sales tricks to their arsenal whenever they find one that provides an edge.

Top performers are always open to getting better. Your bigger sales leadership challenge will come from trickless dogs. If a veteran rep has no track record of continuous improvement, holding grandiose hopes for them to dramatically improve is a false ambition.

Focus on one skill at a time and don't move off that new skill until it has become an "unconsciously competent" technique. Work with your people to eradicate one bad habit at a time, too. For example, many veteran salespeople have a bad habit of jumping to conclusions. Work on contrarian thinking, and nothing else, until positive change is assured.

Appeal to the veteran's ego to provide role model leadership. Remind them: Tenure is good for two things, leadership and performance. Hold them accountable to this higher expectation. In the end, when dealing with vets, you will get what you insist upon.

SUSTAINED PERFORMANCE

HOW TO MAINTAIN CONSISTENT SUCCESS

Consistently winning deals that sustain overachievement requires five things:

1. *Best-in-class sourcing*
2. *Smart onboarding*
3. *Strategic investment*
4. *Calculated retention*
5. *Grooming the next generation*

1. BEST-IN-CLASS SOURCING
2. SMART ONBOARDING
3. STRATEGIC INVESTMENT
4. CALCULATED RETENTION
5. GROOMING THE NEXT GENERATION

BEST-IN-CLASS SOURCING

There are two sales pools to draw from, the fledglings and the experienced. In both cases you must know someone's true motivation for wanting to join the team. Their reasons will fall into one of two categories: Either they are they running *from* something or they are running *to* something. Pass on all the "running froms." Hire the "running to's."

Fledglings are people who haven't sold before but are willing to try. To a fledgling, selling is a job they'll try, not a career they've embraced. Fledglings come in two categories: What's-In-It-for-Me self-purposed hires and Crossovers. Their success is largely dependent on what they sell. If they rep something (like pharmaceuticals, for example), they do not need to get a customer to sign on a line to spend money. They just show and tell. Call activity is what matters. Face time.

TO A FLEDGLING, SELLING IS A JOB THEY'LL TRY, NOT A CAREER THEY'VE EMBRACED.

But if they have to *sell* something with signed contracts and risk factors involved, you are dealing with an entirely different attribute set.

Today's younger workers enter the force more concerned than the Boomers they replace about what a job will do for *them*. They are not emotionally committed to strengthening an organization. Their loyalty is typically one-way.

For many, the work career is a colorful mosaic of different tiles from various jobs and experiences, many of which are unrelated. If they like it, they'll stay. If not, they'll go do something else, often unrelated. The art of a skilled staffing manager, of course, is ferreting out each candidate's interview motivation. Bad sales hires are expensive. Depending on the sales responsibility, a reasonably quick failure exodus costs between six-and-eighteen months' pay, not counting the irritation caused to customers.

DEPENDING ON THE SALES RESPONSIBILITY, A REASONABLY QUICK FAILURE EXODUS COSTS BETWEEN SIX-AND-EIGHTEEN MONTHS' PAY, NOT COUNTING THE IRRITATION CAUSED TO CUSTOMERS.

Although newbies will always play a role in sales force hiring, more emphasis is placed on finding people with sales *experience*. The logic is that at least they bring a realistic view of the life to the workplace.

Career Crossovers are workforce experienced but arrive on the door looking to switch into a new line of industry. The first interview challenge they must hurdle is why they're sitting there in the first place. What is it about *this* opportunity that makes it significantly more compelling than the job they just left, or the one before that? If they hurdle this probe cleanly, the second hurdle deals with realistic expectations as revealed from both sides of the desk.

EXPERIENCE ≠ GOOD

EXPERIENCE ≠ GOOD

Never assume experience equals proficiency. It doesn't. A lot of people play a guitar but few are good enough to be merit a cover charge. The same holds true in sales. A lot of people will tell you they've sold. Very few are worth risking your bonus or career on.

"Trust but verify," my friend Tracey Whittaker says. There's a lot more gold-plated jewelry than pure gold, a lot more cubic zirconias than diamonds. The majority of "salespeople" out there have not been formally trained in selling, much less trained in *value creation*. Don't make the mistake of tagging experience to professionalism or skill level. This is especially true when drafting hiring criteria. Remember: Your success is riding on their performance. Your bonus hinges on their overachievement.

With experienced candidates, the sourcing challenge starts with ferreting out why someone is interested in joining your team. Is he or she running from failure, or running to a better opportunity? Experienced or not, don't waste time on the *running froms* because they cannot, and will not, outrun whatever it was that caused them to flee. Whatever they are running *from*—their "baggage"—will be waiting wherever they go next. With a six-to-eighteen month expense penalty hanging over your head for every wrong guess, why pay for anyone's old baggage to be delivered into a positive new environment?

Source only the *running to's*. If convinced that someone's reason for fleeing the last sales position might be legit, put that person through the second filter screen. What is his or her professional ceiling? Is that person destined to mediocrity? If so, investing KSA development dollars in them will net you loyalty but no additional horsepower. Pursue more aggressively the candidates with upside "stretch." Being motivated to get better is an admirable attribute; having the talent to do it is vital.

SMART ONBOARDING

As attention spans shorten, the amount of cerebral-processing time new hires spend before making a *commit* or *de-commit* decision shortens, too. More than ever, MAXIMUM HORSEPOWER sales teams recognize this. They smartly integrate new talent with strategic precision, recognizing that the emotional journey their new reps go through en route to becoming effective contributors is an important organizational burden that must be shouldered. Companies owe new people a positive assimilation. Smart companies make sure it happens.

On the chart below are two different onboarding trails. Path One is typical of organizations who hire people and onboard them in an unstructured, slipshod fashion.

Path Two is typical of smarter firms who nurture the positive emotional experiences of all new hires. Path Two is the MAXIMUM HORSEPOWER approach.

COMPANIES OWE NEW PEOPLE A POSITIVE ASSIMILATION.

MANAGING THE EXODUS CURVE

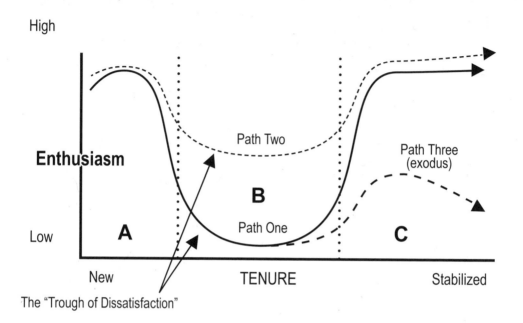

High

Enthusiasm

Low

A

B

Path Two

Path One

Path Three
(exodus)

C

New

TENURE

Stabilized

The "Trough of Dissatisfaction"

GUIDE THE EMOTIONAL EXPERIENCE

A. THE HAPPY STAGE
Everyone is thrilled with a new opportunity. Each interaction creates thoughts. As time passes, thoughts accumulate, both positive and negative. Newness gives way to reality, which diminishes enthusiasm. MAXIMUM HORSEPOWER sales teams strategically assure their people are on Path Two *(above)*. Shallower frustration helps a new rep accelerate toward the effectiveness stage. The quicker he or she succeeds, the less the turnover risk.

B. THE REALITY STAGE
Work sets in. There's much to learn and pressure to bear. Frustration drives a negative emotional experience. MAXIMUM HORSEPOWER sales teams manage this significantly better than ordinary organizations. Path Two *(above)* is shallower.

C. THE 'FLOURISH OR FLEE' STAGE
Sales performers commit emotionally as they assimilate or they don't. If they make it up the learning curve, they feel good about their work as they reach a level of continuous contribution *(Paths One & Two)*. If discouraged, they check out emotionally and de-commit. Leaving *(via Path Three, the exodus)* is inevitable. MAXIMUM HORSEPOWER sales teams have much less flight risk than others.

STRATEGIC INVESTMENT

Accelerating new hire competency is the goal of every onboarding experience. Until a rep is paying for him or herself all he or she has been to this point is a drag on earnings. Creating a sense of urgency for the rep to succeed is most effective when it's positive, not threatening. Fueling that motivation should be an orchestrated series of moves designed to begin bridging the KSAs of the rep with the KSAs required to consistently deliver sufficient results. *Very important:* Make sure that the right people are shaping the new hires' first impressions of your organization. You don't want someone who's disengaged emotionally from the soul of the business to be interfacing with new employees. It's frightening to think that this happens far more often than most sales leaders realize.

MAKE SURE THAT THE RIGHT PEOPLE ARE SHAPING THE NEW HIRES' FIRST IMPRESSIONS OF YOUR ORGANIZATION.

Everyone assimilating into the sales organization should have his or her own customized developmental action plan, complete with check-ups and milestones. Having the plan is worthless, however, unless someone cheerfully monitors its progress. Typically that would be the hiring manager, although some MAXIMUM HORSEPOWER sales organizations assign it as a coaching opportunity to a next-gen promotable. Ownership is vital, as is monitoring each new hire's progress against expectation. Interactions with the new hire should be positive and supportive.

If progress is slower than desired, circle back to these three barriers to performance to figure out why: Either they (1) can't do it, (2) won't do it, or (3) are prevented from doing it.

Don't horse around with developmental shortfalls. Knowledge can be taught and skills can be developed. Hard work addresses both. Hard work, in fact, solves a whole lot of problems and cures a whole lot of ills.

CALCULATED RETENTION

If the other steps are science, this one is art. Calculated retention means you keep the salespeople you want and jettison the mistakes. There are street smarts involved here, since reading people and influencing behavior requires management of the unspoken as much as it does the spoken.

The four impact factors that help with calculated retention are:

- Company culture
- Proactive management of the emotional experience
- Staying connected, especially during times of substandard performance
- No surprises.

Company Culture

Which best describes your company sales culture: Rule by fear, or rule by recognition and reward?

A few years ago, I worked with a company that exceeded 35% annual turnover in its 1,000+ person sales force. When I asked why, the answer was: "Because that's the way it is in our business."

Again I asked why.

"We hire too many bad people."

Phooey, I thought. The problem wasn't an incredible string of bad people. The company didn't know why people where bailing like paratroopers and didn't seem to care. The existing culture said it was okay to accept 400 turnovers a year, costing an average of six months' pay plus benefits. The *culture* said the revolving door of salespeople was a fixed cost of doing business. When the company finally decided to put a pencil to it, the leadership team was alarmed to see the cost of turnover (conservatively calculated) totaled $24 million annually. Suddenly the merry-go-round of exiting salespeople was a problem worth solving.

Spurred financially to take action, the company reconfigured its approach to onboarding and assimilation. Within the first year, they shaved six percentage points off the turnover rate. The cost to do so was virtually nothing, since their new approach utilized existing resources. The improvement value was over $1.5 million, gained just by doing things differently.

A company's culture is a funny thing, since every company has one but line employees tend to see it and describe it differently than executives. For example, does the sales organization fear "quick court-marshaling," managing by fear, with people hearing footsteps as soon as they fall below plan? If so, expect random, surprising, and often excessive turnover. Senior execs are usually insulated from the stress of the battlefield. Their view might be as simple as sales being at or below plan for the year. *How* those numbers come about is typically too granular to bother with. The line managers own the fix.

Unfortunately, a discouraging number of sales organizations motivate this way. Fear can net short-term results but will not motivate a good rep for very long—perhaps only as long as it takes to find another job. Talented salespeople will not tolerate the hostile stress of a punitive climate, nor should they. Dueling customers and competitors day after day is tough enough. Returning to a negative office environment compounds the stress.

> **FEAR CAN NET SHORT-TERM RESULTS BUT WILL NOT MOTIVATE A GOOD REP FOR VERY LONG—PERHAPS ONLY AS LONG AS IT TAKES TO FIND ANOTHER JOB.**

These types of sales cultures also discourage referral hires, since no solid professional takes pride in representing this type of infrastructure and no one trapped in it will encourage a friend to come be miserable, too. Consequently, the recruitable talent pool these companies draw from is typically beneath the caliber interviewed by other, more positive companies. In sales, the number one source of high-performance talent is referral hires from other successful reps. Take that off the table and what do you have? An empty pipeline.

Since top performers will not be soliciting referral candidates, the only referrals the company will get will be from survivor talent. The people they bring in will be similar in nature. Organizations like this will never lead their market space, since most are doomed to mediocrity or worse.

There is, of course, a staggering cost associated with replacing talent. The dichotomy between this type of fear-based sales organization and a thriving one is often revealed by *how* that cost is perceived. Fear companies have high turnover cost and invest less in people because they expect their talent to sneak out the door. High performance sales cultures invest more in the people they have selectively recruited, and reap the benefits of expense savings due to a lower turnover rate. In their view, talent development is as much a proactive retention strategy as it is means to nurturing a better sales force. A stronger, more stable sales force obviously drives better absolute performance.

As often happens, the company culture often boils down to how senior staff perceives developing talent. When it's an expense, they go on the cheap, cut corners, and blame mediocre people for mediocre results. When sales talent development is perceived as an investment, positive changes happen and better things occur.

AS OFTEN HAPPENS, THE COMPANY CULTURE OFTEN BOILS DOWN TO HOW SENIOR STAFF PERCEIVES DEVELOPING TALENT.

Having the correct attitude toward talent development, along with a correct commitment, are two very big cultural components of every successful revenue-driven organization.

Positive cultures that reward overachievement are great for motivation as long as you don't create an entitlement environment in which rewards are expected for delivering as expected. Draw a line clear line at your minimum expectation. Pay fairly for it. Reward those who perform above the line with incentives commensurate to their contribution. Don't be chintzy about paying your top revenue-generators. After all, it's the customer's money that's funding those earned incentives, not the company's.

Proactive Management of the Emotional Experience

What salespeople think shapes how they feel. How they feel determines what they do (or don't do). If you want someone to stick around, they must feel valued. There is a positive reciprocity you should strive to communicate: that's it's mutually beneficial for both sides to help the other succeed, and that the good parts of the job outweigh any noise and inconvenience. Making salespeople feel this way can come by accident or design. MAXIMUM HORSEPOWER teams accomplish it as a course of business, thanks to the orchestrated execution of a series of reinforcing behaviors.

Remember the top three reasons good salespeople choose to leave a company: (1) they feel as though they aren't growing; (2) problems with their manager; (3) money.

Feed the first two head-on by investing in your rep's growth while insisting on an open communication climate in a positive coaching environment. If you do that, you are two-thirds of the way home.

Money, of course, is the third piece. Never lose a good talent over nickels and dimes. If the need arises, mediate to a satisfactory conclusion compensation issues as they arise.

Staying Connected, Especially During Times of Substandard Performance

Here's another culture question: What's your attitude toward non-performance? Is it: (a) Innocent until proven guilty, or (b) Guilty until proven innocent?

A growing number of companies are paranoid of employee lawsuits and give the rep the benefit of a thousand doubts before pulling the trigger on a performance termination. Sales managers despise the process. Human Resources detests having to monitor the process. The man or woman going through the process derides the CYA pettiness of it all. Let's face it: *Everybody* involved in tracking and administering the endless rolls of wallpaper it takes to document the final days, weeks, and months of someone's employment abhors it.

The upside is that the process keeps you out of court. The downside is that it's a crippling managerial burden that is twice the weight of what's comfortable to bear.

From a sales management point of view, if you live with this reality try to free up your sales leaders from getting bogged down by it. Delegate the detail trail. If you're too buried under processes and procedures to delegate it, Six Sigma the current process and find a better way. Free up your sales leaders from the cumbersome tedium of what's legally necessary. Devise a better way to cut through the nonsense.

Usually the best way out is the front door, not the back door. Being sincere in helping redeploy mismatched talent by routing them toward jobs that are better KSA matches often convinces the targeted low performer to pack his or her own bags and catch their own bus out of town. Always seek a win/win, while always respecting the view from both sides of the non-performance lens.

Since fear's forefather creates a schism of distrust between management and reps, polarization must be avoided. Once you alienate sales from sales leadership, you have zero chance of having a MAXIMUM HORSEPOWER sales organization.

The antidote, of course, is staying connected. Connection does not mean blizzards of BlackBerry pings. It means being *emotionally* connected; staying close to what people are thinking and how they are feeling. Not just about the sales cycles they're immersed in but their jobs in general. Their careers in particular. Their lives overall.

Nothing substitutes for two-way face-to-face dialogue. Use the telephone only when face-to-face opportunities are impractical. A phone call is better than no call.

Digital exchanges, by nature, are depersonalized. Easy, yes, but dreadful when it comes to accurately transmitting emotion (like concern).

What smart sales leaders want in these "staying connected" reach-out sessions *is* emotion. Do whatever it takes to treat your people even more respectfully than *you* would like to be treated.

No surprises

MAXIMUM HORSEPOWER sales teams flourish in an open communication environment, which is why you rarely find high performance sales cultures in companies with a CYA mentality.

> **MAXIMUM HORSEPOWER SALES TEAMS FLOURISH IN AN OPEN COMMUNICATION ENVIRONMENT, WHICH IS WHY YOU RARELY FIND HIGH PERFORMANCE SALES CULTURES IN COMPANIES WITH A CYA MENTALITY.**

The lucky seven "no surprises" elements of great sales organizations include:

1. *Open, honest communication* in good times—but especially in bad. Selling is a tough business, a difficult way to make a living that is fraught with frustration and disappointment. Winning communication includes carefully listening to, seeking to understand, and respecting multiple and/or contrary opinions. Understand more, judge less, and support relentlessly. It's the champions' creed.

2. *No secret or hidden agendas.* Zero tolerance for spiteful retribution. Easier said than done, since personal politics and personal agendas always seem to be what drives someone's actions and too often mucks up what is best for an organization. Rare is the leader who puts company good ahead of personal gain. Leadership must show the way.

3. *KSA progress checks.* Inspire development, coach positively, foster loyalty.

4. *Zero rumor tolerance.* The walls have ears. The walls also gossip. Confront it. Then crush it.

5. *Aggressively deal with conflict,* and aggressively work to resolve the conflict in an above-board manner. Harbor no grudges. Selling is a competitive profession, chock full of competitive people. It's okay to disagree from time to time; without passion you'd be a milquetoast bunch who's easy to beat. Separate the issues and

views from the people involved. Depersonalize conflicts however possible, and work to resolve them. Don't let them fester.

6. *Issue rewards, when appropriate.* Never fail to fill a promise or commitment. This is a mortal sin to salespeople. They follow the cheese. If you dangle it, and the catch it, let 'em eat it.

7. *Recognition, when deserved, both formal and informal.* Salespeople have an inborn need to feel appreciated. There's so much rejection in the job that positive recognition is like oil to a motorcar. You have to add it from time or time or your delivery vehicle will grind to a halt.

GROOMING THE NEXT GENERATION

Keep your salespeople who have career aspirations on an escalator of development. Succession-plan graduates model all good things to the rest of the organization.

MAXIMUM HORSEPOWER organizations have no fear of promoting people up and out. No one is irreplaceable yet many ordinary organizations operate under a selfish misconception that a great player cannot be replaced. Phooey. *Everyone* can be replaced.

NO ONE IS IRREPLACEABLE YET MANY ORDINARY ORGANIZATIONS OPERATE UNDER A SELFISH MISCONCEPTION THAT A GREAT PLAYER CANNOT BE REPLACED. PHOOEY. EVERYONE CAN BE REPLACED.

Inspire your people to earn the right to succeed or to fail at things that matter to them. Succession planning involves KSA mapping against a new set of high-performance criteria, a set different than their current job and tailored toward their next one.

Aggressively build those KSA bridges now, frontloading their key transitional assignment—before they actually need that expanded talent set. Hold your next-gen leaders to a higher standard than your general line, and demand that they model their behaviors against those greater expectations.

As you develop your roster of next-gen talents, know who's destined to manage and who is destined to lead. Managers manage, leaders lead and there's a world of difference between the two. Visionary businesses need good managers to succeed, yes. Managers keep track of the day-to-day logistics and the details of running a thriving business.

But what companies really need are leaders, because it is leaders who inspire others to deliver the great work, which creates a sustained MAXIMUM HORSEPOWER environment and relentless success.

Few things inspire a workforce more, or more quickly, than watching those around them being rewarded for great work. Create an escalator environment for motivated people and you'll never run out of individuals who are eager to step aboard.

LEAD MORE, MANAGE LESS

Leadership—*the process of influencing people to direct their efforts toward the attainment of specific objectives.* Whereas management *tells* people to do good work, leadership *inspires* people to do good work.

American clothing designer Ralph Lauren built an empire based on his leadership belief.

"A leader," he said, "has the vision and conviction that a dream can be achieved. He (or she) inspires the power and energy to get it done."

President Dwight D. Eisenhower's view was undoubtedly shaped by his brilliant career in the military, which springboarded him to the White House in 1953 for the first of two terms during the Cold War as our 34th U. S President.

When asked about his leadership style, Ike replied, "You do not lead by hitting people over the head. That's assault—not leadership."

Management—*the process of coordinating human, informational, physical, and financial resources to accomplish organizational goals.* Whereas leadership is inspiring people to do good work, management is *telling* people to do good work.

In the words of Hall of Fame baseball manager George "Sparky" Anderson, "No manager ever won no ballgames." What Sparky sold every day was the need for his players to play hard, from the first pitch to the last. They did, and because they did, many of them now have plaques alongside his on the walls of baseball's Hall of Fame in Cooperstown, New York.

TEN WAYS TO BE A LEADER

1. Begin with praise and honest appreciation.

2. Call attention to people's mistakes indirectly.

3. Talk about your own mistakes before criticizing the other person.

4. Ask questions instead of giving direct orders.

5. Let the other person save face.

6. Praise the slightest improvement and praise every improvement.

7. Give the other person a fine reputation to live up to.

8. Use encouragement.

9. Make the fault easy to correct.

10. Make the other person happy about doing the thing you suggest.

DALE CARNEGIE

AMERICAN WRITER AND SPEAKER

1888-1955

ADAPTING TO CHANGES OVER TIME

MAINTAINING MAXIMUM HORSEPOWER IS NEVER AN ACCIDENT

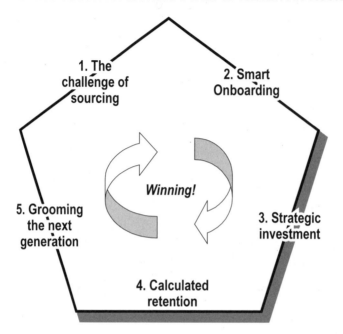

THERE ARE FIVE TIGHTLY INTERWOVEN COMPONENTS

1. *Sourcing.* You can hire purple squirrels or grow them. Growing them is cheaper. A bullpen full of them will win deals others normally wouldn't. They'll do it individually and they'll help each other do it collectively.

2. *Smart onboarding.* Manage the emotional experience, minimize any negative emotional trough. Commitment to the passionate pursuit of accelerated performance starts here.

3. *Strategic Investment.* As the KSAs of the team grow stronger, so does the team. People buy from people; the KSAs define the quality of the person.

4. *Calculated Retention.* Attribute investment protects against unwanted and unexpected attrition. Loyalty and experience provide a competitive edge. Excessive turnover gives it all back.

5. *Grooming the next generation.* Keep talent with career aspirations on an escalator of development. Succession plan graduates should role model all good things to the rest of the organization.

STEP BY STEP BREAKDOWN

OF THE SUSTAINED PERFORMANCE PENTAGON

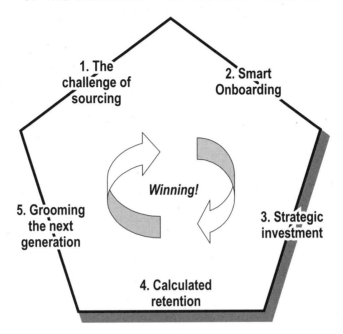

BREAKING DOWN THE ESSENTIAL SUCCESS ELEMENTS

The following pages expand on all five elements of this sustained performance pentagon. Each step is vital to successfully maintaining a MAXIMUM HORSEPOWER sales environment. Have your people work hard to customize the success factors of each step to the intricacies of your performance-based sales culture.

After the step-by-step text explanations are a series of strategic pyramids, one for each pentagon step. The plans break down each step into its necessary success elements.

Closing out this chapter is a summary chart that explains what works and what doesn't when trying to sustain a MAXIMUM HORSEPOWER environment. Chances are you'll recognize traits on both sides of the fence.

BEST-IN-CLASS SOURCING

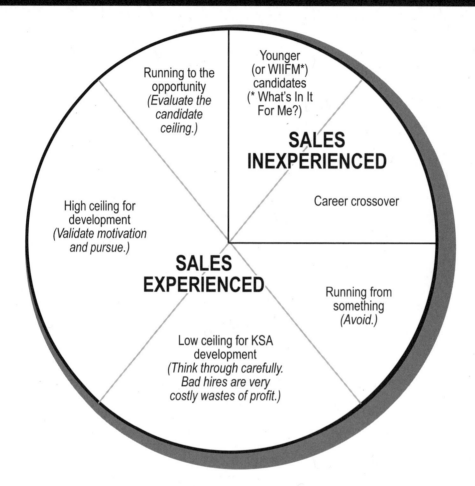

WHERE ARE YOUR BEST PLAYERS COMING FROM?

Smart hiring is a team sport. In high-performance sales organizations, everyone makes the time to find, recruit, hire, onboard, and retain high-performance talent. These sales organizations think smart, work smart, and take action.

Good sales talent will always have job options. Don't miss out because your team is too slow to follow-through.

The Emotional Dip: Guarding Against New-hire Attrition

There are four important things to do to minimize a quick exodus by newly hired salespeople. Hiring reps is expensive and losing them is wasteful, so have your team stay on top of these important stages of onboarding success:

1. Evaluation & Experience Processing

Behaviors result from the culmination of emotional experiences that are shaped by a compilation of thoughts. These thoughts start accumulating as soon as the candidate begins interfacing with the organization. The percolation of these singular ideas comes during the "Happy Stage," when everything is new and great, everyone is *so* nice, and all things are possible.

Who isn't excited by a new job? During the onboarding phase, every experience is new and emotionally validated as a good experience (an emotional plus) or a bad one (an emotional minus). Over time, these tiny pluses and minuses create either a positive or negative outlook. When the experiences overall are positive, reps are happy and motivated. When the experiences are negative, enthusiasm wanes. The more the negatives outweigh the positives, the faster the new hire's enthusiasm plummets. This negative attitude formation ends the Happy Stage and deepens the "Trough of Frustration."

2. Expectation Matching

No one expects the new car smell of a new job to last forever, so the transition from the Happy Stage to the Trough of Frustration is to be expected. The Trough will be shallow or deep, depending on how positive or negative the onboarding experience has been. When the job matches its expectations, the Trough is shallower than when there's a huge disconnect. Sales reps find that gap—between what was sold and what was delivered—as deceitful. Once distrust replaces excitement, you are vulnerable to a quick exodus. The rep will "check out" emotionally and look around for an escape hatch from what he or she perceives is a bad situation. After all: If you can't trust them when they hire you, why should you trust them when they need to pay incentives or assign an achievable budget?

The Happy Stage collects thoughts. The reality of the job takes hold and digs the Trough of Frustration. How deep it goes depends on how many of the reps' early opinions are negative.

When reality meets expectation, there are no surprises and the Trough is minimized, because it is disjoints between the two that cause negative emotional experiences. Make sure your sales team proactively manages its behavior in order to mirror realistic expectations. The truth fosters loyalty. Deception fosters more deception.

Misleading a candidate in order to get him or her to join the organization is foolish. For example, dangling a pie-in-the-sky compensation exaggeration that probably won't happen, or making a cheery promise of future advancement in a flat company stacked with lifers and no upward mobility, is misleading. Shoot straight with people. Salespeople want to know the facts, and they respect hiring executives who share the good *and* the bad. Never "perfume the pig." If you do, a good rep will bolt.

3. *Processing the Assimilation Experience*

Have a structured onboarding process that goes far beyond one assigned "babysitter." More people and touch points are better than fewer. New reps want to do good work, so make sure there is a clear line of sight between what's expected and the rep's mileposts of progress.

A "fend for yourself," do-it-yourself experience sends the message, "You're on your own." This is a four-alarm warning that this new environment is all about "me" as a survivor and not about "us" as a team. If the rep feels the company is making no front-end investment, why should he or she commit? Would you?

4. *Reaching an Emotional Conclusion*

People take action based upon feelings and emotions, which means that the decision to quit is made after the rep has processed everything they've seen, heard, and experienced. Once the accumulated onboarding experiences are weighed, an emotional conclusion is reached and rep's behavioral action is determined. In this case—in the context of onboarding new hires—the sale reps opts to either invest emotional equity and join the team . . . or check out and bolt.

A strong, positive accumulation of experiences will produce a "stay-and-play" behavior. The rep will invest emotional equity in the job, team, and company; he or she will commit in a very inspired way. They will work with discipline and passion, doing their best to perform.

But negative onboarding leads to Bailout City. The new hire quits, causing your organization to swallow a red number loss. Erratic experiences, in addition to negative ones, can cause this, too. When there is too much unpredictability with high amplitude swings of erratic good and bad experiences, a rep's confidence in his or her decision and this new company are quick to erode. These erratic swings are symbolic of CYA environments. Since nobody worth a hoot thrives in a cesspool of blame, anyone with other options will quickly consider them.

HOW MAXIMUM HORSEPOWER TEAMS GUARD AGAINST DISAPPOINTMENT

- *Prolong the Happy Stage as long as possible.* Make the onboarding experience a people-centric, family event where your sales team's culture says to each new team member, "You are valued."
- *Set and deliver realistic expectations.* Check in more than you think is

necessary in order to maintain an accurate pulse reading. Self-centered WIIFM hires ("What's In It For Me?"), especially, tend to internalize. Check their pulse often.

- *Execute a structured KSA development process that methodically invests in a valued hire.* The goal is three-fold: teach the knowledge they need, tighten up skills, and invest positive emotional equity into their new corporate relationship. Leave none of these to chance. The goal is to get every revenue generator to the Effectiveness Stage of solid performance as quickly as possible. You want them to flourish, not flee. MAXIMUM HORSEPOWER sales teams work *together* to help each other get there. Theirs is an "elephant herd" mentality.

- *Relentlessly nurture a positive emotional experience.* This responsibility falls on all MAXIMUM HORSEPOWER team members, not just the hiring manager. Great teams celebrate each other's successes with a confident swagger. Someone else's talent or big win does not threaten anyone's confidence. These teams work together; they are not a collection of individuals who work apart.

To nurture the new hire's feeling that he or she made the right choice to join the team, send the message that once the rep reaches the effectiveness curve, team support waits. The way the team wins deals it isn't favored to win is by pooling the KSAs of everyone. The sum total of all will always outperform the individual efforts of a loner. This sends a powerful invisible message to the rep: *On this team you will grow, and on this team you will succeed. You are not alone. You are part of a team. You are lucky to be on the team and the team is lucky to have you.*

Great teams expect to win—they are confident, not arrogant—and they celebrate each other's successes. The cultural value of *success through teamwork* should be instilled at the onset of the every rep's career, echoed throughout the onboarding process, and remain a vital part of his or her professional life.

Success starts with people, is attained by people, and sustained by people. Stay in touch with their emotional journey and you will build a MAXIMUM HORSEPOWER culture. Do that, and you will continually outperform your rivals.

THE CULTURAL VALUE OF SUCCESS THROUGH TEAMWORK SHOULD BE INSTILLED AT THE ONSET OF THE EVERY REP'S CAREER, ECHOED THROUGHOUT THE ONBOARDING PROCESS, AND REMAIN A VITAL PART OF HIS OR HER PROFESSIONAL LIFE.

WHY BEHAVIORAL DIPS OCCUR

UNDERSTANDING THE "WHY" OF QUICK SALES ATTRITION

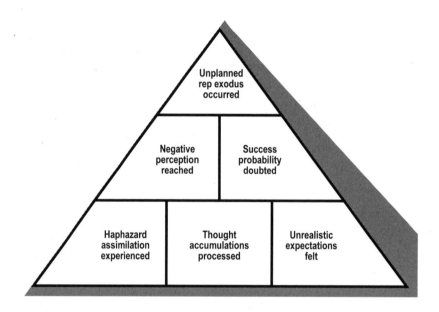

PUT YOURSELF IN THEIR SHOES

Reps leave due to the manifestation of accumulated negative experiences, which shape an emotional reaction that triggers a conscious decision to leave. The brain weighs the job's pros and cons, stacking each experience on either the good side or the bad side of its scale. When the negatives outweigh the positives to the extent the scale touches emotional bottom, those negative thoughts convert to a negative emotion that is strong enough to act upon.

That negative perception, coupled with the belief that success probability is slight, creates an actionable conclusion that causes the rep to seek another opportunity.

MAXIMUM HORSEPOWER sales organizations realize the vulnerability these negative emotional experiences create, so they work proactively to minimize them. The payback is a greater ROI, thanks to: better onboarding, stronger loyalty, quicker success, higher performance, maximum retention, and increased referrals of similar talents.

PROTECTING NEW HIRES FROM NEGATIVE EMOTIONAL ASSIMILATION

HOW TO MINIMIZE UNNECESSARY TURNOVER

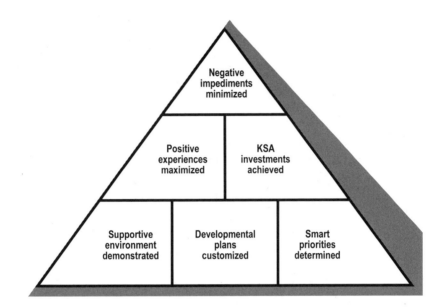

SHALLOWING THE TROUGH OF DISCOURAGEMENT

Minimize negative experiences, maximize positive ones, and quickly (and methodically) invest in the KSA development of newly hired salespeople. Customized development plans should be timelined for each new rep, each element appropriately sequenced.

The surrounding work environment and program owner must be relentlessly positive. Smartly manage who owns the success of the new rep's assimilation. When possible, cross-pollinate different people into the new rep's onboarding experience. By sharing the responsibility, everyone involved brings a new friendship and something special to the new teammate. Guard against discouraged workers being involved in the assimilation. One critical, negative salesperson can wipe out the positive efforts of a half-dozen.

A steady blizzard of positive emotional experiences will fuel motivation, build loyalty, and accelerate the new sales rep's ascension to the effectiveness stage of performance.

THE CHALLENGE OF SOURCING TALENT

PENTAGON STEP 1 OF 5:

* KSA – Knowledge, Skills, and Attributes

UTILIZE YOUR RESOURCES

Staffing and recruiting are integral to success, yet usually ignored during the sales talent hunt. Hiring managers should rely on the expertise of recruiters to fill and stratify the candidate pool. Unfortunately, many sales organizations don't work that way.

More frequently, a hiring manager prattles off a list of things he or she would like (sales experience usually topping the list), but rarely explains why those features matter. Job description finished, the manager then hides behind multiple priorities and disengages from the hunt. Too often the hiring manager allows limited access for interviews.

Personal biases during the candidate stratification process cause too many teams to settle for mediocre, easy-to-manage reps in lieu of top performers who may be job threatening or difficult to manage. A protracted search will lose top candidates, too, since sales professionals have options. Good ones don't like waiting for interviews, decisions, and offers. You must hustle to attract and secure top-shelf talent.

MAXIMUM HORSEPOWER sales cultures use staffing as a strategic resource, tightly engaged, in order to maximize the quality of every hire. Benchmark recruiting is very much a team sport, especially when hunting for a purple squirrel. When you find one, support the recruiting team's efforts with a grateful sense of urgency.

SMART ONBOARDING

PENTAGON STEP 2 OF 5:

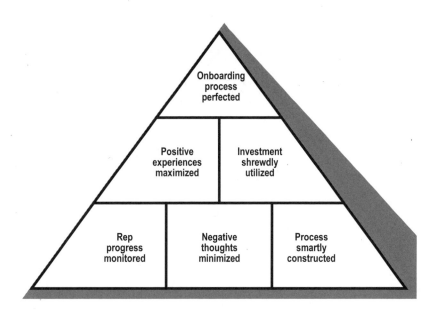

KEEP TABS ON EMOTIONS

The goal of smart onboarding is to assure that the handpicked individuals you've hired have the best possible assimilation experience. A secondary objective is to have these salespeople quickly reach the contributory effectiveness stage, at which they are more than paying for themselves.

The Happy Stage, the Reality Stage (featuring the Trough of Discouragement), and the Flourish or Flee Stage are the three phases of onboarding assimilation. Shoddy onboarding produces negative emotional experiences that can plunge the rep into a negative conclusion that may lead to quitting.

Minimize the Trough of Discouragement's emotional plummet by staying in close touch with each rep throughout their assimilation experience. Protect against unrealistic expectations. Take a constant pulse. Never let attrition be a surprise.

Turnover is an expensive—very expensive—drain on profits. Tighten this area of your sales organization as much as possible.

STRATEGIC INVESTMENT

PENTAGON STEP 3 OF 5:

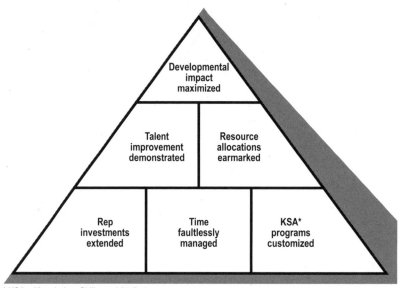

* KSA – Knowledge, Skills, and Attributes

YOU MUST COMMIT!

KSA development is an investment process, not a whimsical, "flavor of the month" sales tactic. Reaping its harvest requires blending investments in talent with investments in resources, while executing against a solid, well-designed plan.

Each rep should own the demonstrated mastery of his or her personalized developmental action plan. The plan is jointly crafted with the manager or coach who will oversee the rep's progress.

Time investments are vital, since selling time is expensive. Development time must be maximized, not wasted. The programs must be relevant, prioritized, completed, and monitored.

When it makes sense to do so, save money by utilizing internal resources. If what you need is outside your local areas of expertise, go outside. Research and validate best-in-class providers. Hire a resource that will mesh with your corporate culture. Whatever you choose to do, engage the right people to do it well. Otherwise, don't waste everyone's time and money.

CALCULATED RETENTION

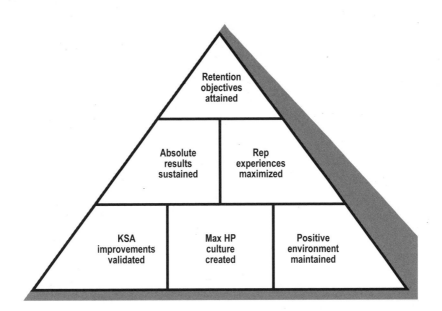

SATISFIED SALES PROS DON'T LEAVE

It's too hard to find and develop good talent to let them go without doing everything possible to create a high performance work environment that's tough to match anywhere else. Success fuels job satisfaction, as does feeling valued. Managing the positive emotional experiences of your people deepens their loyalty. Loyalty grows deep roots.

The loyalty keys: professional development coupled with a positive, vibrant culture that celebrates the contributions of its valued constituency. When people are growing, succeeding, and surrounded by skilled people with pure and positive intentions, there's not much lacking that will cause them to disengage. Money can be benchmarked and equalized.

All people in a company work in one of four job commitment phases, two of which are vulnerable to turnover. Employees are either: actively engaged, engaged, disengaged or actively disengaged. MAXIMUM HORSEPOWER cultures are actively engaged. When you take the time to build one, invest in it and protect it. Strategic retention is a vital element in the ongoing success of great sales cultures.

GROOMING THE NEXT GENERATION

PENTAGON STEP 5 OF 5:

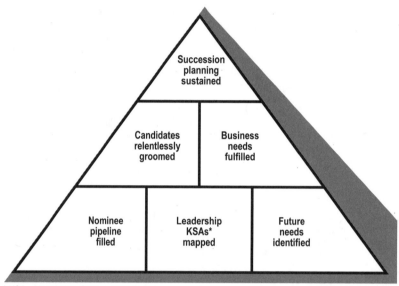

* KSA – Knowledge, Skills, and Attributes

CREATE A TALENT ESCALATOR

Powerhouse rosters come from an escalator of motivated talent who, month after month, grow better on the job. Their enhancement comes from more Knowledge, better Skills, and inspired Attributes. Reps earn the right to tackle more responsibility by being adequately prepped for new roles that are congruent with their desired career path.

The number one reason sales reps leave is lack of growth. A positive environment of skill development and succession planning addresses that exodus vulnerability head on. Matching business needs with talent grooming keeps the promotion pipeline full. Success elements include lining up improvable talent and matching the KSAs of the people to the KSAs of future responsibilities.

A reputation for developing and promoting talent draws new sources of external talent into the organization via referral hires and industry reputation. Referral hires from top performers are precisely who you want. A company with a reputation for deep talent is no secret to the marketplace, its competitors or potential customers. Success begets success.

SUSTAINING A MAXIMUM HORSEPOWER SALES ENVIRONMENT

What Works & What Doesn't

Priority	What Works	What Doesn't
Sincerity & Focus	Care about your people and they'll care about you. If you don't, they won't, either. Why should they? Relentlessly create positive emotional experiences. Look at your team as a collection of individuals. Celebrate the individual. Treat personal interactions as an "audience of one." Total focus, no distractions.	Talent development is a building-block business. Avoid a "blur of many." Don't be too general, too grandiose or attempt too many simultaneous initiatives. Without strategic focus, it's tough to become truly great at anything; your attention is diffused in too many directions. Keep it simple: Prioritize KSA learning points and focus on one at a time. Try too many things at once and you'll fail. Nor will there be a systematic way to objectively gauge the progress of your talent.
Relevance	Customize strategic messaging so that it's personally and professionally relevant. Salespeople live in a world of "What's in it for me?" Tell them, point blank. Use precise execution of relevant talent-strengthening strategies via the KSA approach. Exert no wasted motion.	The shotgun approach to hopeful performance assumes that reps will get better on their own. Will not happen! An employee number doesn't sell; the *person* sells. Build a KSA map that is relevant to the person, to the position, and to the organization. P.S. Never assume that a job title guarantees competence, experience or a KSA match commensurate with the title. Sometimes you'll need to bridge job titles to higher levels of skill and competence.
Follow-up	Relentlessly follow-up. Recognize progress. Doing so enables you to create ongoing positive emotional experiences for your salespeople, and reinforce gaps and shortfalls before they become problems.	Without follow-up or reinforcement, you send the unspoken message that improved skills are optional, not mandatory. Follow up, inspect, and test in order to maximize positive change. Don't tolerate slackers. Praise improvement as you see it. Sales reps thrive on recognition (formal and informal). Don't underestimate its importance.

Motivation	Inspire personal motivation in those who work for you. Motivation is an attribute that does not sustain when injected solely by external catalysts. *Remember: No perspiration without inspiration.* People who live with passion, work with passion. Stoke that passion.	Once or twice a year *rah-rah* motivational speeches are like hot showers. They make you feel good at the time but are not sustainable. If your troops are worn down or beaten, inflating them for a day doesn't solve the reasons they got that way in the first place. Do a root-cause analysis. Pin down the causes and take decisive action.
Role-modeling	Demonstrate positive role-model leadership on macro and micro issues. Locate subject-matter experts who are willing to own specific KSAs. *No one is too young or too old to be a role model!* Everyone in the organization should have a role model to inspire them.	Make sure that your inventory of role models matches the demographics of your sales force. Everyone must be inspired by someone to whom he or she can relate: young, old, male, female, gay, straight, Hispanic, Asian, African-American—*everybody*. Role models inspire attributes that motivate the want and need and that drive performance. Strive to build a robust, inspired sales organization that has lots of role models. Role models should showcase diversity. Homogenous clones don't do it.
Passion & Energy	Lead by example. Live and work with a sense of urgency. Be positive, supportive, relentless, and accessible. Every day offers a new world of electric possibilities. Salespeople find, in life and business, what we look for. All marvelous achievements require some degree of pursuit. Passion is what fuels the chase.	Listless, boring, and/or uncaring yields two very predictable things: A loser's environment and a winner's exodus. Winners work with passion and energy and expect their co-workers to work that way, too. If they find them surrounded by people who don't care, they flee. Salespeople tend to feed off of their leaders. Great leaders inspire great effort and great victories. Uninspiring leadership creates a feeling of malaise.
Great Communication	When your people master all four elements of great communication—*sender, receiver, channel, message*—they sell a whole lot more than ever before.	Every great leader is a great communicator, even though they can communicate in various ways (e.g., a dynamic speaker, a visionary, very people-centric, relentlessly positive). Weak communicators struggle to inspire. Without inspiration, sales efforts suffer. So does loyalty. Not only will the reps not run through a brick wall for the boss, they won't even climb over it, unless someone else leans a sturdy ladder against it.

CHAPTER

VALIDATING SALES EFFECTIVENESS

"Whoever said, 'It's not whether you win or lose that counts,' probably lost."

—Martina Navratilova, tennis legend

The 1932 New York Yankees fielded a team of nine Hall of Famers, among them Babe Ruth and Lou Gehrig. The team's record that season was 107-47, after which they defeated the Chicago Cubs and won the World Series. Game three in Chicago featured Babe Ruth's legendary "called shot" home run to centerfield. Ruth homered twice that game, as did Lou Gehrig. The win put the Yanks up three games to none, setting up a final game rout and a four-game sweep. Many baseball historians consider this ball club, the 1932 Yankees, the greatest baseball team of all time.

Flash-forward thirty years to 1962. Baseball expands, adding a second team in New York. Manager Casey Stengel's beloved Mets fumble their way through a season in which the team hits a measly .240. Their fielding is atrocious; the Mets lead the majors in errors. Two starting pitchers lose twenty or more games; a third drops nineteen. The team's other two starters combine to win four games . . . and lose twenty-nine.

The Mets finish the season with a win-loss record of 40-120, last in the National League, *sixty games* behind the first place San Francisco Giants. This team, the 1962 New York Mets, remain—in the eyes of many—the most inept Major League Baseball club the world has ever seen.

The lesson, of course, is simple. Baseball, in many ways, is like selling: Regardless how good or bad you are, no one wins or loses them all.

The very best team in history—the 1932 Yankees—lost more than one-fourth of its games. The worst team of all time, the Mets, managed to win one-fourth of its games. When the best team, and the worst team, *lose* a fourth and *win* a fourth just by showing up—what defines an organization's greatness (or ineptitude) is what happens during the half-season in-between.

Baseball is a hard game to play well, fraught with frustration and disappointment. Every ballplayer soon learns that some days you win, some days you lose, and some days it rains. Selling is similar to baseball because the same thing happens: you win some and you lose some. But in our case, when it rains we have to keep working.

One question I'm sometimes asked by salespeople is whether or not they are any good at what they do. I respect anyone who has the nerve to ask. It takes courage to walk up to someone who develops sales talent for a living and to ask how he or she stacks up.

I ask one question: "Do you win the ones you're supposed to win, and some of the ones you're supposed to lose?"

Without waiting for a reply, I add: "When you win the ones you're supposed to win, and some of the ones you're supposed to lose, you're good."

That's what Maximum Horsepower sales organizations do. They win more than their share, just like Babe Ruth's 1932 New York Yankees. They win the ones they are supposed to win plus many others, including the vast majority of close ones. Winning becomes a habit, an expectation. They do not take the field happy to play; they take the field playing to win.

There is no jubilation from winning deals we're supposed to win. Anybody can sell the easy ones. The art of the sales profession—the truly magnificent soul of this great, wonderful, and maddening profession—comes from winning the deals we're supposed to lose. When you win as the underdog—steal one away—the feeling is euphoric.

ANYBODY CAN SELL THE EASY ONES. THE ART OF THE SALES PROFESSION—THE TRULY MAGNIFICENT SOUL OF THIS GREAT, WONDERFUL, AND MADDENING PROFESSION— COMES FROM WINNING THE DEALS WE'RE SUPPOSED TO LOSE.

Those great wins are special. When the word comes—learning from the customer that they've picked you—it's magic. Every great salesperson remembers deals that reshaped their career for the better. It is the competitor in you that makes you proud that you've just outsold someone, or a team of someones who woke up that morning whistling, a bounce in their step because they thought *they* were going to outsell *you*—only to learn they've lost. Winning in selling is fabulous. In my opinion, closing a big deal is the greatest feeling in business. Big wins flood endorphins through every capillary in your body. Once people feel victory's elixir, they never forget it. They want to feel it again and again and again.

If your people have experienced what I'm describing three times or more, they are good at what they do. Three great wins is significant: One is an accident, two a coincidence. Three or more is a trend.

WIN THE ONES YOU'RE SUPPOSED TO WIN AND SOME OF THE ONES YOU'RE SUPPOSED TO LOSE

"Nobody remembers who finished second in the Kentucky Derby."

—Steve Cauthen, 1978 winner aboard Affirmed

Winning deals as an underdog doesn't happen by accident. Winning is a byproduct of a customer's cognitive journey through the evaluation stage. Great wins lift entire organizations. Crushing defeats sink them.

GREAT WINS LIFT ENTIRE ORGANIZATIONS. CRUSHING DEFEATS SINK THEM.

Any deal worth pursuing should be pursued only as long as it's worth winning. Every opportunity requires an investment in resources. Because resources are finite, as is time, winning big starts with picking the right spots. Know when to ante in; know when to fold and find another game.

Winning smart starts with knowing when to compete. If a potential deal's price point or its terms and conditions degrade to diminished returns, draw a line and invest no more. If the customer is unyielding, leave the deal for the jackals to fight over. Know when to walk away. Smart sales teams invest in fair deals that work for both sides.

Winning is orchestrated, not accidental, so every deal worth winning deserves its own unique and airtight strategy. The solution is customized and wrapped around a clever, creative, value-laden equation that is competitively unpredictable.

It's what we don't know that is more likely to beat us than what we do—so the hard questions have to be asked, answered, clarified, and understood. The value proposition has to be clearly explained, with a dissected analysis of benefits (tangible and intangible) and cost (direct and indirect). Nothing can be vague, ambiguous, or missing. The proposal must be complete, hard-hitting, clear, and to the point. Everything in it must showcase creative thinking.

Winning plans are idea-rich, impeccably presented, and of maximum relevance to every influence-wielding customer involved in the decision-making process. Winning sales teams believe that an educated customer is a good thing, not a bad one. So, the reps listen brilliantly and, when they speak to fill in the gaps the customer needs to know, they speak to be understood; they don't "perfume the pig." Professional reps are comfortable selling by teaching, rather than pounding the hard sell. They do not lie, deceive, mislead, minimize or neglect germane issues. Risk is openly discussed, as are realistic expectations. Critical success factors are shared, illuminated, discussed, and resolved.

WINNING PLANS ARE IDEA-RICH, IMPECCABLY PRESENTED, AND OF MAXIMUM RELEVANCE TO EVERY INFLUENCE-WIELDING CUSTOMER INVOLVED IN THE DECISION-MAKING PROCESS.

In addition to coupling a great business understanding with a smart, fairly priced business solution, sales champions understand the importance of feeding political stakeholders. Politics is as much a part of business deals as budget dollars, so maximizing political impact often involves candid dialogue that professionally deals with the realities of a contemplated change. Bringing the political discussion from the invisibility of the unspoken background to the front-and-center foreground of frank discussion is a strength, not a weakness. In big deals, it is also essential.

Preparation drives confidence. Confidence fuels a positive, aggressive, and proactive posture when working through tough issues such as value, risk, and politics. Opening up the discussion arena to in-depth exchanges on all things that matter enables winners to create actionable interest and, when the time is right, to ask confidently for the business.

MAXIMUM HORSEPOWER sales organizations listen to win, sell to win, negotiate to win, close to win, contract to win, and implement to win again. They stay positive through every stage of the cycle. If a deal stalls at an executive decision-making level, they engage supportive executive resources (or other customer references) to join the fray and push things past the tipping point.

> **MAXIMUM HORSEPOWER SALES ORGANIZATIONS LISTEN TO WIN, SELL TO WIN, NEGOTIATE TO WIN, CLOSE TO WIN, CONTRACT TO WIN, AND IMPLEMENT TO WIN AGAIN.**

High-performance salespeople do not bask or gloat when they win. They subscribe to the belief that their real work starts with "Yes," because real winners aren't done until the sold promise has been implemented flawlessly. Having earned the right to trumpet that reputation throughout the marketplace, they go and hunt for another deal.

Winning begets winning. "Yes" is the ultimate validation but it is not the end of the sale. The end of the sale is the first step of the next, and all the greats know it.

WIN THE ONES YOU'RE SUPPOSED TO WIN

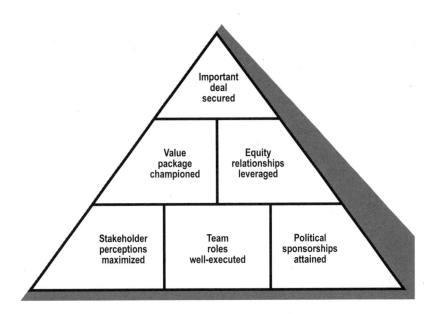

EXECUTE WITH DISCIPLINE. DON'T GET SLOPPY.

MAXIMUM HORSEPOWER sales teams win the ones they're supposed to win—and some of the ones they're supposed to lose. Nobody wins them all.

Remind your team to stay disciplined. Don't let them take shortcuts or assume they'll win. Two things to closely manage: the politics tied to the decision, and the value proposition, as perceived by the customer's decision-influencers and stakeholders. Make sure your people deliver value and feed the politicians. Smart positioning requires getting an accurate reading of the customer landscape, securing the right political sponsors, and then brainstorming what everyone on the sales team knows about the opportunity. Let no one operate in a vacuum. A collection of loners will not outperform a smart team.

Utilize resources and urge the team to work as if they're behind. When they do, they'll win. They will earn the business you deserve. Don't let the team get sloppy, lazy, or careless. When they do, they will lose.

There is a temptation to cut corners when we assume we'll win a deal. Guard against it. Competitors who outwork us will steal business. Stay disciplined, work smart, work hard, and execute professionally.

WIN SOME OF THE ONES YOU'RE SUPPOSED TO LOSE

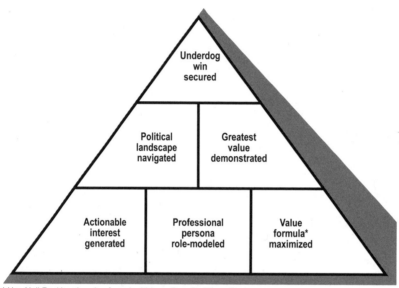

* Use Neil Rackham's value formula: *Value = Benefits Minus Cost*

THESE ARE THE DEALS THAT DEFINE CAREERS.

Stealing a deal away from a competitor requires strategic value-mapping and political savvy. You need to assess the client's key influencers, political winners and losers, and their differing political motivations. You must also sell what matters most to multi-tiered influencers, in order to build, package, and flawlessly deliver a solid proposal that is chockfull of maximum value.

All of the tasks along the bottom row of this pyramid model are the behaviors and sales techniques your people must emulate. Clowns do not win unexpected deals. Pros do. Big deals aren't won by accident. Pros work smarter and harder than mediocre salespeople. By doing so, the pros earn the reward of the customer's trust.

THE PERFORMANCE WHEEL

THE BIG CHALLENGE: MAINTAINING TOP PERFORMANCE WHILE STEADILY INCREASING SALES PROFICIENCY.

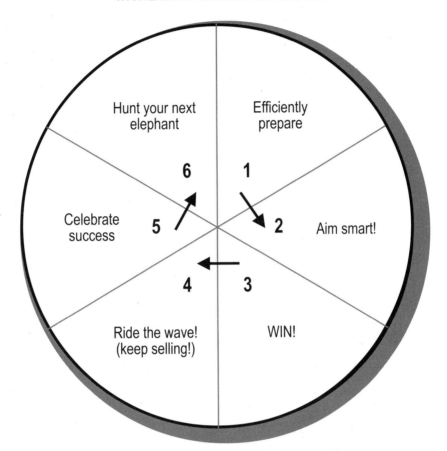

HOW FAST DO YOUR PEOPLE WANT TO GO?

Remind them:

- *Effort and smarts drive clockspeed.* Relentlessly learn! Live with a daily discipline that seeks new ideas, greater insights, and better methods.

- *Invest in your profession.* Sharpen your skills. Practice where you are strong, improve where you are not. Seek critique. *Great pros do not practice on their customers!* They practice on their friends, family, and co-workers. They *perform* for their customers.

- *Embrace your attributes.* Challenge yourself to live in hot pursuit of your dreams. Mediocre performers sell themselves short. Stars don't. To a star, *winning* matters. Winning more deals than the competition *matters*. Ascending to the pinnacle of the profession *matters*.

DISSECTING THE PERFORMANCE WHEEL

The revenue validation of a MAXIMUM HORSEPOWER sales team comes when they consistently win deals they are not expected to win. The adage "One is an accident, two a coincidence, three or more a trend" holds true for individuals as well as organizations. Winning creates a championship swagger and MAXIMUM HORSEPOWER teams have it.

Six sequential steps help teams to maintain the momentum it takes to keep winning more than their expected share of profitable deals:

1. Efficiently prepare.
2. Aim straight!
3. *Win!* Winning matters and winners fight every inch from start to finish. The reason winners work so hard and win so often: they absolutely hate to lose.
4. Ride the wave.
5. Celebrate success.
6. Hunt your next elephant.

1. *Efficiently Prepare*

Work smarter up front and you'll preserve extra time to work harder late in the cycle when the time investment payoff is greatest. Efficient preparation includes thorough pre-call prep, discussing and mapping a sound strategic approach, scripting and rehearsing the presentation. This is a closed-loop process, with little left to chance.

WORK SMARTER UP FRONT AND YOU'LL PRESERVE EXTRA TIME TO WORK HARDER LATE IN THE CYCLE WHEN THE TIME INVESTMENT PAYOFF IS GREATEST.

Few questions are asked of the customer when the answer isn't already known or intuited, unless these questions are investigative; in which case, each is scripted to gain information, clarify something important, or test understanding.

Three things drive the velocity of winning deals: smarts, effort, and urgency. In MAXIMUM HORSEPOWER organizations, a sales opportunity's prep stage is very disciplined. There is minimal wasted time or motion.

2. *Aim Straight!*

Focus is everything. Grandiose scope-creep (of all things possible) is an ever-present temptress—but not something to which a smart sales pro falls prey.

Stars zero in on specific success keys, and build plans precisely aimed at delivering those objectives. Deals worth chasing (investing time, energy, and resources in) always have a commensurate payoff. They assess "winnability" factors (such as risk/reward, upside/downside, best case/worst case), read the political landscape, and accurately analyze each side's best alternative to no deal being made. Feeding every customer stakeholder a highly relevant value proposition is part of their equity-building sales process.

Value propositions are judged by customers to be high impact, low impact, or no impact. Until they are high impact, they remain under construction. Zeroing in on crafting the maximum impact solution for the customer at hand gains a competitive edge early in the comparative selling cycle; the customer never sees a mediocre or boilerplate effort.

This stage of the sale (working hard to gain advantageous differentiation right out of the chute) is where being a student of the sales profession pays maximum dividends. Sharp skills unleashed with strategic purpose drive home powerful messages that pique customer interest in a competitively advantageous way.

THIS STAGE OF THE SALE (WORKING HARD TO GAIN ADVANTAGEOUS DIFFERENTIATION RIGHT OUT OF THE CHUTE) IS WHERE BEING A STUDENT OF THE SALES PROFESSION PAYS MAXIMUM DIVIDENDS.

Great salespeople separate from the pack right here. They demonstrate strategic excellence, while their competitors use generic approach calls.

3. WIN!

Don't assume that winning matters to everyone who sells for a living. I have worked with companies whose people actually wanted to *lose* expansion opportunities, because winning would mean additional work for little or no additional pay. This is typical of hamster-wheel companies that go round-and-round and never seem to grow. Culturally they do not possess the killer instinct of high-performance organizations hungry to win.

Smart victories matter to MAXIMUM HORSEPOWER teams. A smart victory is one with a greater reward than the investment required to secure it. That reward may be immediate, longer-term, or in the form of a strategic marketplace parlay. Great salespeople know when to close and they look forward to it; they close hard the instant they sense that they have earned the right to ask. Nothing beats winning, and winning feeds everything else, including the need to win more.

Weak organizations don't close worth a hoot. They wait for the customers to buy, rather than escort them to the decision point and ask for their business as soon as they have earned the right.

Sales verdicts are court trials, some decided by a judge and others decided by a jury. Someone wins, someone loses. The winner gets the champagne. The loser straggles home to lick his or her wounds and decide when and where to compete again. A loser's time is never recoverable; whatever was spent is gone for good. To a true dyed-in-the-wool *winner*, losing absolutely stinks. He or she *never* gets used to it. Wallowing in the post-defeat cerebral quagmire of being outsold is a toxic dump to anyone who lives to win.

Not all deals are the same, of course. The biggies take extract time and blood. They sap overtime hours, steal weekends, sometimes causing people to be locked in a hotel room spooning with a pillow instead of home with a loved one. Winning these deals happens because the need to win fuels a passion to do whatever it will take to be selected.

Lower performers do not pay that price.

Several other winning traits, tangible and intangible, differentiate the work habits of stars versus mediocres. Stars better understand and thrive in the corporate political arena; mediocres flounder. Stars work strategically and execute flawlessly; mediocres work tactically and execute erratically. Stars take zero for granted; mediocres take face value as fact. Stars realize the game is beneath the surface; mediocres can't see it. Mediocres see only above the waterline. Stars stay productive; mediocres stay busy.

In the end, regardless of deal size, a battle between two quasi-equal solutions is awarded to the person who differentiates him or herself from the competition. The one who best exemplifies the professionalism the customer would love to see in their own salespeople will earn the nod; hence, the advantage of the will to win. There is no substitute for it. Waking up each day with the will to win is the attribute of a champion.

IN THE END, REGARDLESS OF DEAL SIZE, A BATTLE BETWEEN TWO QUASI-EQUAL SOLUTIONS IS AWARDED TO THE PERSON WHO DIFFERENTIATES HIM OR HERSELF FROM THE COMPETITION.

4. Ride the Wave!

When things are going well, keep after it. Follow the same success formula. Success is infectious both individually and collectively. The talk track is working, the time management decisions are working, the value propositions are on target. A smart manager knows to help hot reps stay unencumbered. Free your people to do what they do best: Close business.

Jim Graham taught me the importance of this early in my Xerox career. He was my first manager and helped mold me into a competitive pro.

"The best time to make sales calls is right after you sold something," he said. "You are so excited from the sale, customers read and reward your enthusiasm."

As straightforward as Jim's advice is, guess what a lot of reps do after closing a deal? They knock off the day. Mission accomplished. Time to go relax.

That, of course, is a middle-of-the-bell-curve trait. Diving right back into the fray is a high-performance trait.

5. *Celebrate Success*

Everyone appreciates the recognition of a great win, but not everybody takes the time to celebrate. One of the best ways to inspire your troops to continue their great work is to dwell on the positive emotional space that's fed by statistical achievement.

Three development components fuel MAXIMUM HORSEPOWER behaviors: Knowledge, Skills, and Attributes. Winning comes from applying all three under pressure, and better than the competition. Celebrate big wins, formally when appropriate, informally often. Attributes run on nuclear energy. Recharge those fuel cells in your people and they will self-propel themselves. Selling is a hard business a lot more often than an easy business. When things are going well, *celebrate!*

ATTRIBUTES RUN ON NUCLEAR ENERGY RECHARGE THOSE FUEL CELLS IN YOUR PEOPLE AND THEY WILL SELF-PROPEL THEMSELVES.

6. *Hunt Your Next Elephant*

Great performers know that winning an unexpected deal is no cause for complacency. Stung competitors retaliate. They aggressively reconfigure their strategies, determined to exact revenge. The best way to tie up your competitors' resources is to make them defend the pillar accounts of their customer base. Do that, and they're too busy to attack yours.

Preach the sales leadership mantra: Winning one is an accident. Two is a coincidence. Three or more is a trend. Show me you're a trendsetter.

Stars internalize the affirming emotions that come from a big win and quickly re-channel their focus toward the *next* mountain they are determined to climb. They set out on that trek with purpose and determination, following the same success formula of hard work and professionalism that keyed victory for them the last time.

The two greatest salespeople I've ever worked with—Xerox legend Jerry Moore and British financial services expert Russell Jones—never tire of climbing mountains. Physically and stylistically, the men have nothing in common. What separates them from other salespeople is their determination to keep climbing higher peaks. They live for it, thrive on it, and never tire of it. These men inspire others through their sheer determination to succeed. They want to be so far to the right side of the performance bell curve you have to turn the page to find them.

Motivation in all great performers comes from within. Great managers relentlessly refuel their champions' self-motivating egos. In a high-performance environment, every day is a new challenge and a new opportunity.

Great sales organizations, therefore, are a mosaic of like-minded winners, and every one of those MAXIMUM HORSEPOWER cultures was constructed from the bottom up. They do not fall from the sky. Work hard, work smart, and commit to building your own. When you do, you will drive your business forward.

GREAT SALES ORGANIZATIONS, THEREFORE, ARE A MOSAIC OF LIKE-MINDED WINNERS, AND EVERY ONE OF THOSE MAXIMUM HORSEPOWER CULTURES WAS CONSTRUCTED FROM THE BOTTOM UP.

CHAPTER 15

VALIDATING SALES EFFECTIVENESS

YOU WILL HARVEST WHAT YOU GROW

Every company—and every sales organization—faces the same three choices:

"What if I train and they leave?

"What if I train and they stay?

"What if I train, they stay, and help recruit others who also stay?"

This oft-quoted industry mantra cuts to the core of the people development decision.

At its essence, a company is nothing more than a collection of people who are paid to pursue independent goals that eventually converge into something good. Better people, theoretically, should produce better results.

Stepping outside the sales world, take a minute to look around at performers who intrigue you. In every walk of life you see a different version of the same truth: When inspired, ordinary people can do extraordinary things.

Sir Edmund Hillary was a beekeeper who decided to climb Mount Everest. Oprah Winfrey wanted to be on TV—but got fired from her first job as a newsreader in Baltimore because she cried on the air. Joanne Murray Rowling was a French tutor and teacher struggling to pay rent before thinking up *Harry Potter* during a train ride from Edinburgh to London.

The world of professional selling works the same way: When inspired—and coached—diamonds in the rough will soon sparkle. When they do, these super salespeople become company gemstones. They are precious and valuable, because without a growing business, the company has no long-term future.

It has been my experience that a company's future prospects are linked directly to the strength of its revenue-generators. A strong sales force portends a bright future. It provides the backbone to a positive and vibrant culture.

A weak sales force foreshadows problems. Doubt, worry, and a lack of confidence permeate the halls. People are more likely to jump ship than bail or help repair a leak.

The best answer to this chapter's three-question opener is the third. When you build and invest emotional equity into a high-performance sales organization—a MAXIMUM HORSEPOWER sales organization—your diamonds stick around. They also attract other solid salespeople, who aspire to join because winners like to win and want to play for a team for whom winning is important.

The investment you make in your salespeople—or choose not to make—will become a self-fulfilling prophecy. If you make none, you will get what you deserve: continual pummelings from companies that do.

THE INVESTMENT YOU MAKE IN YOUR SALESPEOPLE—OR CHOOSE NOT TO MAKE—WILL BECOME A SELF-FULFILLING PROPHECY.

But if you make a consistent effort to build a prideful sales culture, your organization will strengthen; for the same reason Ed Hillary climbed Everest, Oprah wallpapered America, and J. K. Rowling got kids to read: When inspired, ordinary people can do extraordinary things.

Good luck, and good selling. Thanks for honoring our great profession.

HOW TO STRENGTHEN YOUR SALES FORCE QUICKLY

(The end goal is at the top. The middle row enables you to achieve the end goal. The baseline row identifies your first steps. The strategic plan reads from the top down. The plan is executed from the bottom up.)

GREAT SALES ORGANIZATIONS MAKE THE RIGHT THINGS HAPPEN.

Helping your people sell better doesn't need to cost a lot of money or take a lot of time. Improvement comes quickest when process-driven, so think through and map out your change strategy. This book steps you through that process.

Without guidance, a salesperson may improve on his or her own—usually by trial and error. Progress will be slow and erratic. Reps tend to learn more from the frustrations of losing than the joy of winning, so a fend-for-yourself sales culture typically experiences many costly defeats. A lot are due to poor selling.

It is much quicker—and smarter—to build a sales culture that inspires winning and professional growth. This book explains how to do that, what works and what doesn't, and why.

There aren't enough MAXIMUM HORSEPOWER sales organizations out there, which means there are significant market rewards for companies who teach their people sell better. Do yourself a favor: *Be one!*

RESOURCES & RECOMMENDATIONS

All of these resources and organizations do great work.

NEIL RACKHAM

Neil Rackham is a global thought-leader on issues of interest in sales and marketing. Three of his books have appeared on *The New York Times* bestseller list. Below is bio information abridged from his website, www.NeilRackham.com:

> "In the 1970's Neil led the largest ever research study of successful selling. This massive project, supported by major multinationals including Xerox and IBM, involved a team of 30 researchers who studied 35,000 sales calls in over 20 countries. The research took 12 years at a cost of $30 million (in today's dollars). From the results of these studies he published the groundbreaking classic *SPIN® Selling* (McGraw-Hill, 1988) and *Major Account Sales Strategy* (McGraw-Hill, 1989). His recent book *Rethinking The Sales Force* has received industry acclaim.
>
> Neil has worked closely with and been an advisor on sales performance to several of the largest American Fortune 100 companies. More than half the Fortune 500 train their salespeople using sales models derived from his research."

Neil is a personable and entertaining fellow. Contact him through his website.

HUTHWAITE, INC.

Huthwaite now owns the training administration of SPIN® Selling, and complements Rackham's work with some nice intellectual capital they've developed on their own. Huthwaite customizes its programs to the intrinsic needs of its client companies. They are a very professional group and do terrific work. Huthwaite is headquartered in Northern Virginia, with offices in Canada, China, Australia, Singapore, and the Middle East.

I am a strong advocate of SPIN® Selling methodologies, and a big supporter of Huthwaite's fine work. Contact information:

Huthwaite United States
22630 Davis Drive, Suite #100
Sterling, VA 20164-6400
Tel: 800-851-3842
Website: www.huthwaite.com

HARVARD PROGRAM ON NEGOTIATION

This is a terrific interactive program that's available to corporate clients, taught on an as-available basis by a team of Harvard Law's top professors. Shared below is information abridged from the program's website, with its address mentioned at the bottom.

"The Program on Negotiation (PON) is a university consortium dedicated to developing the theory and practice of negotiation and dispute resolution. Founded in 1983 as a special research project at Harvard Law School, PON includes faculty, students, and staff from Harvard University, Massachusetts Institute of Technology and Tufts University.

Business leaders, government officials, corporate trainers, and corporate counsel participate in short PON training courses in partnership with the Center for Management Research. These two- to three-day workshops are described in detail at: www.pon.execseminars.com."

I have worked several times with Bob Bordone, Gillien Todd, and Florrie Darwin and recommend the PON team highly. Each is an outstanding facilitator. All three live near Boston.

Robert Bordone is the Thaddeus R. Beal Assistant Clinical Professor of Law, Director of the Harvard Negotiation and Mediation Clinical Program. Tel.: 617-495-9194. Email: rbordone@law.harvard.edu.

Gillien Todd is a Lecturer on Law at Harvard Law School, where she received her J.D. She also teaches the negotiation workshop for outside professionals and is a partner with the Triad Consulting Group, Inc. Tel.: 617-495-1684. Email: gtodd@law.harvard.edu.

Florrie Darwin, Lecturer on Law, is also a teaching faculty member and integral member of the PON team. Tel.: 617-495-9389. Email: fdarwin@law.harvard.edu.

CORPORATE EXECUTIVE BOARD (SALES EXECUTIVE COUNCIL)

"The Corporate Executive Board provides best practices research, decision-support tools, and executive education to a membership of the world's leading corporations and not-for-profit institutions [from its website, www.ExecutiveBoard.com]." Companies with similar challenges exchange ideas for mutual benefit. These reports are thorough, comprehensive, and well written. If your company isn't a member, you might want to join. Contact:

Corporate Executive Board
1919 North Lynn Street
Arlington, VA 22209
Tel: 571-303-3000
Website: www.ExecutiveBoard.com

SHEROD MILLER, PH.D.

A teacher/coach, Dr. Miller serves companies that want to strengthen leaders and teams by developing stronger, more impactful interpersonal effectiveness. I found his listening skills workshop illuminating—and especially valuable for salespeople. I recommend him highly. Contact information:

Sherod Miller, Ph. D., Chairman
Interpersonal Communication Programs, Inc. (ICP)
30772 Southview Drive, Suite 200
Evergreen, CO 80439
Tel: 800-328-5099
Website: www.comskills.com

RECOMMENDED REFERENCE BOOKS:

GETTING TO YES by Roger Fisher. The basis for the Harvard negotiation program, this simple but comprehensive read is a great backbone for improving your sales closing techniques.

SPIN® SELLING by Neil Rackham. A seminal work in the profession. Basic principles still relevant. Adaptation to current buying climate maximizes success. Still a terrific book for salespeople, because it's still the largest research work of its kind.

RETHINKING THE SALES FORCE by Neil Rackham. Read *SPIN*, then this one.

TO REACH THE AUTHOR

Ocean Palmer is author Ted Simendinger's pen name. To contact Ted with questions or comments:

Tel. 877-611-6222 (toll-free)
Website: www.SalesTalentDevelopment.com
Email: ted@SalesTalentDevelopment.com